UNEMPLOYMENT AND THE GREAT DEPRESSION IN WEIMAR GERMANY

Also by Peter D. Stachura

NAZI YOUTH IN THE WEIMAR REPUBLIC

THE WEIMAR ERA AND HITLER 1918–1933: A Critical Bibliography

THE SHAPING OF THE NAZI STATE (*editor*)

THE GERMAN YOUTH MOVEMENT 1900–1945: An Interpretative and Documentary History

GREGOR STRASSER AND THE RISE OF NAZISM

THE NAZI MACHTERGREIFUNG (*editor*)

Unemployment and the Great Depression in Weimar Germany

Edited by

Peter D. Stachura, M.A., Ph.D., F.R.Hist. S.

Reader in History, University of Stirling

M

MACMILLAN

PRESS

First published 1986

Published by
THE MACMILLAN PRESS LTD
Houndmills, Basingstoke, Hampshire RG21 2XS
and London
Companies and representatives
throughout the world

Typeset by Latimer Trend & Company Ltd, Plymouth

Printed in Hong Kong

British Library Cataloguing in Publication Data
Unemployment and the Great Depression in
Weimar Germany.
1. Unemployment—Germany—History—
20th century
I. Stachura, Peter D.
331.13'7943 HD5779
ISBN 0-333-37646-3

To the Memory of my Uncle
Jan Stachura (1916–1985) R.I.P.
An Inspiring Leader in the Polish Wartime
Resistance (Home Army);
a hero for Poland,
with respect and admiration

Contents

List of Abbreviations

ADGB	Allgemeiner Deutscher Gewerkschaftsbund – General Federation of German Trade Unions
AVAVG	Gesetz über Arbeitsvermittlung und Arbeitsversicherung – The Law on Labour Exchanges and Unemployment Insurance
BAK	Bundesarchiv Koblenz – The German Federal Archive in Koblenz
DDP	Deutsche Demokratische Partei – German Democratic Party
DNVP	Deutschnationale Volkspartei – German National People's Party
DVP	Deutsche Volkspartei – German People's Party
FAD	Freiwilliger Arbeitsdienst – Voluntary Labour Service
GG	Geschichte und Gesellschaft
HAK	Historische Archiv der Stadt Köln
HZ	Historische Zeitschrift
KJVD	Kommunistische Jugendverband Deutschlands – Communist Youth Association of Germany
KPD	Kommunistische Partei Deutschlands – German Communist Party
NSDAP	Nationalsozialistische Deutsche Arbeiterpartei – National Socialist German Workers' Party (Nazi Party)
RABl	Reichsarbeitsblatt
RAM	Reichsarbeitsminister – Reich Labour Minister
RdF	Reichsminister der Finanzen – Reich Finance Minister
RDI	Reichsverband der Deutschen Industrie – Reich Association of German Industry
RGBl	Reichsgesetzblatt – the official legal gazette issued by the Reich Ministry of the Interior
RK	Reichskanzlei – Reich Chancellory
RT	Stenographische Berichte der Verhandlungen des Deutschen Reichstages
RWWAK	Rhenisch-Westfälisches Wirtschaftsarchiv zu Köln
SA	Sturmabteilungen – Stormtroopers
SPD	Sozialdemokratische Partei Deutschlands – Social Democratic Party of Germany

StAB	Staatsarchiv Bremen
StAH	Staatsarchiv Hamburg
USPD	Unabhängige Sozialdemokratische Partei Deutschlands – Independent Social Democratic Party of Germany
VfZ	Vierteljahrshefte für Zeitgeschichte
WTB	Woytinsky, Tarnow, Baade
ZAG	Zentralarbeitsgemeinschaft
ZStW	Zeitschrift für die gesamte Strafrechtswissenschaften

Notes on the Contributors

Jürgen W. Falter is Professor of Political Science and Comparative Fascism at the Free University of Berlin. In 1977–8 he was a Kennedy Research Fellow, Harvard University, and in 1980–81 Visiting Professor at The Johns Hopkins University, Bologna Center, Italy. Professor Falter's most recent major publications are: *Zur Kausalanalyse qualitativer Daten* (with Kurt Ulbricht) (Frankfurt/Berne, 1982); *Der 'Positivismusstreit' in der amerikanischen Politikwissenschaft* (Opladen: 1982); *Politische Willensbildung und Interessenvermittlung* (ed. with Christian Fenner and Michael Th. Greven) (Opladen: 1984); and *Wahlen und Abstimmungen in der Weimarer Republik* (Munich: 1985).

Conan J. Fischer is a Lecturer in History at Heriot-Watt University, Edinburgh. He is the author of *Stormtroopers: A Social, Economic and Ideological Analysis 1929–35* (London: 1983), and of various articles on Nazism and Communism in interwar Germany. Dr Fischer is currently writing a history of Communist–Nazi relations during the Weimar era.

Karin Hausen is Professor of Economic and Social History at the Technische Universität, Berlin. She has published on the history of German colonialism, the history of technology, and on family and women's history; she is also editor of *Frauen suchen ihre Geschichte* (Munich, 1983).

Michael H. Kater has been Professor of History at York University in Toronto since 1973, and in 1985–6 was Visiting Professor of the History of Medicine at McMaster University, Hamilton. His main research interest is the social history of modern Germany. Recently he has moved into the area of German medical history in the nineteenth and twentieth centuries. He has published numerous articles and books, his latest monograph being *The Nazi Party: A Social Portrait of Members and Leaders, 1919–1933* (Cambridge, Mass: 1983). Professor Kater is presently working on a book about physicians in the Third Reich.

John A. Moses is Associate Professor of History at the University of Queensland. Dr Moses has published extensively in the fields of German colonial history in the Pacific, German historiography, and chiefly in German labour history, and is the author of *Trade Unionism in Germany from Bismarck to Hitler, 1869–1933* (2 vols, London/New York, 1982). He is currently preparing a study of the trade union policy of the German Communist Party (KPD) 1919–33.

Dietmar Petzina is Professor of Social and Economic History at the Ruhr University, Bochum. He is the author of many articles on modern German social and economic history, and his most recent books include: *Konjunktur, Krise, Gesellschaft. Wirtschaftliche Wechsellagen und soziale Entwicklung im 19. und 20. Jahrhundert* (ed. with Ger van Roon) (Stuttgart, 1981); *Deutsche Wirtschaftsgeschichte im Industriezeitalter. Konjunktur, Krise, Wachstum* (ed. with Werner Abelshauser, 1981); and *Wirtschaftspolitik im britischen Besatzungsgebiet 1945–1949* (ed. with W. Euchner, 1984).

Michael Schneider is on the academic staff of the Friedrich-Ebert-Stiftung in Bonn. He has published widely in German trade union and labour history and his recent books are: *Aussperrung. Ihre Geschichte und Funktion vom Kaiserreich bis heute* (Cologne, 1980); *Die Christlichen Gewerkschaften 1894–1933* (Bonn: 1982); and *Streit um Arbeitszeit. Geschichte des Kampfes um Arbeitszeitverkürzung in Deutschland* (Cologne: 1984).

Peter D. Stachura is Reader in History at the University of Stirling. He has published extensively on the history of the Youth Movement in Germany, the Weimar era, and the development of National Socialism. Dr Stachura's books include, most recently: *The German Youth Movement 1900–1945. An Interpretative and Documentary History* (London: 1981); *Gregor Strasser and The Rise of Nazism* (London: 1983); and *The Nazi Machtergreifung* (ed.) (London: 1983). He is presently completing a monograph on the social and economic history of the younger generation in Weimar and Nazi Germany.

1 Introduction: The Development of Unemployment in Modern German History

Peter D. Stachura

In recent years mass unemployment has emerged as a leading social and economic problem and has been accorded, in consequence, the highest political priority in Western European countries. The issue has become the subject of extensive public debate, which is hardly surprising, given that in EEC countries unemployment has risen from a modest 2½ million on the eve of the 1973 oil crisis to over 12 million by the end of 1982, and then to nearer 14 million in 1985. But a curious dichotomy is to be observed: the existence of millions of jobless workers contrasts sharply with high levels of prosperity for many of those fortunate to be in full employment, and in view of the well-developed welfare support systems available in industrialised European nations, the discussion among public and politicians alike about the causes and possible remedies for unemployment have at times taken on a rather unreal flavour. Public concern apparently goes hand in hand with a considerable amount of toleration of the problem.

The length and severity of the current recession inevitably invites comparisons to be made with the Great Depression of the 1930s and the large-scale unemployment it produced, though most commentators agree that such comparisons can be taken only to a limited degree.[1] For instance, the jobless 50 years ago had nothing like the welfare and insurance support that is available in Western Europe nowadays, and while the problem of the 1980s came after almost 40 years of rising prosperity following the end of the Second World War, the Europe of the 1930s had barely recovered from the economic, political and international upheavals of the First World War. None the less, there is clearly some validity in the analogy, particularly when many of the basic social effects of mass unemployment are as intrinsically disturbing now as they were during the Depression. Now, as before, it is the long-term unemployed on whom most of the suffering falls. Not only does unemployment invariably result, despite welfare provision, in a lower standard of living for the worker and his family, it can also produce tensions in married and family life – hence the frequency of the breakup of homes in these circumstances – an acute loss of morale and self-esteem, a growing disinterest in work and atrophy of working skills, and feelings of resentment against society in general. Health can be adversely affected also, and there are often psychological problems to be confronted. Down the years unemployment has been linked to rising crime rates, especially in large industrial cities, civil unrest, political radicalism and racialism. The special situation of the young unemployed has attracted considerable interest, as it did in the 1930s.[2] Indeed, the response of governments at the present time to unemployment reveals a marked similarity in several respects to that during the Depression. In the Federal Republic of Germany, for example, among the schemes adopted since the mid-1970s, have been work-creation projects, vocational training and further education courses and amenities – mainly directed at younger people – curtailments in working hours in order to spread work among a larger number, reductions in civil service staff, and other public expenditure cuts. More modern measures have been introduced alongside these, of course, including investment and tax concessions for private companies, direct wage subsidies, and schemes to encourage greater regional mobility.[3] On a broader scale, many economists are convinced that there is only a certain amount any single national government can do to alleviate, let alone solve, unemployment, because of the world-wide nature of the current recession, and the close, complicated system of economic and financial interdependency among the industrial powers of the world: in the 1930s government spokesmen in many of the countries worst affected by unemployment made precisely this point in self-defence against mounting political criticism. Whatever the truth of this argument, there is no denying that the passage of time has not seriously diminished the complexity of the unemployment problem, and even if its social and political implications are not as drastic now as they used to be they remain pressing and just as demanding of energetic and constructive remedial action.[4]

Those attempting to come to terms with the phenomenon of unemployment are immediately faced with a definitional problem: what exactly is 'unemployment'? Definitions of the term, which itself did not come into general usage until the late nineteenth century, have varied considerably at different times and from one country to another, though it has come to be associated with industrial capitalist society in the modern era. But it covers a wide range of possibilities. For a start, Saitzew distinguishes between 'objective' unemployment, that is, unemployment brought about as a direct result of circumstances in the labour market, of a lack of available work, and 'subjective' unemployment, which is caused by a physical or mental inability to work, by an unwillingness to work despite being able-bodied, by a lack of necessity to work on account, perhaps, of private wealth, or by a number of other factors such as industrial action by one side or the other (strike, work-to-rule, lockout, dismissal).[5] This statement is helpful but is not meant to be a comprehensive definition.

The most easily identified and understood form is 'open' unemployment, where the jobless are visible and can be officially counted, but unemployment can just as easily be 'hidden' or 'invisible' and thus not revealed by official statistics – which, in any case, were somewhat deficient in most countries until the 1930s. Agriculture and related industries are traditionally characterised by this type of unemployment, which undoubtedly reached serious proportions in the interwar period. Also difficult to quantify is what might be termed a limited form of unemployment, namely, underemployment, where a worker is employed in a job for which he is overqualified, or where his labour is not as productive as it could be because of inadequate training or inefficient machinery. Closely analogous to this is short-time and temporary employment, where the worker is again under-utilised.

Prior to the period of rationalisation in industry during the mid-1920s in industrial Europe, unemployment was mainly of a cyclical nature: it was occasioned by the ups and downs of the business cycle, so that when depression set in, and demand for a particular product declined, the workers in the industry concerned could be laid off until an upturn in the cycle was forthcoming. In the 1920s, however, structural or technological unemployment, arising as a direct result of the replacement of labour by machines and mass production techniques, was added to cyclical unemployment. Not as serious is frictional unemployment, the period of idleness experienced by workers changing jobs with an unavoidable, if brief, time-lag involved. The perennial incidence of seasonal unemployment, however, comes into a different category. Due either to the seasonal nature of certain occupations, or to adverse weather conditions in winter months, workers in construction, catering, and agriculture were vulnerable. Superfluous labour was simply shed during periods of inactivity. Related to this type of unemployment was casual work, experienced by those unable or unwilling to hold down a regular job even if given the opportunity to do so. The existence of these two latter forms of joblessness was explained by Marx in *Das Kapital*: he was convinced that 'involuntary idleness' (*Unbeschäftigkeit*) was a permanent and inevitable feature of the industrial capitalist economic system, which needed 'a disposable industrial reserve army' of labour to be engaged or dismissed from employment according to prevailing circumstances at any time, thus allowing employers a free hand to pay low wages.[6] The existence of residual unemployment in every industrial society even during times of high and sustained growth seems to add weight to this argument, though perhaps it can be more straightforwardly accounted for by demographic influences: heavy population expansion at certain periods can produce a pool of labour in excess of the number of jobs available.[7]

The interwar years added several new dimensions to the nature of unemployment. For the first time then a large number of long-term jobless appeared – workers without employment for six months or more – a category which increased substantially during the Depression. Until the early 1920s unemployment had invariably been a short-term, temporary experience and one which, while uncomfortable enough, was not characterised by massive material deprivation, as happened in the 1930s. The class nature of unemployment also underwent significant change after 1918. No longer was unemployment more or less confined to the industrial proletariat, for sections of the white collar and artisanal middle classes also became affected in large numbers. The scale and intensity of unemployment during the Depression in Europe proved in this regard to be something of a social leveller. For the middle classes out of work there was not merely material loss to be confronted but also, and more importantly in the eyes of many of them, the loss of social status through the dreaded process of proletarianisation. In addition, what made unemployment so different during the 1930s was the unique coming together at the one time of many or all of the various types and characteristics of unemployment, which produced unprecedented numbers of jobless from both sexes and from all ages and social backgrounds.

Finally, the post-1918 era was notable for a widespread change of attitude on the part of governments and general public towards the plight and status of the unemployed, of whatever kind. Until a relatively late date in the nineteenth century, unemployment was usually seen in European society as an extirely personal and self-induced condition: an individual was out of work because of his own personal failings, and he was lumped together with sinners, miscreants and even criminals, in fact, part of the milieu of society. This view had been reinforced by the connection between unemployment and revolutionary disturbance in nineteenth-century Europe. Politically, unemployment seemed to play a not insignificant role in periodic challenges to established authority in various countries. In France, the unemployed had figured in the Revolutions of 1830 and 1848 (the 'June Days' and the National Workshops experiment) and later in the Paris Commune. The revolt of the Silesian weavers in 1844 was celebrated by Engels as heralding the beginning of a recognisable industrial proletariat that would threaten the status quo in Germany. On this sort of evidence it was easy for officials everywhere to denounce the unemployed as dangerous scoundrels. This ill-informed, negative outlook only began to change fundamentally once it became more widely recognised that industrialisation and the mechanics of capitalism created economic conditions over which the individual worker had no control: everyone was vulnerable to the vicissitudes of the business and trade cycles. The attendant large-scale social problems of urban industrial society which became more obvious in the second half of the century also helped to concentrate minds and change attitudes. Furthermore, the efforts of socialist and labour movements, as well as of social reformist circles, at last began to make a wider impact in many countries. By the 1880s, therefore, the beginnings of a more humane, sympathetic view of the jobless became discernible, though much uncertainty about how to deal with the causes and consequences of unemployment persisted. Schemes of work relief and the creation of labour colonies were tried out in a number of countries without noticeable success.[8] It took a while longer for the changing climate to produce substantive legislation offering a measure of protection to the unemployed. Britain took the initiative when she passed the Unemployed Workmen Act in 1905 which distinguished between those put out of work through no fault of their own, and those who were workshy. The National Labour Exchange Act followed four years later, and the National Insurance Act in 1911 which contained an element of unemployment insurance for workers in certain trades. Before the war labour exchange systems appeared in many countries to facilitate the placing of labour in employment and to make available up-to-date information about vacancies and training opportunities. Trade unions operated welfare services for jobless members. As in so many other social matters, the First World War exercised a decisive and benign influence on official attitudes to the jobless, and the postwar period saw governments creating comprehensive schemes of unemployment insurance. Germany was no exception in this respect.

Before 1914 attitudes in Germany to unemployment and the jobless followed the pattern set in the rest of industrial Europe, and a more informed appreciation of the problem emerged under the same social, economic and political influences that were changing views more generally. The shockwaves generated by the depression of the 1870s, when the numbers out of work in Germany increased substantially, and then the considerable social issues thrown up by the sheer pace of industrialisation and urbanisation compelled a degree of official rethinking. The connection between the occurrence of unemployment and recession could no longer be ignored.[9] The state had entered the sphere of social legislation in somewhat spectacular fashion – by contemporary standards – during Bismarck's chancellorship, but while legislation provided for sickness, accident, old age and invalidity insurance, unemployment was not covered. Those political and reformist groups who wanted unemployment included in the state social security edifice faced formidable opposition from the traditional liberal view of social affairs that self-help and not governmental intervention was the answer, and also from the vulgarised social Darwinist outlook which stressed 'the survival of the fittest': society, according to this harsh philosophy, was no place for the weak or unemployed. After all, it was argued, were there not schemes of poor relief administered by the churches and private bodies to which the jobless, like everyone else in need, could turn for assistance? However, the fact that the problem of unemployment had become an apparently permanent, rather than a diminishing, feature of modern industrial society convinced an ever-widening audience as time wore on of the need for special measures of relief.

The scale of the unemployment problem in Wilhelmine Germany is impossible to gauge precisely because there was not the machinery to collect reliable and comprehensive statistics. In view of the over-all expansion of the economy before 1890, it is certain that unemployment was then of little importance, but afterwards the often violent fluctuations in the business cycle did give rise at times to more serious numbers of jobless. The census conducted by the Reich Office of Statistics (the *Berufszählung*, or Occupational Census, of June 1895 and the *Volkszählung*, or Population Census, of December 1895) indicated an unemployment figure of just under 300 000 in mid-1895 and 771 000 at the end of the year.[10] This was the first set of statistics of unemployment on a national scale in Germany to be made available, though it was far from detailed and not entirely accurate. Only those jobless who fulfilled certain criteria were listed in the census: to be included a worker had to be physically fit, in need and in active pursuit of a job, and to have a previous record of regular employment. Whole categories of workers, those seeking their first job, those returning to the labour market after a prolonged absence (through illness, for example) and those changing jobs involving a time-lag, were not counted. Neither were those in 'hidden' unemployment or underemployment. Between 1895 and 1914 jobless statistics were provided by the trade unions, but they recorded only their own members who were out of work, and given that unionised workers constituted a mere 24 per cent of industrial workers as late as 1901,[11] the limitations of this source are obvious. Taking all factors into acount, the best-informed estimate of the average rate of unemployment in Germany 1890–1913 is around 3 per cent. During periods of cyclical depression, as in 1892–3, 1901 and 1908–9, the rate was probably closer to 6 or 7 per cent, with the textile and metal industries worst affected. In 1907–13, the rate dropped to between 1.2 and just over 3 per cent.[12] The network of locally organised Labour Exchanges (*Arbeitsnachweise*) which expanded after 1890, became even more useful in helping job-seeking workers when an umbrella body, the *Verband deutscher Arbeitsnachweise*, was established in 1898 to provide co-ordination throughout the country.[13]

It is interesting to note that whereas some trade unions set up reasonable unemployment relief schemes for their members before the war – thus during a time when unemployment was a relatively infrequent and transient condition for the average German worker – the Social Democratic Party (SPD) was ambivalent about the entire issue of unemployment and certainly did not share the opinion of a large cross-section of contemporary middle-class observers that the problem could provide the seed-bed for revolution. A basic reason for the party's approach was that the unemployed were usually drawn from sections of the male industrial working class not conspicuously represented in its membership. Older workers, very young unskilled, single and low-paid workers, and itinerant workers engaged in seasonal employment in catering, construction and agriculture – most of them non-unionised – constituted the bulk of the jobless.[14] In other words, the unemployed were usually not of that skilled and semi-skilled 'labour aristocracy', the politically-conscious groups of the proletariat, who came to predominate in the SPD before 1914; they came instead from the rough, non-respectable working class, a sort of sub-proletariat.[15] Consequently, unemployment was not a particularly urgent social or political concern for any established vested interest in the *Kaiserreich*, working class or not. For its part, the Reich government was likewise reluctant to become too involved, therefore, and refused to unequivocally commit itself in the debate about a national unemployment insurance scheme at that time. Despite a sudden upsurge in unemployment at the beginning of the First World War (it reached 22.4 per cent in August), the average low level of unemployment during the conflict ensured that the government's attitude held firm. There was no pressure to change. Only with Germany's defeat, the November Revolution, and the establishment of the Weimar Republic with which the SPD and labour movement were closely identified, did the question of unemployment policy come to the forefront of politics. The days of limited, short-term unemployment were over, now to be replaced in Germany and elsewhere in Europe by an era of mass and enduring unemployment. In these drastically changed circumstances the role of the state could no longer be peripheral.

The reversion to peacetime brought formidable tasks to all the former belligerent powers, but Germany was immediately more susceptible than others to the profound stresses that this metamorphosis inevitably entailed. The political unrest that persisted until 1923 made economic and social reconstruction all the more difficult to accomplish, especially also as it was to take place within the framework of a new state. Amidst the instability, however, there existed a powerful awareness on the moderate Left that the Republic should pursue an energetic *Sozialpolitik*. The SPD and trade unions, representing a majority of the working class, needed, for reasons of basic humanitarianism and of political credibility, to invest the state with a clear commitment to meaningful social welfare reform. An embryonic foundation for this endeavour had been laid during the war. It had seemed essential in the government's eyes to secure the support of organised labour and of the working class as a whole for the war effort, and to this end a series of measures to help the sick, elderly, widowed and the few unemployed were passed. More importantly, the unions were granted official status as negotiating partners by the 1916 Auxiliary Service Law (*Hilfsdienstgesetz*).[16] It was a limited but welcome step in the right direction, and consequently, the early years of the Republic were noteworthy for several reformative initiatives which improved the material conditions and standing of the working class. An auspicious beginning had been made by the inclusion in the Weimar Constitution of a clause (Article 163) guaranteeing the right of every German to work. The Constitution further accorded labour a new, enhanced status in the life of the nation, and stipulated that the state had a responsibility to look after and protect its working population. This was followed up by the introduction of the 8-hour working day, the Labour Law, which recognised the practice of collective bargaining, the Factory Council Law (*Betriebsrätegesetz*) regulating worker representation on the factory councils of private firms, and the creation of a system of state arbitration in wage disputes leading to binding settlement on both sides of industry. The state increased expenditure on housing, health and education, and old age, sickness and accident insurance benefits were raised. For the younger generation, the Republic adopted an unmistakably enlightened attitude, which was epitomised by the passing in 1922 of the National Youth Welfare Act (*Reichsjugendwohlfahrtsgesetz*).[17] Even if in the event the practical implementation of these measures did not satisfy certain sections of the working class,[18] the good intentions which lay behind them are not in doubt. There is no denying either that at the heart of this over-all advance in social legislation lay the question of the state's responsibility for the unemployed, which was brought sharply into focus by the process of demobilisation in 1918–19.

The homecoming of millions of soldiers occasioned an acute crisis of unemployment for the fledgling Republic. In December 1918, 5.4 million were out of work, a figure that rose to 6.6 million the following month. The government was understandably alarmed and acted swiftly to bring the situation under control. Considerable funds were allotted to industry for work creation, incentive schemes for employers to rehire soldiers formerly in their employ were set up, and a special office was created to co-ordinate the payment of unemployment relief. A crucial additional factor helping the government was the inflationary trend of the early 1920s. As a result, the jobless figures tumbled to 620 000 in June 1919, to 370 000 in March 1920, and to a mere 150 000 in late 1921. Compared with Britain and the United States, Germany's drive to overcome early postwar unemployment was spectacularly successful, if shortlived, for with the onset of hyper-inflation in 1922–3, and the complications arising from the political situation at home and abroad (right-wing and Communist risings, Ruhr occupation), unemployment shot up once again. Between November 1922 and November 1923 it rose from 2 per cent to over 23 per cent, while an even larger number of workers were put on short-time.[19] The Republic came close to economic and political collapse, but decisive steps to end the campaign of passive resistance in the Ruhr, and to stabilise the currency through the creation of the *Rentenmark*, restored equilibrium, which was further consolidated by the Dawes Plan to ease reparation payments. Unemployment levels returned to pre-1922–23 levels, in consequence, and between April 1924 and October 1925 averaged under 5 per cent. But by that latter date long-term unemployment for those willing and able to work had already become for the first time in German history a permanent feature of the labour market: there were 195 000 unemployed in this category.[20] For them unemployment signified a protracted period of real material want, for the traditional institutional and personal support systems could not provide sufficient cover or protection. Further evidence of this developing trend in unemployment was furnished by the severe recession in winter 1925–26 when a relatively high percentage of the $2\frac{1}{4}$ million jobless had been out of work for a lengthy time.[21]

For many of those campaigning for the state to finally set up a national relief scheme for the unemployed, an added imperative came in the shape of the intensive process of rationalisation in German big industry in the mid-1920s – the drive by employers, encouraged by the American example, to eliminate uneconomic plant and promote all-round efficiency, and increase productivity through the introduction of modern machinery and technology (including the conveyor belt) and the standardisation of production and finishing procedures. Labour, including highly skilled blue collar and white collar workers in older trades, became more expendable than before. The only rising demand here was for cheap, unskilled female workers. Rationalisation created yet another new form of unemployment – structural unemployment, which for those affected often meant an extended period out of work. Radical leftist writers referred to a 'new quality' of unemployment – a type caused by a planned offensive by capitalism. None the less, both the SPD and trade unions accepted rationalisation and its labour consequences as the necessary price to pay for maintaining Germany's competitiveness in world markets.[22]

By the mid-1920s there was more unanimity than at any time previously in government, and among the public at large, about the requirement for measures to deal effectively with the social implications of unemployment. The question of a state-sponsored national insurance scheme for the jobless, which had been the subject of discussion since before the war, could hardly be postponed any longer. The state, of course, had not been entirely inactive in this general sphere since the end of the war. In 1919 it had taken over the network of labour exchanges that had developed since the 1890s and in 1922 the Labour Exchange Act set up labour exchanges in all localities under public control. In the early postwar era, also, the state had passed legislation relating to unemployment relief, beginning during the demobilisation process and followed by the *Verordnung über Erwerbslosenfürsorge* in February 1924.[23] This created a very modest form of state aid, though applicants had to undergo a means test. The principal source of support for the jobless still remained the unions and local welfare agencies. Draft plans for a comprehensive national scheme had been drawn up by government since 1919 but they had all run up against opposition of one kind or another. In September 1925, however, the Reich Labour Ministry finally produced the blueprint of a plan which formed the essential basis of what was to be approved by the Reichstag nearly two years later. The Law Concerning Labour Exchanges and Unemployment Insurance (*Gesetz über Arbeitsvermittlung und Arbeitsversicherung*, abbreviated to AVAVG) of 7 July 1927 was widely acclaimed as the crowning glory of the Weimar Republic's social welfare policy.[24]

The Act, which took effect in October 1927, combined a series of innovations with elements already established by previous legislation in this field. Thus, the establishment of an independent, central body – the *Reichsanstalt* – to co-ordinate the nationwide system of local labour exchanges, was a logical extension of the 1922 Labour Exchange Act. The *Reichsanstalt*'s creation now made it possible to collect reliable data on unemployment for the first time in Germany. Moreover, while the Act linked compulsory contributions (payable by those insured against sickness) to unemployment insurance and the *right* to benefit irrespective of any other means of support, provided the worker was able and willing to work and had been made redundant through no fault of his own, claimants had to have made contributions for at least 26 weeks during the preceding year. Employers and workers contributed equally to the fund – about 3 per cent of average earnings. The weekly-paid benefits, which became payable following a waiting period of between 3 and 14 days after application, were granted for a maximum of 26 weeks, with further extension to 39 weeks possible in exceptional circumstances, usually long-term unemployment. The level of benefit was determined for each worker according to a rather complicated system of wage categories, previous wage level, number and age of dependants, marital status, gender, and type of locality in which resident: on average between 35 per cent and 75 per cent of a claimant's previous wage was paid in benefit, plus 5 per cent family supplement if applicable. Some 17 million workers were covered by AVAVG, but not included were agricultural, fishing and forestry workers, casual workers, domestic piecetime workers, and certain categories of apprentices. Indeed, the Act was not particularly generous in its treatment of workers under 21 years of age.

The scheme was designed to accommodate a maximum of 800 000 unemployed on average per year, a not unreasonable figure at a time of relative economic and labour market stability. When benefits ran out for the unemployed worker and he was still without a job, there was a second fallback position for him to turn to in the form of Emergency Aid (*Krisenfürsorge*), which was set up in November 1926. It was granted for up to 32 weeks, with a possible extension to 45 weeks in certain cases; benefits were paid at a lower level than unemployment insurance and only after a means test had been applied to claimants. Finally, when both these forms of aid had been exhausted, the unemployed had recourse to a third tier of support, parish-administered poor relief; benefit was paid at a level regardless of former wage or job and was just sufficient to sustain the bare essentials of life. In some areas the able-bodied jobless had to perform work in return for assistance. All things considered, the schemes of aid available to the unemployed after 1927 were welcomed as signifying advancement for the cause of social justice. Unfortunately, AVAVG had hardly become operational when changing economic circumstances and pressure from powerful interest groups such as the big industrial employers made it liable to important amendment.

Seasonal factors explained to a large extent the 1 896 274 jobless in winter 1927–8, most of whom drew unemployment insurance benefit,[25] thus putting the kind of pressure on AVAVG it was not designed to have. Even more demand was exerted on the system the following winter when around 3 million were officially registered as out of work. In an attempt to bring revenue more into line with expenditure under AVAVG the government passed amendments to the law in December 1928 and October 1929 which, on the one hand, reduced the period of support for workers in occupations badly affected by seasonal unemployment to a mere 6 weeks, and on the other, reorganised the machinery to promote efficiency and eliminate abuses. Even before the advent of sustained mass unemployment after 1929, therefore, the advantages of AVAVG had been visibly eroded.[26]

Although 1926–8 was a period of general economic recovery in Germany, marked by an increase in average real wages and a reduction in working hours, the problems of a labour market already coping with the impact of rationalisation and the expansion of female employment were compounded by demographic changes caused by the high prewar birth rate. Hence more workers joined the labour pool. These developments obviously carried important implications for both the unemployment situation and AVAVG, and also for the political balance in government. The continuing financial difficulties of the Reich in 1929–30 inevitably generated disagreements within the Hermann Müller-led Grand Coalition about how to make further changes to AVAVG that would bring the unemployment insurance into line with what the government felt was affordable. Matters finally came to a head in March 1930, when the registered jobless was 3 million. The collapse of the coalition was ultimately occasioned, of course, by the irreconcilable views of the German People's Party (DVP), acting under the influence of its big business wing, and the SPD, striving to uphold the basis of Weimar's *Sozialpolitik*, over the future method of funding AVAVG.[27] The Depression had claimed its first important political victim. More ominously, with Müller's successor as Chancellor, Dr Heinrich Brüning unable to command a working majority in the Reichstag, government had to rely on the emergency powers granted President von Hindenburg under Article 48 of the Constitution. Parliamentary democracy was pushed aside, never to return. The onset of the Depression in Germany coincided, therefore, with a decisive swing towards political authoritarianism. The implications for social welfare soon became clear.

The Great Depression was the severest economic crisis ever experienced by modern captitalist society, and in no other European country were the wider social and political consequences more devastating than in Weimar Germany.[28] Here it was an unprecedented catastrophe from virtually every standpoint, at the centre of which stood the problem of mass unemployment. The German economy had enjoyed only a very limited recovery on insecure foundations during the 1920s. High interest rates at home led to an overdependence on short-term capital investment from abroad, principally the United States, and because of the considerable importance of exports to the economy the decline in world trade affected Germany rather badly: the value of her exports fell further after 1929. International obligations, especially reparations payments, the significant international influence over the *Reichsbank*, and the deep-rooted fear in government of inflation after the experience of 1923, all combined to exercise an adverse material and psychological effect on Germany's financial system which came to the brink of total collapse in 1931.[29] The intrinsic health of the economy had never been restored since the end of the First World War, and already by 1929 the fluctuating unemployment rates, declining level of investment in industry, and the crisis in agriculture were graphic indications of inherent weaknesses in the economy. After the Wall Street crash, the hasty and large-scale withdrawal of foreign capital, the rapid contraction of industrial production, and a substantial decline in demand at home and abroad, produced a three-dimensional crisis of epic proportions in Germany: industry, agriculture and finance all nosedived at more or less the same time, piling social, economic and political problems on top of one another. From an international perspective, the Depression emphasised the seriousness of the so-called 'German problem' that had arisen after 1918, for the course and outcome of the crisis in Germany sooner or later profoundly affected the rest of Europe, and beyond, as well.

Among Europe's industrial powers, Germany was the hardest hit by unemployment in both absolute and proportionate terms.[30] It lasted longer, and for a larger number of people, than elsewhere in Europe, and only the United States fared worse. The registered number of unemployed rose from 1.6 million in October 1929 to 6.13 million at the highpoint of the Depression in Germany in February 1932, meaning about one-third of the working-age population. In January 1933, as Hitler was on the threshold of power, the figure was still 6 million. There were also the 'invisible' unemployed in sectors such as agriculture, those who did not bother to register because their period of entitlement to benefit had elapsed, and those who were excluded from receiving benefit following successive changes to the rules (various categories of female workers and younger workers, for instance): altogether these groups amounted to between one million and three million additional unemployed, giving a total in 1932 of seven to nine million.[31] Moreover, there were approximately 400 000 itinerant jobless at that time. When the dependants of the unemployed are taken into account it can be appreciated that a very substantial proportion – some 23.3 million or 36 per cent – of the German population was directly hit by the ravages of unemployment.[32] The longer a person was out of work the more difficult it became to re-enter employment, either because his attitude to work had changed or, if this had not been adversely affected, because his skills had been blunted, lost or outdated during the layoff period. Alongside 'open' and 'hidden' unemployment, Germany had extensive under-employment and short-time working in the early 1930s, and for those in work there was the all-pervasive fear of being made redundant.

The reasons why Germany's unemployment was greater than that in other European countries are not to be found exclusively in the severe nature of the Depression. She had traditionally a higher rate of seasonal unemployment because of the magnitude of her agrarian sector and her harsh winters: the construction industry was a major casualty. Germany's labour pool had expanded during the 1920s due to high prewar birthrates and female employment, which was proportionately larger than elsewhere in Europe. Also, there was a carryover into the early 1930s of long-term structural unemployed, who in December 1929 constituted 12.8 per cent and in September 1931 20.3 per cent of the registered jobless.[33] No other European industrial economy had this type of unemployment on such a scale. In short, it was a unique combination of both long- and short-term factors which produced Germany's extraordinary levels of unemployment.

Germany in the early 1930s presented a picture of unremitting social and economic gloom, a society characterised by long dole queues outside the labour office (*Stempelstelle*) and groups of shabbily dressed, sullen men hanging about street corners. The Depression was no respecter of class barriers: all sections of society were caught up in the unemployment vortex. The 'old and 'new' *Mittelstand*, the white collar employees, small businessmen and farmers, the professional groups, and others, experienced considerable hardship and loss of status.[34] But the bulk of the misery fell on the industrial proletariat, particularly in the heavily industrialised regions of the country – in the Ruhr, Rhineland, Berlin, Brandenburg, Saxony and Silesia. In 1932, 44.3 per cent of registered unemployed lived in the 50 largest towns and cities.[35] Mainly agricultural areas such as East Prussia, Pomerania, Bavaria, and especially Württemberg, escaped comparatively lightly. The worst affected sectors of the economy were the metal, mining, timber, textile and construction industries. Older, as well as younger, single, and unskilled workers were more vulnerable to dismissal than most, and a large majority in all categories of unemployed were males.[36]

The immiseration of the industrial proletariat, and especially of the vast numbers of jobless among them, was deep and comprehensive. The extensive data relating to declining income, food consumption, clothing standards, indebtedness, and health, permits no other conclusion. Family tensions and marital problems, rising criminality, suicides, and increases in mental and psychological problems were the result; widespread despair, hopelessness and angry resentment was the reaction.[37] For those workers still in employment the balance of power shifted inevitably in favour of the employers, particularly as opposition from the debilitated trade union movement was ineffective.[38] For some time before the Depression, the big industrialists and landowners, the backbone of traditional right-wing politics, had been determined to roll back the social and welfare gains of the early 1920s. The Depression afforded them a golden opportunity to dismiss shopfloor militants, reduce wages to below the legal minimum on many occasions, abolish bonus schemes, neglect working conditions, and extend working hours. Despite these developments, and a remarkable reflection of the reality of the capital–labour power relationship, was the steep decline in the number of workers involved in strikes 1930–32.[39] The onslaught of the employers, however, did nothing to heal the deep divisions that had existed in the German working class since the beginning of the Weimar Republic over socioeconomic and political priorities. Indeed, the Depression deepened these rifts by dividing the working class into the employed and unemployed, a development of telling significance for working-class politics in general, and the respective constituencies of the SPD and German Communist Party (KPD) in particular.[40]

Whatever the pros and cons of the recently revived controversy over Brüning's policies,[41] there is no doubt that his deflationary strategy, in which the aims of balancing the budget and protecting large-scale agriculture (*Osthilfe*) at home, and of seeking a final solution to the reparations problem in foreign affairs, took top priority, intensified the economic and financial crisis, and thus also the social distress and political instability. The policy of increasing taxes and duties, reducing wages, salaries and other areas of public expenditure meant that no effective checks, not to mention solutions, to mass unemployment were forthcoming from government. Brüning did not accept that a deficit-financed work-creation programme, for example, would materially improve the jobless situation, but more to the point, he was more concerned that a scheme of this type would prove inflationary and hence wreck his resolve to balance the budget at all costs. Recovery and the easing of unemployment, he was convinced, was not a matter primarily for the state but for the private sector of the economy. Above all else, Brüning's approach ensured that the welfare system, constructed in the 1920s largely to protect the working class, would, in conjunction with the actions of employers previously referred to, be systematically dismantled as the Depression wore on: by 1932 it was but a pale shadow of its former self. The disintegration of Weimar's *Sozialpolitik* was epitomised by the fate of the unemployment insurance system.

As the number out of work soared after 1930 and contributors to AVAVG plummeted, the system had to give way in the absence of governmental intervention. What Brüning did do was to change the rules of entitlement, the level of benefit, and the period during which benefit was paid through a succession of amendments incorporated in emergency decrees 1930–32.[42] Seasonal and agricultural workers, domestic servants, and many categories of female and younger workers were eliminated from entitlement by mid-1932, the level of benefit was substantially reduced, and the time for which it was granted was finally cut from 26 to 6 weeks. During the same period the level of contributions doubled. Worst of all, perhaps, was the reintroduction for all claimants of eligibility assessment (*Hilfsbedürfsigkeit*) in place of the legally guaranteed right to benefit. The fundamental principle on which AVAVG had been originally built was thus broken. The outcome was that as more and more unemployed were debarred from benefit, emergency aid and poor relief were left to bear the brunt of their welfare support: by late 1932 AVAVG catered for only a small minority of the jobless. Both the Emergency Aid and poor relief schemes were also drastically scaled down, and because of the numerous restrictions and exclusions a considerable percentage of the unemployed were receiving no support of any kind during the last six months of the Republic.[43]

The prodigious material deprivation created by mass unemployment during the Depression was bound to contribute to political unrest and the rise of extremism on the Left and Right. This is not to say that all the unemployed took to the streets in violent political or paramilitary protest: many did, but others slumped into an attitude of despairing apathy – the Marienthal syndrome, it might be called.[44] This is not the place to delve into the relationship between unemployment and the emergence of the National Socialists and KPD as powerful forces in Weimar politics. What can be said with certainty, however, is that from whatever perspective it is viewed, the cardinal importance of mass unemployment to the history and eventual failure of the Republic is undeniable. This basic fact provides the *raison d'être* of the present volume of essays.

The contributions presented here are not meant to provide a comprehensive history or analysis of unemployment during the Depression in Germany. There are aspects of the problem which are obviously not dealt with, such as the attitude of the major churches and some of the leading political parties. Neither does the volume attempt to pursue a conceptual uniformity or methodological consistency: it includes a variety of different approaches to the central theme, mass unemployment and the social and political responses it stimulated among social groups, the main totalitarian movements, the trade unions and government. However, a central feature of all contributions is the acceptance of a deep relationship between social, economic and political influences and developments, using this basis to explain the problem of unemployment in the Weimar Republic. By probing in this manner it is hoped that a clearer understanding of a crucial issue in one of the most turbulent periods in modern German and European history will emerge.

In the opening essay Professor Petzina is primarily concerned with an analysis of the fundamental causes of German unemployment. He adduces the paradigm of reconstruction as a more convincing means of explaining the inherent crisis nature of the economy than the more popular theories of stagnation. Accordingly, he argues, the 1924–9 period was one of 'unfulfilled' reconstruction during which a variety of factors, but especially the modest volume of investment in industry and agriculture, conspired to push up levels of unemployment. The lack of investment can be attributed to particular circumstances in the national and international financial and economic systems over which successive German governments were unable to exercise significant influence. The detrimental implications of low investment for the labour market were compounded by the rationalisation process in industry and by a demographically-inspired expansion of the pool of workers before 1931–2. In other words, concludes Petzina, structural and cyclical unemployment combined with a labour surplus to produce millions of jobless in the early 1930s.

The ubiquitous impact of the Depression on Weimar society makes it appropriate to examine in some detail how particular social groups were affected. This forms the underlying theme of the contributions by Michael Kater, Karin Hausen and Peter Stachura. The increasingly difficult position of an important middle-class professional group, medical doctors, is explained by Professor Kater. Problems relating to increases in the number of practitioners and the consequences of this for income levels – a situation which quickly took on the appearance of a generational conflict between older, established doctors and younger, newly-qualified ones – were exacerbated by the onset of the Depression and the spectre of unemployment. Before 1933, therefore, many doctors, unhappy with their financial status and career prospects,and resentful of the sociopolitical climate of the Republic, had gravitated towards National Socialism.

Difficulties of a rather different kind – those encountered by working women – form the subject of Professor Hausen's paper. The large-scale employment of German women in the 1920s generated tensions at home, in the workplace and in society at large, especially during periods of high unemployment, thus putting severe pressure on them. They had to cope not only with social prejudice, but also with mounting discrimination in the labour market and threats to the integrity of family life. The Depression only made the situation worse because traditional views in society that the 'proper' place for women was at home with her family were reinforced, while campaigns against 'double earners' (*Doppelverdiener*) were stepped up. Even the unemployment insurance scheme was not applied fairly to women. Taking all of these factors into account, Professor Hausen concludes, women were hit just as harshly as men during the early 1930s, albeit in different ways.

Another section of Weimar society in crisis, the younger generation, is analysed by Dr Stachura, with particular reference to the marked vulnerability of industrial working-class youth to unemployment during a period of radical cutbacks in welfare provision for them. The social consequences during the Depression were deeply disturbing: rising levels of juvenile delinquency and criminality, a steep increase in suicides, deteriorating health and educational standards, vagrancy, vice and the appearance of scruffy street-gangs, all testified to the increasingly desperate situation of youth. Both the middle- and working-class young lost hope in the future and often drifted out of the mainstream of society. The theme of *Jugendverwahrlosung* (waywardness) was widely debated by shocked contemporaries, and the attraction which many younger Germans developed for political extremism before 1933 was regrettable but not entirely surprising in these circumstances.

Two themes raised by Stachura regarding the younger generation, namely, the nature of official and institutional reaction to mass unemployment, and the links between large numbers of jobless and the growth of political radicalism in the Depression, are discussed in their broader context by the remaining contributions in this book.

Turning to the first of these themes, John Moses examines the response of the free trade union movement (ADGB) to the problem of mass unemployment. The pragmatic, non-revolutionary attitude to economic and social matters of the union leadership from the beginning of the Weimar Republic, and how this approach influenced the ADGB's handling of the unemployment issue in the 1930s, is fully analysed. Having failed to protect the unemployment insurance system from savage governmental cuts, the ADGB then addressed itself to the question of job creation, producing the famous WTB-Plan (Woytinsky, Tarnow and Baade) in 1932. Unable to secure the co-operation of Chancellor Brüning or his successors, however, the union, already badly weakened by loss of members and funds, could merely look on helplessly at the army of unemployed as the Republic moved towards final disaster.

Picking up the question of job creation during the Depression, Michael Schneider offers a detailed assessment of the role of government from Brüning to Hitler in this sphere. While acknowledging that Brüning had to operate under a number of important constraints, including a legacy from previous administrations of restrictive economic and financial policies, prevailing conservative concepts of economic policy, and reparations – plus the fact that he was confronted by a crisis of unparalleled severity – Dr Schneider is none the less critical of the Chancellor's traditionalist adherence to the primacy of foreign policy which, after all, resulted in a disastrous insensitivity to the wider implications of his deflationary policies at home. Although the Depression and unemployment were by no means the only factors that caused the Republic to fall, Brüning's lack of serious interest in job creation only gave comfort to the anti-democratic political extremists. His successors, Papen and Schleicher, on the other hand, did pay more attention to job creation and between them laid the foundations for initiatives subsequently taken by Hitler after 1933. Ironically, therefore, it was the National Socialists who derived political benefit from schemes that might have helped stabilise the Republic.

The growing threat of political radicalism to the Republic was exemplified, of course, by the spectacular rise in electoral popularity of the National Socialists and Communists. It is the specific relationship between mass unemployment and the unemployed, and political extremism, in 1929–33 that is scrutinised by Jürgen Falter. He applies to available aggregate data on electoral behaviour bivariate correlation analysis as well as more sophisticated statistical models, including multiple and pooled regression analysis. Ecological regression techniques are also used to produce more refined conclusions about individual and group voter responses. On the basis of significant determinant variables, such as religion, urbanisation, and the class nature of unemployment, Professor Falter produces a series of conclusions which, while confirming a number of established general notions about the relationship between unemployment and the Nazi Party (NSDAP) and KPD, offers a remarkable degree of specification and differentiation. Mass unemployment, he argues, did contribute to the NSDAP's electoral success, but only indirectly: that is, the Party benefited from the fear and despair induced by the threat, not the reality, of unemployment among those from a conservative, right-wing political background who had lost confidence in the traditional nationalist parties.

The final contribution by Conan Fischer evaluates the complex causal link between unemployment and the KPD during the early 1930s. Focusing initially on the different ways historians have understood the impact of unemployment on the feelings and outlook of individuals, he then proceeds to an analysis of the nature and extent of the KPD's appeal to the jobless, particularly those of the younger generation, who constituted the bulk of its membership. While agreeing with the conventional view that the KPD benefited considerably from the large pool of young, working-class unemployed, Dr Fischer argues further that working-class unemployment also helped the NSDAP. Indeed, there was a process of drift from one side to the other, especially in 1932, of which the NSDAP was the principal beneficiary, and the trend was accelerated after Hitler was in power. Fischer concludes, therefore, that the political radicalism of the young working-class jobless was intense, but not rooted in ideological conviction. As free floaters, so to speak, they represented a new and distinctive type of political radicalism.

From these essays it can be readily appreciated that mass unemployment and its myriad social and political ramifications was a crucial factor in the historical process that eventually destroyed the Weimar Republic and made possible the establishment of the Third Reich. It gnawed away at Germany's social fabric, undermining relations between different sections of the population, destroyed confidence in the present and hope for the future and promoted political extremism. Few other single factors in Weimar's tortured history can claim to have had such a devastating impact.

Finally, it would be appropriate, perhaps, to conclude with a few words about the treatment of the unemployment problem following the National Socialist *Machtergreifung*. Before 1933 the NSDAP had made a good deal of noisy propaganda about the need to restore 'Work and Bread' to the millions of unemployed, and Gregor Strasser's widely-noticed speech on this theme in the Reichstag in May 1932 certainly appeared to underline the Party's serious commitment in this sphere. Yet neither Strasser nor anyone else in the Party had formulated a carefully thought-out, comprehensive policy on unemployment: after all, the *Sofortprogramm* hardly came into this category.[45] There was merely generalised support for work-creation schemes and the concept of labour service, with which Konstantin Hierl was identified. Having come into power, however, the NSDAP was immediately compelled, for reasons of political expediency if nothing else, to give urgent attention to the problem. During the course of 1933 Hitler emphasised in a series of speeches his concern to solve unemployment which would come about, he was convinced, not only through state intervention but also through the efforts of private enterprise and, equally important, 'the originality of the German people'.[46] None the less, state deficit-spending on a massive scale was channelled into the public and private sectors in different ways and with remarkable success, for unemployment dropped from 6 million in January 1933 to 3 714 000 in November 1933, 2 226 000 in October 1934, 1 876 000 in June 1935, 1 035 000 in September 1936, and a mere 469 000 in September 1937.[47] By the latter date, therefore, Hitler had eradicated the scourge of unemployment – the 'First German Economic Miracle' (*Wirtschaftswunder*), according to one historian.[48] After 1937–8 the regime was faced with a shortage of labour.

The efficacy of particular measures to relieve unemployment is still a matter for considerable debate among historians, especially as the decline in the number of jobless was not as rapid or dramatic as might seem at first sight from the figures. There were ups and downs between 1933 and 1936, though the over-all trend was clear. Only in mid-1936 did unemployment finally fall below the level of 1928–9. How important were each of the major elements in the regime's campaign against unemployment?

The so-called *Reinhardt-Programm* of public works, which was sanctioned by the Law to Reduce Unemployment (June 1933), spearheaded the state's direct contribution to the 'Battle for Work' and essentially involved expanding schemes originating with the Papen and Schleicher administrations.[49] It was soon followed by *Landdienst* (service in the countryside) for younger workers under the direction of the Hitler Youth, the broadly similar *Landhilfe* (Rural Aid) and *Landjahr*, and then Labour Service (*Reichsarbeitsdienst*), which was made compulsory in 1935. The impact of such schemes on the over-all jobless figures should not be overestimated, though they did contribute quite significantly in conjunction with the low birth rates of the First World War to the relatively sharp drop in youth unemployment by 1935.[50] Also a limited success was the campaign to push female workers out of the labour market through an odd mixture of propaganda (against 'double earners' and for *Kinder*, *Küche*, *Kirche*) and bribery in the shape of state marriage loans and other financial baits. Before long, and particularly after the inauguration of the Four Year Plan, women workers actually increased in number with encouragement from the state in view of labour shortages.[51] The much-vaunted construction of new motorways and improvements to the road and canal network as a whole absorbed fewer workers than National Socialist propaganda claimed: 85 000 in 1934 and 130 000 in 1936.[52] On the other hand, it does appear that the expanding state and party bureaucracy after 1933 did bring relatively large numbers, predominantly male, into employment.[53] The state's assistance to private industry included, apart from political and moral support, generous tax incentives, loans and flexible credit arrangements, direct wage subsidies, contracts, wage controls, and special regional aid policies, though these must be balanced against the upturn in the business cycle which first appeared in late 1932 and continued more or less until the recession in 1938. The most important aid to industry, however, was the state's subjugation and then regimentation of the labour force, many of whom experienced low standards of living in 1933–6.

When all the evidence is reviewed, it is difficult not to conclude that the primary factor which substantially reduced unemployment came from the military sphere, in two connected ways: through the introduction of universal male conscription in March 1935, which took about one million off the unemployment rolls within two years and, simultaneously, through the relatively large-scale programme of rearmament and the resultant expansion, in particular, of the iron, steel and chemical industries.[54] This interpretation can be supported by considerable statistical data, and it also fits very well into the wider context of the nature of the Third Reich, that of an aggressively militaristic regime aiming for wholesale territorial expansionism by force of arms and ultimately world domination. Hitler's solution of Germany's unemployment problem, therefore, was motivated by evil, not by genuine social, or humanitarian, considerations, and involved through the Second World War the highest possible price for Germans and non-Germans.

Notes

1. Cf. Christian Saint-Etienne, *The Great Depression, 1929–1938: Lessons for the 1980s* (Stanford, 1984); Hermann Van der Wee (ed.), *The Great Depression Revisited. Essays on the Economics of the Thirties* (The Hague, 1972); Mark Casson, *Economics of Unemployment: an historical perspective* (London; 1983); A. Steinherr, *The Great Depression. A Repeat in the 1980s* (Brussels, 1982); Jeremy Seabrook, 'Unemployment Now and in the 1930s', in Bernard Crick (ed.), *Unemployment* (London,

1981), pp. 7–15; Karl Holl (ed.), *Wirtschaftskrise und liberale Demokratie. Das Ende der Weimarer Republik und die gegenwärtige Situation* (Göttingen, 1978), Introduction.

2. Organisation for Economic Co-operation and Development, *Youth Unemployment. The Causes and Consequences* (Paris, 1980); Mark Casson, *Youth Unemployment* (London, 1979); T. L. Rees and P. Atkinson (eds), *Youth Unemployment and State Intervention* (London, 1982); Hans-Christian Harten, *Jugendarbeitslosigkeit in der EG* (Frankfurt, 1983); Michael P. Jackson, *Youth Unemployment* (London, 1985).
3. Douglas Webber and Gabriele Nass, 'Employment Policy in West Germany' in Jeremy Richardson and Roger Henning (eds), *Unemployment. Policy Responses of Western Democracies* (London, 1984) pp. 167–92.
4. Adrian Sinfield, *What Unemployment Means* (Oxford, 1981); Bill Jordan, *Mass Unemployment and The Future of Britain* (Oxford, 1982); Edmond Malinuaud, *Mass Unemployment* (Oxford, 1984).
5. Manuel Saitzew (ed.), *Die Arbeitslosigkeit der Gegenwart*, Erster Teil (Munich, 1932) pp. 10ff.
6. David McLellan, *The Thought of Karl Marx. An Introduction* (New York, 1974) pp. 73f.
7. John A. Garraty, *Unemployment in History. Economic Thought and Public Policy* (New York, 1978) p. 6ff.
8. Ibid., pp. 119f, 129f.
9. Paul Berndt, *Die Arbeitslosigkeit. Ihre Bekämpfung und Statistik* (Halle, 1899) p. 33; John Schikowski, *Über Arbeitslosigkeit und Arbeitslosenstatistik* (Leipzig, 1894) pp. 20ff.
10. Kaiserliches Statistisches Amt, *Die beschäftigungslosen Arbeitnehmer im Deutschen Reich* (Berlin, 1896). Only from the date of this census did the term *Arbeitslosigkeit* become commonly used in Germany.
11. Frank Niess, *Geschichte der Arbeitslosigkeit. Ökonomische Ursachen und politische Kämpfe. Ein Kapitel deutscher Sozialgeschichte* (Cologne, 1979) p. 80.
12. Linda A. Heilman, *Industrial Unemployment in Germany, 1873–1913* (Doctoral Dissertation, University of California, 1982) p. 68. See also the unemployment table in Jürgen Kuczynski, *Die Geschichte der Lage der Arbeiter in Deutschland von 1800 bis in die Gegenwart* (East Berlin, 1947) Band 1, p. 215.
13. Anselm Faust, 'State and Unemployment in Germany 1890–1918 (Labour Exchanges, Job Creation and Unemployment Insurance)', in, W. J. Mommsen (ed.), *The Emergence of the Welfare State in Britain and Germany, 1850–1950* (London, 1981) pp. 151ff.
14. Heilman, *Industrial Unemployment in Germany, 1873–1913*, pp. 277ff.
15. For a discussion of the distinctions in the working class see Richard J. Evans (ed.), *The German Working Class 1888–1933. The Politics of Everyday Life* (London, 1982), esp. Dick Geary, 'Identifying Militancy: The Assessment of Working-Class Attitudes Towards State and Society', pp. 220–46.
16. Ludwig Preller, *Sozialpolitik in der Weimarer Republik* (Stuttgart, 1949)

pp. 4–81; Hans-Joachim Bieber, *Gewerkschaften in Krieg und Revolution* (Hamburg, 1981) pp. 306–23.

17. Preller, ibid., pp. 249ff; Wilhelm L. Guttsman, *The German Social Democratic Party, 1875–1933* (London, 1981) pp. 188f.
18. For a critical assessment see Dick Geary, 'Welfare Legislation, Labour Law and Working-Class Radicalism in the Weimar Republic' (unpub. paper presented at Warwick University, September 1983). I am grateful to the author for giving me a copy.
19. Cf. Gerald D. Feldman *et al.* (eds), *The German Inflation Reconsidered. A Preliminary Balance* (Berlin/New York, 1982); Gerald D. Feldman, *Iron and Steel in the German Inflation 1916–1923* (Princeton, 1977); Karsten Laursen and Jørgen Pedersen, *The German Inflation 1918–1923* (Amsterdam, 1964); Carl-Ludwig Holtfrerich, *Die deutsche Inflation 1914–1923. Ursachen und Folgen in internationaler Perspektive* (Berlin, 1980); Lothar Wentzel, *Inflation und Arbeitslosigkeit* (Hanover, 1980).
20. Helmut Druke *et al.*, *Spaltung der Arbeiterbewegung und Faschismus. Sozialgeschichte der Weimarer Republik* (Hamburg, 1980) p. 86.
21. Fritz Blaich, *Die Wirtschaftskrise 1925/26 und die Reichsregierung* (Kallmünz, 1977) *passim*; Dieter Hertz-Eichenrode, *Wirtschaftskrise und Arbeitsbeschaffung. Konjunkturpolitik 1925/26 und die Grundlagen der Krisenpolitik Brünings* (Frankfurt, 1982).
22. Robert A. Brady, *The Rationalization Movement in German Industry (Berkeley, Calif, 1933) passim*; Eva C. Schöck, *Arbeitslosigkeit und Rationalisierung. Die Lage der Arbeiter und die kommunistische Gewerkschaftspolitik 1920–1928* (Frankfurt, 1977) pp. 75ff, 162ff, 169ff; see also Gunna Stollberg, *Die Rationalisierungsdebatte 1908–33* (Frankfurt, 1981).
23. Frieda Wunderlich, *Die Bekämpfung der Arbeitslosigkeit in Deutschland seit Beendigung des Krieges* (Jena, 1925); Michael T. Wermel and Roswitha Urban, *Arbeitslosenfürsorge und Arbeitslosenversicherung in Deutschland* (Munich, 1949) Band 1, pp. 24ff.
24. Walter Bogs, *Die Sozialversicherung in der Weimarer Demokratie* (Munich, 1981) pp. 104ff, 110–22; Preller, *Sozialpolitik in der Weimarer Republik*, pp. 363ff; Niess, *Geschichte der Arbeitslosigkeit*, pp. 176ff.
25. National Industrial Conference Board, *Unemployment Insurance and Relief in Germany* (New York, 1932) p. 13; Dietmar Petzina, Werner Abelshauser and Anselm Faust, *Sozialgeschichtliches Arbeitsbuch III. Materialien zur Statistik des Deutschen Reiches 1914–1945* (Munich, 1978) p. 119.
26. Bernd Weisbrod, 'The Crisis of German Unemployment Insurance in 1928/1929 and its Political Repercussions' in Mommsen, *Welfare State*, pp. 188–204, esp. pp. 191ff; Ilse Maurer, *Reichsfinanzen und Grosse Koalition. Zur Geschichte des Reichskabinetts Müller (1928–1930)* (Berne/Frankfurt, 1973) for the detailed background.
27. Helga Timm, *Die deutsche Sozialpolitik und der Bruch der Grossen Koalition im März 1930* (Düsseldorf, 1952) *passim*.
28. From the extensive literature on the topic see, for general background, Charles P. Kindleberger, *The World in Depression 1929–1939* (London,

1973); Karl Brunner (ed.), *The Great Depression Revisited* (Boston, 1981); Peter Fearon, *The Origins and Nature of the Great Slump 1929–1932* (London, 1979). For Germany in particular see Fritz Blaich, *Der Schwarze Freitag. Inflation und Wirtschaftskrise* (Munich, 1985); Werner Conze and Hans Raupach (eds.), *Die Staats – und Wirtschaftskrise des Deutschen Reiches 1929/33* (Stuttgart, 1967); Wilhelm Treue (ed.), *Deutschland in der Weltwirtschaftskrise in Augenzeugenberichten* (Munich, 1976); Wilhelm M. Breuer, *Deutschland in der Weltwirtschaftskrise 1929/32* (Cologne, 1974); Ursula Büttner, *Hamburg in der Staats – und Wirtschaftskrise 1928–1931* (Hamburg, 1982); Ursula Büttner and Werner Jochmann, *Hamburg auf dem Weg ins Dritte Reich. Entwicklungsjahre 1931–1933* (Hamburg, 1983); Gerald D. Feldman (ed.), *Vom Weltkrieg zur Weltwirtschaftskrise. Studien zur deutschen Wirtschafts – und Sozialgeschichte 1914–1932* (Göttingen, 1984) and Willi A. Boelcke, *Die deutsche Wirtschaft 1930–1945. Interna des Reichswirtschaftsministeriums* (Düsseldorf, 1983).

29. Cf. Karl E. Born, *Die deutsche Bankenkrise 1931* (Munich, 1967).
30. Walter Galenson and Arnold Zellner, 'International Comparison of Unemployment Rates', in *National Bureau of Economic Research: The Measurement and Behaviour of Unemployment* (Princeton, 1957).
31. Preller, *Sozialpolitik in der Weimarer Republik*, p. 394, estimates one million 'invisible' jobless; Niess, *Geschichte der Arbeitslosigkeit*, p. 40 puts it at two million, and Druke *et al.*, *Spaltung der Arbeiterbewegung*, p. 88 at three or four million. The contemporary Institut für Konjunkturforschung made it two million.
32. Blaich, *Schwarze Freitag*, pp. 60, 69.
33. Saitzew, Erster Teil, pp. 43ff, 118ff.
34. In 1932 on average 13.6 per cent of *Angestellte* were unemployed, compared with only 2.4 per cent in 1927. This group constituted only 6.7 per cent of the registered jobless total in March 1930 and 10 per cent in September 1932 (Preller, *Sozialpolitik in der Weimarer Republik*, pp. 167–8).
35. Blaich, *Schwarze Freitag*, p. 62. For more details on the regional pattern of unemployment see Bruno S. Frey and Hannelore Weck, 'Hat Arbeitslosigkeit den Aufstieg des Nationalsozialismus bewirkt?', *Jahrbuch für Nationalökonomie und Statistik*, 196, 1981, pp. 1–31, and Petzina, Abelshauser and Faust, *Sozialgeschichtliches Arbeitsbuch III*, p. 121.
36. Saitzew, Zweiter Teil, pp. 1–8, 35ff, 83ff.
37. Wladimir Woytinsky, *The Social Consequences of the Economic Depression* (Geneva, 1936) pp. 88ff, 135–80; Treue, *Augenzeugenberichten*, pp. 138ff, 245ff, 336ff; Bruno N. Haken, *Stempelchronik. 261 Arbeitslosenschicksale* (Hamburg, 1932); Eckhard G. Wandel, 'Germany's Political Morale and Morals During the Great Depression', *Leo Baeck Institute Year Book*, XXVIII, 1983, pp. 11–17; Timothy W. Mason, 'National Socialism and the Working Class 1925 – May 1933', *New German Critique*, 4, 1977, Spring, pp. 49–93.
38. Cf. John A. Moses, *Trade Unionism in Germany from Bismarck to Hitler*, vol. 2 (1919–33) (London, 1982); Manfred Scharrer (ed.), *Kampflose Kapitulation. Arbeiterbewegung 1933* (Reinbek, 1984); Frank Deppe and

Witich Rossmann, *Wirtschaftskrise, Faschismus, Gewerkschaften. Dokumente zur Gewerkschaftspolitik 1929–1933* (Cologne, 1981).

39. Preller, *Sozialpolitik in der Weimarer Republik*, pp. 408–18, 473–83, 540–64; Woytinsky, *The Social Consequences of the Economic Depression*, pp. 164f. On industrialists see Henry A. Turner, *German Big Business and The Rise of Hitler* (Oxford, 1985); Bernd Weisbrod, *Schwerindustrie in der Weimarer Republik. Interessenpolitik zwischen Stabilisierung und Krise* (Wuppertal, 1978); Reinhard Neebe, *Grossindustrie, Staat und NSDAP 1930–1933. Paul Silverberg und der Reichsverband der deutschen Industrie in der Krise der Weimarer Republik* (Göttingen, 1981); Michael Grübler, *Die Spitzenverbände der Wirtschaft und das erste Kabinett Brüning. Vom Ende der Grossen Koalition 1929/30 bis zum Vorabend der Bankenkrise 1931* (Düsseldorf, 1982).

40. Woytinsky, *The Social Consequences of the Economic Depression*, p. 135; Eve Rosenhaft, *Beating the Fascists? The German Communists and Political Violence, 1929–1933* (London, 1983) pp. 5, 28f.

41. Knut Borchardt, 'Zwangslagen und Handlungsspielräume in der grossen Weltwirtschaftskrise der frühen dreissiger Jahre. Zur Revision des überlieferten Geschichtsbildes' in Knut Borchardt (ed.), *Wachstum, Krisen, Handlungsspielräume der Wirtschaftspolitik. Studien zur Wirtschaftsgeschichte des 19. und 20. Jahrhunderts* (Göttingen, 1982). For further references see Blaich, *Schwarze Freitag*, pp. 151–2.

42. Preller, *Sozialpolitik in der Weimarer Republik*, pp. 418–48.

43. Mason, 'National Socialism and the Working Class', p. 86, puts it at 1.3 out of 5.8 million registered unemployed in December 1932; Woytinsky, *The Social Consequences of the Economic Depression*, p. 175, states that in August 1932, 47 per cent of *all* jobless – 7 590 000 in his estimation – were without support.

44. Marie Jahoda, Paul F. Lazarsfeld and Hans Zeisel, *Die Arbeitslosen von Marienthal* (1933 – new edn, Bonn, 1960). The English version is, *Marienthal. The Sociography of an Unemployed Community* (Chicago: 1971; London, 1974).

45. Peter D. Stachura, *Gregor Strasser and the Rise of Nazism* (London, 1983) pp. 98f, 103f.

46. Akten der Reichskanzlei, *Die Regierung Hitler*, Teil 1, 1933–4, ed., Karl-Heinz Minuth (Boppard, 1983) vol. 1, p. 506ff (Doc. 147) (see also vol. 2, pp. 749–805 (Docs. 213, 214)).

47. *Statistisches Jahrbuch für das Deutsche Reich* (Berlin, 1940) p. 380. There was some juggling with the figures by the government. Certain categories such as seasonal and casual workers, some long-term unemployed and some female workers were no longer included in the statistics soon after 1933.

48. Avraham Barkai, 'Die Wirtschaftsauffassung der NSDAP' in *Das Parlament: Aus Politik und Zeitgeschichte*, 25, 1975, pt. 9, p. 3.

49. Fritz Reinhardt, *Die Arbeitsschlacht der Reichsregierung* (Berlin, 1933).

50. Rudolf Wiedwald, 'Die Arbeitslosigkeit der Jugend in den Jahren 1932 bis 1934', *Zentralblatt für Jugendrecht und Jugendwohlfahrt*, XXVI, 1934, no. 8, p. 233; Hertha Siemering, *Deutschlands Jugend im Bevölkerung und Wirtschaft. Eine statistische Untersuchung* (Berlin, 1937) p. 346.

51. Timothy W. Mason, 'Women in Germany, 1925–1940: Family, Welfare and Work, Part II', *History Workshop*, 1, 1976, Autumn, pp. 5–32; Dörte Winkler, *Frauenarbeit im 'Dritten Reich'* (Hamburg, 1977).
52. Karl Lärmer, *Autobahnen in Deutschland 1933 bis 1945* (Berlin, 1975) p. 54.
53. Dietrich Orlow, *The History of the Nazi Party*, vol. 2, 1933–45 (Newton Abbot, 1973) chapter 2.
54. Arthur Schweitzer, *Big Business in the Third Reich* (Bloomington, 1964); R. J. Overy, *The Nazi Economic Recovery 1932–1938* (London, 1982).

2 The Extent and Causes of Unemployment in the Weimar Republic*

Dietmar Petzina

The history of the Weimar Republic, especially the history of its social and economic development, is frequently interpreted as being merely the prehistory of National Socialism. With reference above all to inflation, high unemployment and the Great Depression, the 13 years of the first German Republic are seen as a succession of disasters inseparably linked to Hitler's advent to power. Mass unemployment, in particular, is blamed for the triumph of political radicalism over democratic stability. Although the problem of unemployment was not peculiar to Germany, in no other country was such an explosive combination of social collapse and political instability produced, which was to influence the course of history in such a fateful way. Questions regarding the extent and causes of unemployment, therefore, need to be posed for reasons extending beyond mere historical interest – particularly in view of the experiences of the early 1980s. If history has anything to teach us here, it would be that democracies require a social consensus and job opportunities for everyone if they are to survive on a long-term basis.

The following comments concentrate on the economic implications of unemployment, to be discussed on the basis of three essential questions:

Firstly: How did unemployment develop chronologically?
Secondly: Who was particularly hit by unemployment? Were there noticeable differences between social groups, branches of the economy and geographical regions?
Thirdly: Which causes can be identified? How did contemporaries interpret and react to unemployment?

*German-English translation by Ingeborg Schneider and Peter D. Stachura.

I

Every statistical documentation of unemployment in the 1920s had to contend with considerable deficiencies in methodology and compilation. Reliable and detailed unemployment statistics became available for the first time after 1928, when the newly-founded *Reichsanstalt für Arbeitsvermittlung und Arbeitslosenversicherung* carried out regular, nationwide surveys on the basis of uniform criteria. Previously there had been two principal methods of collecting data: one used Labour Exchange reports which were compiled mainly by the municipalities, but also by private representatives of the Labour Exchange system; the other used, from 1903, the trade union movement's unemployment statistics which, initially on a quarterly and then on a monthly basis (and in conjunction with the Reich Office for Statistics), detailed the number of trade unionists out of work. The unions' statistics served as the main basis of information for assessments of unemployment before the First World War, and between 1919–28 they also constituted the most comprehensive and reliable source of information[1] (see Table 2.1).

A glance over the development of unemployment confirms the considerable differences between the pre-war era and the Weimar Republic. This is very closely linked to trends in the German economy during the 1920s when there was an over-all picture of stagnation. Industrial production and per capita output during that decade did not rise above the level of 1914, and indeed, in most years, lagged behind. Germany shared this experience of 'relative stagnation' with most other European countries since their growth potential was significantly affected by the war and the resultant domestic and international economic dislocation. None the less, it would be misleading to emphasise stagnation as a general feature of the interwar period on the basis of statistically-averaged data, which really indicates widely differing conditions in each country. Non-European countries, particularly the USA, enjoyed a prosperous decade after the war. Germany's development ran counter to that of other industrial countries not only in chronological terms. It also had more periods of particularly intensive growth alongside deeper crises than most other countries which cannot be meaningfully explained as 'stagnation' alone. A comparison of unemployment, as shown in Table 2.2, illustrates the parallels and differences.

The history of the Weimar Republic's economic development falls, like its political history, into three major phases, which also denote important differences in the labour market: the period of post-war

Table 2.1 The percentage of unemployed trade unionists pre-war and post-war

Pre-war

Month (end of)	*1907*	*1908*	*1909*	*1910*	*1911*	*1912*	*1913*
January	1.7	2.9	4.2	2.6	2.6	2.9	3.2
February	1.6	2.7	4.1	2.3	2.2	2.6	2.9
March	1.3	2.5	3.5	1.8	1.9	1.6	2.3
April	1.3	2.8	2.9	1.8	1.8	1.7	2.3
May	1.4	2.8	2.8	2.0	1.6	1.9	2.5
June	1.4	2.9	2.8	2.0	1.6	1.7	2.7
July	1.4	2.7	2.5	1.9	1.6	1.8	2.9
August	1.4	2.7	2.3	1.7	1.8	1.7	2.8
September	1.4	2.7	2.1	1.8	1.7	1.5	2.7
October	1.6	2.9	2.0	1.6	1.5	1.7	2.8
November	1.7	3.2	2.0	1.6	1.7	1.8	3.1
December	2.7	4.4	2.6	2.1	2.4	2.8	4.8
Average	1.6	2.9	2.9	2.0	1.9	2.0	2.9

Post-war

onth nd of)	*1921*	*1922*	*1923*	*1924*	*1925*	*1926*	*1927*	*1928*	*1929*	*1930*	*1931*
nuary	4.5	3.3	4.2	26.5	8.1	22.6	16.5	11.2	19.4	22.0	34.2
ebruary	4.7	2.7	5.2	25.1	7.3	22.0	15.5	10.4	22.3	23.5	34.5
arch	3.7	1.1	5.6	16.6	5.8	21.4	11.5	9.2	16.9	21.7	33.8
pril	3.9	0.9	7.0	10.4	4.3	18.6	8.9	6.9	11.1	20.3	31.9
ay	3.7	0.7	6.2	8.6	3.6	18.1	7.0	6.3	9.1	19.5	30.0
ne	3.0	0.6	4.1	10.5	3.5	18.1	6.3	6.2	8.5	19.6	29.8
ly	2.6	0.6	3.5	12.5	3.7	17.7	5.5	6.3	8.6	20.5	31.1
ugust	2.2	0.7	6.3	12.4	4.3	16.7	5.0	6.5	8.9	21.7	33.7
ptember	1.4	0.8	9.9	10.5	4.5	15.2	4.6	6.6	9.6	22.5	35.1
ctober	1.2	1.4	19.1	8.4	5.8	14.2	4.5	7.3	10.9	23.6	36.8
ovember	1.4	2.0	23.4	7.3	10.7	14.2	7.4	9.5	13.7	26.0	39.0
ecember	1.6	2.8	28.2	8.1	19.4	16.7	12.9	16.7	20.1	31.7	42.4
verage	2.9	1.5	9.7	14.2	6.9	18.1	8.8	8.4	13.1	22.2	34.2

ource: See note 2.

Table 2.2 The percentage of unemployment in selected countries 1919–1938

Year	*Germany*[a]	*UK*[b]	*USA*[c]	*Sweden*[d]	*France*[e]
1919	3.7	5.2	3.4	5.5	
1920	3.8	3.2	5.8	5.4	
1921	2.8	17.0	16.9	26.6	5.0
1922	1.5	14.3	10.9	22.9	2.0
1923	10.2	11.7	4.6	12.5	2.0
1924	13.1	10.3	8.0	10.1	3.0
1925	6.8	11.3	5.9	11.0	3.0
1926	18.0	12.5	2.8	12.2	3.0
1927	8.8	9.7	5.9	12.0	11.0
1928	8.6	10.8	6.4	10.6	4.0
1929	13.3	10.4	4.7	10.2	1.0
1930	22.7	16.1	13.0	11.9	2.9
1931	34.3	21.3	23.3	16.8	6.5
1932	43.8	22.1	34.0	22.4	15.4
1933	36.2	19.9	35.3	23.3	14.1
1934	20.5	16.7	30.6	18.0	13.8
1935	16.2	15.5	28.4	15.0	14.5
1936	12.0	13.1	23.9	12.7	10.4
1937	6.9	10.8	20.0	10.8	7.4
1938	3.2	12.9	26.4	10.9	7.8

a Up to 1932 only trade union members are included.
b Unemployed determined on the basis of the unemployment insurance system.
c The unemployed as a percentage of the non-agrarian working population.
d Trade union statistics.
e The unemployed in terms of employees in mining, construction and industry.

Source: See note 3.

reconstruction and inflation 1919–23, the period following the stabilisation of the currency 1924–28/9, and finally, the Great Depression. By such a division, the years of economic recovery are reduced to the status of an unimportant episode of a crisis which, commencing in 1914, was regarded by contemporaries as lasting continuously for 20 years. However, this periodisation overemphasises the crisis nature of the Weimar Republic, especially in respect of the 'abnormal' years before 1924. Of course, taking only the inflation and its consequences into account, the conventional explanation of the crisis is entirely valid. If, on the other hand, unemployment and employment, industrial production and gross national product, are used as the criteria, the traditional view has to be modified. The proportion of jobless lay close to the full employment level of pre-war times and only in summer 1923, at the height of the inflation, did it reach crisis point. In other words, between 1919–20 and 1922–3 the German economy experienced a boom, and the gross national product seemed to have increased in real terms by 7 per cent a year between 1919 and 1922, only to show a dramatic decline in 1923 of some 10 per cent. The exceptional expansion during the first four post-war years can be interpreted as a specifically German development, a period of continuous economic reconstruction.

In contrast, a distinct slowdown of the economic revival occurred after 1924. Between 1924 and 1929 the average rate of unemployment lay around 10 per cent, with an upward trend. More significant during this time were the extreme fluctuations in the labour market, which can be observed from the figures in Table 2.1. Still, following the stabilisation crisis of 1923–24, there was a surprising improvement from autumn 1924 which led to almost full employment again by summer 1925. This progress lasted only a year, of course, until running into the crisis 'before the crisis' in 1926. The years 1927 and 1928 brought a new, temporary period of improvement – produced and accompanied by rapid industrial growth – but with a structurally higher level of unemployment. And finally, 1929 is to be seen, according to the indices of unemployment, industrial investment and production, as the beginning of the Great Depression in Germany, during which the German employment system came to a catastrophic end.

The unemployment figures (Table 2.2) indicate that, apart from the United States, Germany was hardest hit by the crisis. Between 1930 and 1933 the average unemployment rate was over 30 per cent, and at the height of the crisis nearly every second industrial worker was jobless. The basic pattern of development in the crisis applies also to other industrial countries, albeit with less intensity and different timing. The Depression affected Germany with particular ferocity, however, because economic factors coincided with structural weaknesses, causing the one to exacerbate the other.

The Great Depression was only partly the outcome of a parallel cyclical decline of the economic base in the most important industrial countries. The economic cycle was displaced by structural changes in the private economic sector, which were especially marked in Germany. They gave a crisis regarded as 'normal' and 'solvable by internal control' a direction which to perceptive contemporaries was bound to result in a disastrous collapse of the entire system. To be mentioned in this regard are, above all, the rigidity of the economy which was caused by the noticeably large-scale monopolisation of production and distribution in Germany, the inflexibility of wages and prices because of a largely centralised tariff system, and the destruction of the liberal world trade and currency systems due to the establishment of steadily increasing customs and trade restrictions; finally, the problem of international debt, and the associated movements of capital, led to a pronounced instability in international financial relations. Several of these factors originated during the inflation, which is thus very closely linked to the Great Depression in Germany: the cartelisation and concentration of the German economy, which even before 1913 was more extensive than in other industrial countries, had been considerably strengthened during the inflation. This process of concentration consolidated in turn the rigidity of the economic structure which had been initiated during the First World War by wage and price regulations. In the event of crisis, therefore, every economic and political strategy which relied on the economy being its own remedy, and which was based on the liberal system of the nineteenth century, was doomed to failure.

In the 1920s and early 1930s, German society was affected to widely varying degrees by the problem of mass unemployment. Open unemployment was concentrated in industry, especially in the older 'traditional' industrial areas. In 1932, at the height of the Depression, the highest unemployment rates were to be found in the industrial regions of the Rhine and Ruhr (Westphalia and the Rhineland), Saxony, the Berlin area (Brandenburg) as well as the Silesian textile districts[4] (see Table 2.3).

Industrial districts with a large proportion of industries producing capital goods experienced a particularly severe collapse, but after 1933 had a quicker recovery than regions with a high proportion of consumer goods industries. 'Old' consumer goods regions were Saxony, Silesia and parts of the Rhineland, while especially southern Germany, but also predominantly agrarian districts like East Prussia and Lower Saxony were more resistant to open unemployment. Hidden unemployment, which cannot be statistically reported, did play an important role, of course, in agrarian districts.

The gap between differently structured economic regions was drama-

Table 2.3 The unemployed as a percentage of those in employment (health insurance members)

Labour Office District	*1931*	*1932*	*1933*	*1934*	*1935*	*1936*
East Prussia	15.4	20.8	12.9	3.7	3.6	3.3
Silesia	25.9	34.5	30.5	16.7	15.2	12.2
Brandenburg	25.5	34.2	31.3	16.7	10.8	7.9
Poznan	17.6	24.0	17.3	5.1	5.1	4.0
North (Nordmark)	18.9	29.4	28.2	15.9	10.8	7.5
Lower Saxony	19.1	27.0	22.3	9.5	6.0	3.1
Westphalia	24.3	35.1	27.9	14.1	10.9	7.9
Rhineland	25.6	36.3	32.9	19.7	17.0[a]	11.7
Hesse	23.7	30.3	27.2	14.6	12.1	8.9
Central Germany	22.0	29.2	23.0	10.4	6.8	4.1
Saxony	24.5	33.4	29.0	16.5	13.7	10.1
Bavaria (incl. Pfalz)	19.8	25.7	22.0	11.4	8.6	5.9
South-west Germany	14.9	19.3	16.6	8.2	5.6	3.7
German Reich	22.2	30.3	26.1	13.7	10.5[a]	7.4

a From 1935, including the Saarland.
Source: See note 5.

tically accentuated in large towns and cities. In the capital, Berlin, the largest industrial centre after the Ruhr and Saxony, the number of unemployed rose 1928–32 from 133 000 to approximately 600 000, in Hamburg from 32 000 to 135 000, and in Dortmund from 12 000 to 65 000. In relation to every 1000 inhabitants, however, the cities in the industrial areas of Saxony and Silesia were hardest hit: in 1932 in Chemnitz there were 169 unemployed for every 1000 inhabitants, in Leipzig the figure was 140, and in Breslau 146. Similar levels were reached in the Ruhr, whereas distinctly lower figures obtained in south German cities like Stuttgart, Munich and Augsburg. An even more favourable situation existed in provincial commercial and administrative centres such as Münster and Königsberg where the industrial working class was small in number (see Table 2.4).

As in other industrial countries, the extent and impact of unemployment was extremely diversified, not only in relation to geographical area and economic sector, but also to social class. In Germany, the civil service – those employed by the state and local government – traditionally enjoyed a privileged position. Dismissal was possible only in exceptional cases and usually occurred independently of economic

Table 2.4 The number of unemployed in every 1000 inhabitants of German cities and large towns 1928–1936

City/Town	*1928*	*1929*	*1932*	*1933*	*1936*
Aachen	30.9	21.9	99.6	83.3	60.1
Altona	28.2	23.7	121.7	117.8	42.8
Augsburg	29.6	29.3	96.3	84.7	19.8
Berlin	–	37.2	140.5	137.5	40.8
Beuthen (Upper Silesia)	–	–	–	–	42.5
Bielefeld	–	–	115.5	81.7	23.2
Bochum	33.8	26.0	114.9	83.6	24.9
Brunswick	39.3	43.9	122.6	107.1	12.4
Bremen	24.8	37.4	126.8	106.3	17.7
Breslau	35.7	40.0	145.7	139.3	78.8
Chemnitz	10.0	41.5	168.7	144.1	57.1
Dortmund	26.3	21.0	136.0	119.9	47.7
Dresden	27.7	37.9	136.9	127.5	61.8
Düsseldorf	22.5	28.3	112.4	117.6	33.4
Duisburg-Hamborn	55.1	49.6	145.0	128.6	45.9
Erfurt	31.3	29.5	130.0	116.8	32.0
Essen	35.2	24.8	117.4	109.0	45.5
Frankfurt	19.4	30.0	117.2	109.4	48.6
Gelsenkirchen	32.8	15.7	105.5	104.2	48.4
Gleiwitz	24.7	24.2	96.9	89.2	39.6
Hagen (Westphalia)	20.9	28.8	139.7	110.0	28.1
Halle	15.8	33.0	124.7	110.5	25.4
Hamburg	29.6	31.1	119.4	128.2	55.7
Hanover	26.5	29.3	123.7	118.0	18.4
Harburg-Wilhelmsburg	34.9	36.3	150.0	137.8	44.9
Hindenburg (Upper Silesia)	18.0	16.8	104.4	116.2	42.7
Karlsruhe	16.6	21.8	91.2	91.1	31.5
Kassel	21.1	16.7	113.7	105.4	21.1
Kiel	36.8	40.4	130.2	115.0	10.4
Cologne	24.2	24.2	109.7	104.3	52.8
Königsberg	23.5	30.6	101.2	58.2	10.6
Krefeld	26.4	31.5	92.0	78.9	36.0
Leipzig	18.7	26.8	139.6	131.6	49.8
Ludwigshafen	22.9	32.5	110.9	106.1	37.1
Lübeck	30.4	42.2	153.1	127.5	18.9
Magdeburg	29.3	29.8	113.0	96.4	16.6
Mainz	26.7	36.9	119.0	109.6	42.7
Mannheim	25.9	35.0	122.2	114.3	39.1
Mülheim	26.9	21.5	121.3	100.4	18.9
Munich	28.1	32.2	102.1	98.9	24.8
Mönchen-Gladbach-Rheydt	37.4	36.3	164.2	–	40.6
Münster	14.0	12.8	50.3	38.0	12.3
Nuremberg	29.5	32.6	135.6	116.3	33.1
Oberhausen	29.5	25.5	119.2	111.2	41.8

City/Town	*1928*	*1929*	*1932*	*1933*	*1936*
Plauen	41.2	30.7	176.3	170.8	71.2
Remscheid	–	–	121.9	92.5	17.8
Saarbrücken	–	–	–	–	37.6
Solingen	–	–	167.5	148.8	53.4
Stettin	45.4	43.4	120.8	102.2	29.0
Stuttgart	11.8	14.9	90.5	75.3	6.1
Wiesbaden	24.6	35.2	117.1	113.5	60.1
Wuppertal	47.7	54.8	137.3	123.6	42.4
Würzburg	–				11.2

Source: See note 6.

influences. Manual workers in this sphere did not have the privileged status of a civil servant, but their position was more secure than that of their counterparts in private industry.

Finally, the position of white-collar employees (*Angestellten*) is of special interest. Before the First World War they were, in terms of their social status and job security (mainly confined to men), part of a newly-emerging middle class (*Mittelstand*) which was distinctly separate from the working class. On the other hand, the increase in numbers of white-collar workers during the Weimar Republic signified an important change in German society between the wars. While the proportion of manual workers (*Arbeiter*) fell from 55 to 50 per cent and stagnated in absolute terms at around 15 milion between 1907–25, the number of white-collar employees tripled rapidly between the turn of the century and 1925 to reach 3.5 million.[7] This increase was due mainly to the bureaucratisation of production and the expanding role of pre- and post-manufacturing processes. New methods of goods distribution and a growing need for personnel in commerce and transport, as well as a demand for additional private and public services, led to the creation of a new social class of considerable political and social dynamism.

Despite the material equalisation of white- and blue-collar workers during the 1920s regarding their income and the growing threat of unemployment, a subjective emphasis on their differences was maintained. The attempt by white-collar workers to keep their distance from the 'lower orders' in the interests of maintaining their own superior status created an anti-proletarian sentiment which became susceptible to political radicalisation during the Depression. Together with the 'old' *Mittelstand*, sections of the white-collar employees formed the mass basis of National Socialism because the personal threat of unemployment which many of them felt noticeably strengthened their anti-socialist attitudes. In fact, many white-collar employees, unable to identify with the secure, ideological system of the industrial proletariat or with the traditional values of the pre-war bourgeoisie were, in Geiger's phrase, 'colonists of virgin territory in society'.[8] The formation of a new social identity failed in the Weimar Republic, not least because of the short period of 'normality', especially since this normality was characterised by extreme fluctuations in the employment sphere and a loss of status by a majority of white-collar employees (see Table 2.5).

Table 2.5 The total number of unemployed and of unemployed white-collar employees (1921–1932)

Year	*Total no. of*[a] *unemployed (in 1000)*	*No. of unemployed*[b] *white-collar employees*	*Percentage of unemployed white-collar employees to total no. of unemployed*
1921	354	–	–
1922	213	–	–
1923	751	50300	6,7
1924	978	–	–
1925	636	95900	15.1
1926	2010	234800	11.7
1927	1327	161600	12.1
1928	1368	–	–
1929	1897	–	–
1930	3076	243500	7.9
1931	4559	367100	8.1
1932	5603	511400	9.1

a Annual average calculated on the basis of figures for 13 months.
b Includes commercial, technical and office employees.

Source: See note 9.

II

Under the impact of an apparently inexorable rise in unemployment during the 1920s, a heated discussion arose in Germany about its nature and causes. In particular, the *Institut für Konjunkturforschung* (Institute for Economic Research), which was founded in 1925, attempted to interpret the empirical evidence theoretically and to give advice on the different types of unemployment.[10] In addition, prominent among the plethora of specialised studies on the subject were the publications, in the early 1930s, of the *Verein für Socialpolitik*;[11] and lastly, as early as 1926, the difference between cyclical and structural unemployment was appreciated, even if the causes were still disputed.[12] The differentiation betwen 'cyclical' and 'structural' was based on the experience of a relatively regular cycle in the economy and labour market during the period of intensive industrialisation before 1914. In contrast, the irregularities in Germany's economic development between the wars can be seen:

- in the unusually different trade cycle of 1920–22;
- in the inflationary and politically influenced crisis of 1923 and the subsequent stabilisation crisis before summer 1924;
- in the crisis of Autumn 1925/Spring 1926;
- in the Great Depression 1929–33;
- finally, in the uninterrupted, apparently non-cyclical boom after 1933.[13]

It is not possible to explain in this paper the multiplicity of partly speculative hypotheses concerning the interpretation of economic crisis and unemployment during the interwar era. Whether the crisis of the 1920s and 1930s represents the coming together of several turning points of different-sized cycles, or whether the 1920s altogether are to be seen as part of a falling branch of a 'Kondratieff Cycle', that is, of a long-term economic development, is an intriguing question, however difficult it would be to test empirically. We are obliged, however, to analyse the over-all economic development of the situation in Germany in order to explain the aforementioned peculiarities of unemployment and crisis. For that we use the paradigm of reconstruction, meaning we investigate the consequences of the wartime and post-war influences on economic development. Our thesis is: the paradigm of reconstruction permits a more plausible interpretation of apparently irregular processes in the labour market than the widely accepted theories of stagnation. Consequently, our approach allows the period 1919–1922/3 to be interpreted as a phase of reconstruction after the disruption of war, and 1924–9 as a phase of 'unfulfilled' reconstruction.

The special feature of the first phase was an increase in capital stock of nearly one-third in the German national economy, which was unique by international standards. Despite the demands of war, capital stock might have grown by a third during 1914–18, and in industry at the end of the inflation it may have to be assessed at 10 per cent higher than it was in 1913. The specific dynamics of this investment cycle were produced by the interaction of inflation, government financial policy and rapidly growing profits from falling wage costs caused by inflation. The favourable commercial conditions for capital investment served as a transmission belt between the *potential* for growth generated by the qualifications of people and *actual* growth. The result was the aforementioned full employment of that period.

The situation between 1924 and 1929 was totally different. Unlike perhaps the period after the Second World War, a pattern of reconstruction beyond the first five years of the post-1918 era can hardly be identified. While the time-scale of reconstruction in the economy of West Germany after 1945 stretched into the first half of the 1960s, after 1918 only the years to 1923 correspond to the expected course of development. The crucial structural problem before the onset of the Great Depression, and at the same time, the corollary of rising unemployment, was the low volume of investment. In 1925–9 the net investment quota was only 11 per cent, compared with 15.2 per cent in 1910–13, while in 1920–22 it was probably much more. After 1924 investments in the industrial sector showed substantial fluctuation and reached a new low. The same can be said for agriculture. The state sector had a procyclical restrictive attitude to investment. The proportion of its investments in the gross national product fell from 2.9 per cent in 1913 to 2 per cent in 1925–9, although public expenditure as a whole doubled in comparison with the pre-war era. This break in investment patterns provides the key to understanding the crisis in the labour market in the 1920s. What caused the structural problems in the labour market during the 1920s?

1. The end of the inflation coincided with the disappearance of what had been an especially propitious climate for production (cheap credit, low wage costs, low taxation, high deficit spending). The growth factor of 'state deficit spending' was no longer present after 1924 – the real level of state expenditure for 1925–9 averaged out at considerably less than for 1919–23. The proportion of public expenditure to national income was about 35 per cent in 1919–22 and 26 per cent in 1925–9, while absolute expenditure (prices of 1913 level) was in the first period some 15.5 milliard marks per annum and only 12.8 milliard marks in the second period.

2. The contribution of German exports to the gross national product

remained far lower during the interwar era than it had been before 1914. The export quota dropped from 22 per cent of the gross national product in 1913 to 16 per cent in 1928; the proportion of German exports in world exports fell from 13.2 per cent to 9.1 per cent. This development was not confined to Germany – it applied also to Britain. The one-time balance in the world economy between the industrial powers of Europe and the countries producing raw materials, and between the industrial nations themselves – which was the result of a false protectionist commercial and economic policy – was initially upset by the First World War and then finally and completely ruined in the 1930s. On top of this came the unsolved problem of a system of 'political debts', and also the destabilisation of the international financial and currency system. The result was important: the traditional impetus behind growth in German industry was partly neutralised, without compensation being found in the domestic market. The reasons can be only briefly mentioned here: the new competition from the USA and younger overseas industrial countries in the world market, world-wide protectionism, and an international finance and debt policy destructive of the world economic system; finally, the failure of national governments to agree to even minimal collaboration in the world economy.

3. Since 1924 the low rate of private investment went hand in hand with a distinctly improved position for workers' and employees' real wages. The proportion of earned income to national income between the end of the period of inflation and the beginning of the Great Depression was considerably higher than before the First World War, though was not maintained during the Third Reich or after the Second World War.

This is shown in Table 2.6.

Table 2.6 The proportion of earned income to national income 1910–13 to 1955–59 (in percentages)

Years	%	*Years*	%
1910/13	70.9	1935/38	78.1
1925/29	87.3	1950/54	74.0
1930/34	97.1	1955/59	72.8

Source: See note 14.

There appears to be a significant connection between fears of modest profit and a low rate of private investment. Without doubt, the problem of overloading the private economic system existed before and during the Great Depression, yet the lack of demand in national and world economies was of similar economic importance for the low rate of investment. The extra capacity created largely in the export industries during the inflation was not fully exploited and caused a reservoir of structural unemployment, to which the process of rationalisation also contributed.

The National Socialist economic cycle does not require detailed explanation despite its – even by international standards – unique features of rapid growth and simultaneous concentration on the domestic market. Important economic and political factors which served as security for the development of the labour market in the Weimar Republic went into reverse after 1933. If the second half of the 1920s can be understood with the paradigm of an incomplete reconstruction, the time after 1933 can be seen as an opportunity to tap the unexploited growth potential of the Weimar Republic. The National Socialist 'economic miracle' meant more than simply overcoming the cyclical disruption caused by the Great Depression; it also involved the elimination of 'long-standing obstacles to growth'.[15] What, since the mid-1920s, had had a disruptive effect, became after 1933 a creative growth factor, at least in economic and labour policy, albeit under the political aegis of the National Socialist *Führerstaat* and its preparations for war.

4. What role did the state's economic policy play in this context? Could it have exercised a more decisive influence on the unemployment situation during the late Weimar era? First of all, it has to be remembered that, despite the increase in public expenditure, especially in the consumer sphere, the state's financial policy had an altogether restrictive impact on investment. Public investment developed in a procyclical fashion, that is, it was geared to rising state income in periods of growth, and was then reduced as income dropped in times of cyclical depression. Thus, on the whole, the problem of unexploited capacity in industry was exacerbated, but not caused. However, the opportunities for having a more expansive policy in the 1920s should not be exaggerated. Similar economic and labour market strategies pursued by Reich governments of various political complexions are evidence for the psychological 'predicaments' facing politicians. Even if government had wanted to,

measures limiting investment could hardly be politically influenced in the short-term. The whole *raison d'être* of the Weimar Republic would have been at risk around 1925 had the state sought to side with the employers by interfering with established wage agreements.

Impeding the development of the labour market was the growing inability, during the inflation and following years, of the organised employers and trade unions to agree, thus directly requiring the state to exert a stronger influence on wage and income policy by forcing a settlement. Practically all important wage agreements in 1924–32 came about through state arbitration, indicating that the collaboration between employers and unions on labour matters which was agreed in 1918 was now ineffectual. Until the Depression, the trade unions welcomed this intervention of a socially-aware administration of, and jurisdiction in, labour policy. In wage conflicts there was a tendency for state arbitration to favour the workers rather than the employers, which as early as 1928 led the latter to question their readiness to accept this system. Only during the Great Depression did the system operate to the disadvantage of the workers. These varying experiences in the different phases of the Weimar Republic explain why, in Germany, after 1945, neither employers nor trade unions favoured the re-establishment of compulsory state arbitration.

Whether as a result of state intervention the level of real wages in the Weimar Republic was too high cannot be answered with a simple yes or no. Certainly the aforementioned connection between a high proportion of earned income and a low quota of investment existed. On the other hand, real earnings in Germany lay clearly below the level in Britain (about 30 per cent), whose economic development in the 1920s was in many respects similar.[16]

It seems reasonable to suppose that the actual opportunities available to Weimar governments in the spheres of money, credit and finance policy for solving the problems of the labour market were politically and psychologically very limited indeed. The fear of inflation played a central role in Germany right up to the Depression, thus impeding any state initiative to increase expenditure on the labour market. Moreover, Weimar governments exercised only slight influence over the internationally controlled *Reichsbank* which, to the probable detriment of investment, accorded absolute priority to stabilising the currency through high interest rates. Every suggestion for combating unemployment in the Weimar Republic based on a more expansive monetary and credit policy had to be assessed, therefore, not in economic terms but rather in relation to its political feasibility. Germany's dependence on the international capital market, its extremely high foreign debt of 20 milliard marks (equivalent to one-third of the national income), and the linking of the German reparations problem to questions of domestic economic policy produced a constellation which could only be modestly influenced by Germany.

These points do not refute the criticism made by economists and historians of the labour and economic policies of Weimar governments, particularly in the Depression. But they provoke scepticism about the stated possibility of an alternative economic and social policy which would still have had a chance in the concrete historical situation at the beginning of the 1930s. Ignoring international obligations, Hitler could force the *Reichsbank* to hasten an expansion of credit to finance work creation programmes, and politically he could disregard the obligations imposed by the Young Plan, including the redemption of the *Reichsmark* at the international level. As Chancellor during the Depression, Brüning could not do this, and he imposed further restrictions on himself which possibly also prevented him using the room for manouevre that still existed in social and economic policy. To have overestimated the political and psychological resilience of the German people during the latter part of the Weimar Republic was a matter of grave historical misjudgement, particularly when the aim of this policy had been the salvation of Weimar democracy.

Finally, two other developments may be intimated which, taken together, put an additional burden on the German labour market in 1925–33: the demographically-inspired expansion of the labour pool, and the increase in industrial productivity caused by rationalisation.

5. The age structure of the population, as well as the development of the birth-rate in Germany before 1914 resulted, despite war losses, in there being about 5 million more in the labour pool in 1925 than there was in 1907.[17] According to Reulecke's calculations, the 'countable' labour pool in 1907 was 30.7 million and in 1925 some 35.1 million; the actual number of employable persons (those in employment plus the jobless) amounted to 90.5 per cent of this figure in each case. This demographically-inspired trend intensified between 1925 and 1933, so that at the height of the Depression the number of persons over 14 years of age fit for work surpassed the number in 1925 by 2.6 million (50.2 million in 1933, and 47.6 million in 1925). On the basis of this demographic development, the propor-

tion of men in work consequently rose from 60.5 per cent to 67.6 per cent, while for women the figures were 29.6 per cent and 35.3 per cent respectively. As regards working women, the increase cannot be ascribed exclusively to the demographic factor; a 'structural' rise in the quota of employed persons during the 1920s must also be taken into account. According to the calculations of the *Institut für Konjunkturforschung*, the number of people willing to work rose in 1925–31 from 32.0 million to 33.4 million, of whom 1.2 million alone were in the commercial and industrial sectors. The turning-point of this demographic 'overloading' of the labour market came in 1931–2, because then the distinctly smaller age groups of the war years came of working age.

Without being able to pursue in this paper the links between the demographic factor of overloading and problems relating to the development of regions and specific sectors of the economy, one important conclusion can be made: because of decisive demographic changes, the German labour market had to bear a considerable additional burden for a relatively short period of transition. This would have been the case even if in the Weimar Republic, as before the First World War, extensive industrial growth had led to a corresponding increase in employment.

6. In fact, however, a contrary trend is noticeable in Germany from the mid-1920s. The rise of German industry, which caused a great deal of astonishment abroad, went hand in hand with an intensification of the production process in the most important key industries. Technical and organisational improvements, which contemporaries labelled 'rationalisation', were an attempt to compensate for the pressure of high labour costs that existed after the stabilisation of the *Reichsmark*. In no other country, apart from the United States, were technical improvements in industry as far reaching as in Germany. They went together with the mechanisation of the production process, the intensification of capital investment in industry, concentration into larger units, and more regulation of the market. By increasing productivity, the aim was to remain internationally competitive, particularly *vis-à-vis* the USA, the new competitor in the world market. Indeed, between 1925 and 1929, Germany succeeded in raising productivity in industry by 20–25 per cent, in coalmining by some 35 per cent and in pig-iron by 41 per cent. According to estimates prepared by the *Institut für Konjunkturforschung*,[18] the 'releasing effect' caused by increased productivity in 1926–30

amounted to 1 130 000 workers. Thereupon, an over-all account for industry produced the following balance for 1931:

- an increase in the numbers of those willing to work after 1926 of 600 000.
- a saving through the rise in productivity of one million people.
- the unemployment caused by economic cycles of 2.1 million.
- industrial unemployment in 1931 of 3.7 million.

In other words; approximately half the unemployment in industry was caused by structural factors which fused during the Depression with the consequences of economic decline.

7. Our question about the causes of unemployment in the Weimar Republic has produced, therefore, several answers. Like all European industrial countries, Germany was confronted during the 1920s and 1930s by the problem of long-term high unemployment. Only within the wider context of this basic situation in all industrial countries is it sensible to identify specific characteristics of Germany's development. As our analysis has shown, these are to be found in the particular circumstances in which post-war reconstruction took place, and also in the particular dependence on to which Germany, as the leading debtor nation at this time, was thrown. Germany's economic and labour market policy could change little in the short-term in this area, or as regards the structural factors behind unemployment, even if the causes had been understood. This statement does not signify a relapse into the *ex-post* fatalism of a historian. What it does mean, however, is that the special political constraints which emerged from the multitude of related factors are to be taken seriously.

In another way, the 1920s marked on an international level a profound change in the system of economic control – the transition from a liberal to a tightly-organised system. Every economic and labour market policy based on the liberal economic aims and experiences of the pre-1914 era became a potential factor of crisis itself. It might be worthwhile speculating, not merely from a historical viewpoint, whether the crisis of the 1920s and 1930s can be explained more accurately as a fusing of different political and institutional principles of control in national and international economic policy, rather than through traditional cyclical theories. That might be of considerable value for understanding the crisis in the labour market in the 1980s.

Notes

1. Wladimir Woytinsky, *Der deutsche Arbeitsmarkt. Ergebnisse der gewerkschaftlichen Arbeitslosenstatistik 1919–1929* (Berlin, 1930).
2. Adolf Agthe, 'Statistische Übersicht der Arbeitslosigkeit in der Welt', in *Schriften des Vereins für Socialpolitik*, 185/I, 1932, p. 152; Woytinsky, *Der deutsche Arbeitsmarkt*, p. 9.
3. Stanley Lebergott, 'Annual Estimates of Employment in the United States 1900–1950'; Walter Galenson and Arnold Zellner, 'International Comparison of Unemployment Rates', in National Bureau of Economic Research (ed.), *The Measurement and Behaviour of Unemployment* (Princeton, 1957).
4. Dietmar Petzina, 'Zum Problem des Verlaufs und der Überwindung der Weltwirtschaftskrise im regionalen Vergleich – Materialien und Interpretation', in Friedrich-Wilhelm Henning (ed.), *Probleme der nationalsozialistischen Wirtschaftspolitik* (Berlin, 1976).
5. Compiled from Reichsarbeitsministerium (ed.), *Statistische Beilagen zum Reichsarbeitsblatt* (Berlin, 1932–7).
6. *Statistisches Handbuch von Deutschland 1928–1944*, Länderrat des amerikanischen Besatzungsgebiet (ed.), (Munich, 1949), p. 485.
7. See Heinz-Jürgen Priamus, *Angestellte und Demokratie, Die nationalliberale Angestelltenbewegung in der Weimarer Republik* (Stuttgart, 1979).
8. Theodor Geiger, *Die soziale Schichtung des deutschen Volkes. Soziographischer Versuch auf statistischer Grundlage* (Stuttgart, 1932).
9. Priamus, *Angestellte und Demokratie*, p. 28.
10. Institut für Konjunkturforschung, 'Stand und Ursachen der Arbeitslosigkeit in Deutschland', in *Vierteljahrshefte zur Konjunkturforschung*, Sonderheft 29 (Berlin, 1932).
11. For instance, Manuel Saitzew (ed.), *Die Arbeitslosigkeit der Gegenwart* in *Schriften des Vereins für Socialpolitik*, 185/1, 1932.
12. Bernhard Harms, 'Strukturwandlungen der deutschen Volkswirtschaft', in *Weltwirtschaftliches Archiv*, 24, 1926, Heft 2.
13. Werner Abelshauser and Dietmar Petzina, 'Krise und Rekonstruktion. Zur Interpretation der gesamtwirtschaftlichen Entwicklung Deutschlands im 20. Jahrhundert', in W. H. Schröder and R. Spree (eds), *Historische Konjunkturforschung* (Stuttgart, 1980).
14. Walther G. Hoffmann, *Das Wachstum der deutschen Volkswirtschaft seit der Mitte des 19. Jahrhunderts* (Stuttgart, 1965) p. 87.
15. Knut Borchardt, 'Zwangslagen und Handlungsspielräume in der grossen Wirtschaftskrise der frühen dreissiger Jahre: Zur Revision des überlieferten Geschichtsbildes', in Bayerische Akademie der Wissenschaften, *Jahrbuch 1979* (Munich, 1979).
16. Carl-Ludwig Holtfrerich, 'Zu hohe Löhne in der Weimarer Republik? Bemerkungen zur Borchardt-These', in *Geschichte und Gesellschaft*, 10, 1984, Heft 1.
17. Jürgen Reulecke, 'Veränderungen des Arbeitskräftepotentials im Deutschen Reich 1900–1933', in Hans Mommsen, Dietmar Petzina and Bernd Weisbrod (eds), *Industrielles System und politische Entwicklung in der Weimarer Republik* (Düsseldorf, 1974).

18. Institut für Konjunkturforschung, 'Stand und Ursachen der Arbeitslosigkeit in Deutschland', in *Vierteljahrshefte zur Konjunkturforschung*, Sonderheft 29 (Berlin, 1932).

3 Physicians in Crisis at the End of the Weimar Republic*

Michael H. Kater

The Weimar Republic was not a particularly happy time for German doctors of medicine. Having hardly evolved into a fully-fledged profession when the First World War began, they found themselves in great demand during that conflict, only to be somewhat abandoned by society after their return to civilian life. One problem was that there were now too many doctors in the land, and the young among them were pushing the older ones to retire and make room for them. On the other side, the established doctors resented the large medical student numbers and squarely opposed female students and practitioners, now ever more visible. Because the physician-patient ratio was changing, the doctors' earnings were not what they used to be. In addition, the physicians continued, in many important respects, to suffer from a dependence on the sickness insurance funds, to a degree which outside observers regarded as detrimental to the doctors' interests. Physicians found it difficult to solve all these problems on their own, especially as they considered the sociopolitical climate of Weimar a hostile one. It is not surprising, then, that many of them crossed over to the National Socialists before the Republic had spent itself. What is less certain, to date, is how large exactly this group was, how old its members were, what their detailed expectations consisted of and how they thought the Nazis had fulfilled them after the erection of the Third Reich.

The first serious issue which confronted the physicians as the Republic was ushered in was that of youth recruitment. Until the First World War the professional development of medical doctors in Germany had been characterised by a triangular relationship between three contractual partners: medical insurance funds (*Krankenkassen*), patients, and physicians. After the war the most significant factor that changed the pace and perhaps the quality of this professionalisation

*The research for this article was generously funded by the Social Sciences and Humanities Research Council of Canada, Ottawa.

process was the metamorphosis of the triangular relationship into a quatrolateral one. Because of a growing cleavage within the medical corps, there were now four, not necessarily consenting, parties: the patients, the funds, established older doctors on the one hand, and licensed younger doctors not yet registered to practice medicine on behalf of the state-sanctioned insurance funds, on the other.

Why was this so? It appears that until the First World War German medical faculties had produced just enough young doctors to replenish the stock of practicing physicians in any given year in a natural fashion, to the effect that each physician under contract with a sickness fund (*Kassenarzt*) could make what was considered a decent living.[1] Because of fundamental changes in the structure of society wrought by the First World War there were, at the beginning of the Weimar Republic, suddenly too many young doctors wishing to be registered for practice with the funds.[2] Such registration was becoming increasingly necessary because the revolutionary governments immediately after the war had, as a sociopolitical gesture *par excellence*, raised the average income ceiling, thus making medical insurance compulsory for ever broader sections of society.[3] This meant that more people in the population were now forced to visit insurance fund physicians than in previous times, and fewer people remained to avail themselves of the services of privately-established doctors who would charge them higher fees (*Privatpatientenwesen*). The consequence of this for the medical establishment was that a smaller number of fund-independent physicians (*Privatärzte*) could draw benefits from the still available honoraria offered by a shrunken number of affluent 'private patients'.

It was usually the settled practitioners with long-standing reputations in their medical specialty, not excluding, incidentally, general practice, who were fortunate enough to pursue their profession beyond the pale of the insurance funds. Junior doctors, on the other hand, especially those just graduated from university, were invariably dependent on the fund system, for potential private patients did not know of them. In the turbulent post-war years they became a threat to the fund doctors of long standing who could rely on a reservoir of patients that treasured them usually in the capacity of 'family doctor'. As the potential for private practice, which every fund doctor was permitted to engage in if he so desired, vanished, the physicians' struggle for a share in the existing total of fund patients became one of the dominant themes in the history of medical services during the early years of the Republic. The problem was reducible to a question of ratio: With more doctors per fund patient, the individual doctor's income was bound to decrease. If one restricted the number of licensed physicians registered to practice under the fund system by some form of closure, however, one had the means to control the average doctor's income level.

Insurance fund registration closure, or *numerus clausus*, was the issue which came to divide the established doctors, derisively described as *beati possidentes*, and the incoming licencees, the so-called *Jungärzte*, and made for a rift in the entire profession until well after Hitler's political takeover. By spring of 1921 it could be seen that the number of doctors in the Reich would be rising drastically in the future. Matters were approaching crisis proportions in 1922–3, the months of the inflation which complicated all physicians' existence immeasurably, when the first calls for a *numerus clausus* went out from among established doctors' circles.[4]

On 30 October 1923, the Berlin government responded to the imminent dilemma with an ordinance based on the emergency act of 13 October. Through law it restricted the number of fund-registered physicians by a formula of 1000 insured patients per doctor, without, however, revoking any existing registrations. Incoming applicants – and these included many mature medical men who had interrupted their university education because of war service and had then gone back to the classrooms – were placed on a waiting list for a region of their choice and thus impelled to hold out, until an old doctor retired or died. The initiation process could be speeded up if the new doctor settled in his place of birth or where his closest relatives resided, ideally if his father was a resident fund physician. It remained for regional boards composed of representatives of physicians and insurance funds to decide in any given vacancy case whether a waiting applicant should be inducted into the insurance system; decisionary stalemates could be resolved by appeals to be launched by either contractual partner on the board, for consideration by a government-anchored review agency (*Schiedsamt*). Unsuccessful applicants had no recourse to appeal. As it turned out, newcomer doctors were to wait at least two years in places where they actually resided, and five years if on file for an out-of-town fund practice.[5]

These rigid stipulations had, for the moment, ensured the future well-being of already registered physicians, but at the same time they had blocked the professional career of many highly qualified hopefuls eager to start out on their own. In the years of general economic stabilisation after 1923, the number of would-be registrants grew ever larger, and the animosity between young and old intensified. At the beginning of 1924, 1500 applicants were on the regional board lists, of whom approximately 1200 were known to be war veterans. Two years later the number of candidates had more than doubled, and by 1929 it was close to 4000.[6] Roughly half of the 1926 candidates were doctors who had been licensed for medical practice before the injunction of October 1923.[7] Because this figure could not be significantly reduced, the main organisation of German physicians, the Leipzig-based German Doctors' League (*Verband der Ärzte Deutschlands – Hartmannbund*) in November 1929 directed a plea to the reviewing boards to consider, throughout 1930, all those disadvantaged young physicians for fund registration who had been properly licensed by the end of 1924, and particularly those with a war record.[8] But in 1930, there were still 3500 luckless young doctors waiting for processing, and that number was not likely to decrease swiftly because senior, established, fund doctors were more reluctant than ever to retire early since they, too, suffered economic setbacks in their practices and notably found their pension provisions utterly inadequate. On the whole, the average age of practising fund physicians in the Reich was on the increase as the Great Depression was about to descend.[9]

The plight of the medical profession during the tortuous years of extreme economic upheaval after 1929 constituted only a small part of the over-all structural problems German society was faced with at the Republic's end. As is well known, Chancellor Brüning used emergency legislation in an attempt to allay the difficulties he deemed controllable, and the physicians, like other social groupings, were none the better off for it. As the spectre of a huge academic proletariat loomed on the horizon, it became more necessary than ever to artificially contain the bands of freshly-graduated academics, most of them without proper job prospects, who were threatening their invested elders, often with the aid of newly-formed, belligerent lobbies.[10] But even these lobbies were not able to dispel the aura of inter-generational conflict that began to engulf German society; in the case of the physicians, they increased the rift.[11]

Brüning's erstwhile solution for this sociomedical problem lay in the emergency act of 26 July 1930, which in the fund insurance realm upheld the doctor-patient ratio of 1:1000 indefinitely, but now transferred the decision-making powers of the review boards solely to agencies whose authority rested with the state-aligned Reich Insurance Office.[12] However, because this provision merely perpetuated the ills of non-accommodation for the younger recruits rather than effectively deflating their number,[13] it was followed, on 8 December 1931, by a further act modifying the previously valid *numerus clausus* ratio to

1:600, thus allowing a greater number of fund doctors to participate in treating the same number of insurance patients. Yet an added hardship for the young doctors was seen by many in the new requirement that, before registration with the sickness funds, they had to endure a three-year period of assistanceship, commonly at a hospital. Doctors of all age groups now found themselves between the devil and the deep blue sea, in a situation not dissimilar to the one that had prevailed just before the emergency legislation of autumn 1923: While all of them were faced with ruthless competition amongst themselves with the predictable result that henceforth the average income per doctor would deteriorate, the beginner physicians in future were to be stalled for an additional two to three years before enjoying the full status of professionalism.[14] Moreover, as the records show, the subsequent recruitment of the young insurance scheme doctors proceeded only slowly and haphazardly in 1932, with the result that in some regions of Germany war veterans in their mid-thirties, after frustrating waits of eight to ten years, were still prohibited from joining their older and more successful peers.[15]

At this juncture it would be worthwhile to investigate the collective fate of those young doctors who found themselves barred from fund practice right after leaving university. Generally, five options were open to them. They either risked alienation from their profession because they accepted other jobs, or they became technically unemployed, especially if they had decided to wait it out in their birth places so as not to miss the earliest opportunity for call-up. A second possibility was to join a public hospital or a private or university clinic in a subordinate position, often under miserable conditions, and hold out for better times that way. Yet a third option was to sit in for an established senior colleague who wanted time off for holidays, or was ill, for shorter or longer periods. Fourthly, a junior doctor could still elect to try practising on his own as a 'private physician' without fund privileges, and in this manner keep himself afloat until his permission from the review board would be at hand. And lastly, he could enter the civil service as a health administrator, choose academic teaching or private employment, as a ship's medic, in industry or commerce, or become a consultant for the insurance funds.

As was routinely pointed out during crisis times in the Weimar Republic, it is problematic to speak of 'unemployment' in the free professions because here the rules of supply and demand would regulate the workload, and hence the total income for a professional group, but not automatically lead to job dismissals.[16] Still, one authoritative voice conservatively estimated that, at the end of 1930, well into the Depression, there were approximately 23 000 idle academics, a sizeable portion of whom must have been physicians.[17] Yet it would not be correct to equate this number, as Professor G. Müller of Mannheim intimated, with the nearly 4000 overdue *Jungärzte*, because on the one hand, not all of those were really unemployed, and, on the other hand, this number indubitably included registered fund physicians who had chosen to forsake their professions in despair.[18] Once again, if in Stettin in the autumn of 1924, 20 per cent of all resident doctors existed on some kind of dole,[19] then at least half of those must have been *Jungärzte*. In 1927 it was stated that a junior doctor waiting for access to the funds either had to be independently wealthy, incur horrendous debts, or go hungry.[20] And during the Depression more than one perceptive critic warned the established medical profession of a possible radicalisation on the part of the disenchanted young doctors, whose 'spiritual and material destitution' was vividly conjured up.[21]

An aspiring practitioner was permitted, and sometimes coerced, to work in a hospital in three situations: as a medicinal intern (*Medizinalpraktikant*), a voluntarist (*Voluntärarzt*), and as assistant physician (*Assistent*, short for *Assistenzarzt*). Anyone who wished to fully complete his medical education in the German Reich was compelled to serve in a practical capacity for one year, under the supervision of a chief physician (*Chefarzt*) who was frequently a professor, as part of his curriculum.[22] This activity usually did not earn money, it cost a lot; but if an intern was fortunate, he was offered free room and board in the hospital as well as a meagre stipend of up to 75 marks a month.[23]

If the funds would not admit the young doctor after medical practice and university graduation, he might attempt to extend his practical stint in the form of voluntarist service. Again, as the term implies, little or nothing was paid to this professional-in-training, but commonly he hoped that his situation would be converted to a regularly compensated assistant's berth. Such a voluntarist period could last for three years or more.[24]

One young doctor who succeeded in moving from his voluntarist position straight to an institutionalised assistanceship was Rudolf Neubert who at first, in 1924, was offered the (normal) rate of 400 marks a month, and then the princely amount of 600 marks.[25] Supply and demand for assistant doctors fluctuated during the Weimar Republic, depending on the exact time and place, but generally it was not impossible to secure a moderately well-paid position toward the end of the 1920s and early 1930s, provided an intern had been willing to work himself through the arduous stages of subordinate hospital apprenticeship.[26] Shying away from the tribulations occasioned by these efforts to become a registered fund doctor, countless assistants spent several years at their hospitals in order to attain the status of a specialist (for whose qualifications at least three years of assistanceship were prescribed), hoping thereafter to thrive in private, fund-unrelated practice or to progress to a university lectureship.[27] But while, in the 1920s and early 1930s, the number of resident specialists in Germany was indeed on the upswing,[28] it remained practically impossible for any but the brightest assistants, preferably at university clinics and under the aegis of an influential full professor, to become experts in their field and to advance even to a junior position (*Privatdozent*) in one of the Reich's medical faculties.[29] In some clinics, assistants were in their forties and fifties without any prospects of gaining independence.[30] At the end of the Republic contractually employed assistants were harassed, especially by municipal hospitals, which suffered severely under budgetary cutbacks, with the object of removing them from their posts, after expedient references to the notorious emergency legislation.[31]

To act as deputy for a local, properly registered fund physician temporarily on leave for whatever reason was, all things considered, one of the most popular ways for young medical graduates to eke out a living. Some of these deputyships could be rather profitable, depending on the clientele (such as certain ones in Berlin). At other times a doctor had to work exceedingly hard, notably in rural practices where pedalling a bicycle belonged to the required expertise (even though in some instances motor cars are known to have been offered). It was also not unusual to stand in for more than one senior doctor at a time, although this would increase one's workload.[32] Yet clearly, deputyships were no permanent solution to the problems of the *Jungärzte*, and many juniors were complaining that they were forced to slave during the holiday season when the established doctors took their vacations.[33] One interesting case, perhaps not symptomatic of the rest, was reported from Lower Saxony in the winter of 1931. A young female doctor, who had already tried her skills in an assistant's spot, secured employment in a replacement position, but, evidently disillusioned with her lot, moved on to the Dutch East Indies.[34] The main factor which prevented a young doctor from setting up a private practice was that most well-endowed private patients who remained above the large tiers of fund-insured patients were already committed to some reputable physician – invariably in the towns and cities, for in the countryside the fund system was widespread. The young doctor who dared to establish himself in the urban environment with the intention of luring away some of those committed patients found that the going was rough.[35] Besides, the cost of medical equipment and rent was prohibitive and indebted the beginning practitioner to the tune of approximately 4000 marks in his first year.[36] Added on to those problems was the worry connected with fee collection: whereas the fund administration always paid the *Kassenarzt* automatically, the private doctor incurred great trouble with patients who remained remiss.[37] If one survived all these trials, one might well make a determined effort at private practice till the time of fund registration came around or the number of clients rose, but still the earnings were, more often than not, frustratingly small.[38] So-called 'replacement funds' (*Ersatzkassen*) to which some occupational groups subscribed and which had erected no barriers against *Jungärzte* made little difference in the over-all situation because their contributions were fairly negligible.[39]

There remained, then, the few positions to be had with the government, usually as local or regional health administrator (*Stadtarzt*; *Kreisarzt*) or welfare physician (*Fürsorgearzt*), in private employment, perhaps as a marine physician[40] or in industry, and, lastly, with the funds themselves. Entrance to *Kreisarzt* circles, for example, was governed by the same stipulations that determined other opportunities in the governmental service, and those were also anything but rosy.[41] Well-paying positions in private enterprise were always hard to come by. The funds were in the habit of hiring control physicians in their confidence (*Vertrauensärzte*) who were hardly popular with their freely-practising colleagues;[42] latterly the funds had also switched to employing young graduates for their ambulatory services, that were drawn up in competition with physicians' practices and bordered on illegality.[43] Understandably, few young doctors wanted to penetrate their own professional code by acting as potential strike-breakers against their older peers – a distasteful role which had been prefigured during the incipient years of altercation between the sickness funds and contracting doctors fighting for acceptable professional embursements.[44]

But the problem of *Jungarzt* recruitment also appeared to lie with the medical faculties which were overflowing with students. Towards the close of the Republic many self-interested physicians, not excluding *Jungärzte*, were arguing in favour of a *numerus clausus* for students of medicine at the universities.[45] In the end the view prevailed that closure in the classrooms and seminars was not consonant with Germany's tradition of freedom in learning and research. As far as the medical faculties themselves were concerned, they preferred to speak of raising the teaching standard and toughening-up examinations, although, as far as one can make out, nothing ever came of it.[46] For reasons to be explained below, the absolute frequency of medical students in the Reich rose from just over 16 000 in 1914 to 22 474 in 1919.[47] After that, it declined, to reach its nadir during the summer semester of 1925.[48] Between 1925 and 1928 the figures rose again slightly, and after that they accelerated with enormous speed. While in summer 1928 the frequency stood at 11 935, it had climbed to 24 808 exactly four years later. What frightened the established doctors especially was the explosion of student figures at the lower end of medical studies, namely, during the first semesters. Thus, during the Depression years, 3454 new students entered the medical faculties in summer 1929, 3929 in summer 1930, and 4346 in summer 1931.[49]

Such figures as these become meaningful only after a comparison with similar figures for registered physicians. Whereas there had been 34 136 practitioners of all specialties in 1913, there were 33 230 in 1919 and 47 904 in 1925. By 1928, 49 152 physicians were residing in the Reich, and in 1932 that figure had jumped to 52 518.[50]

What impressed statisticians about these numbers at the end of the Weimar Republic was that from the beginning of the 1920s to the middle of the 1920s (1925), the total of doctors had increased, while the total of students had declined.[51] This trend reflected the absorption into the medical profession of the masses of returning military physicians to civilian life as much as of repatriated medical people from the former colonies and surrendered German territory.[52] But it also bespoke the initial run on the medical faculties by military officers who were immatriculated still during or right after the war under preferential conditions – conditions that did not obtain after 1919, so that the student frequency was precipitously down.[53] After 1925 the doctors' corps grew only moderately, because closure, decreed in autumn 1923, was having its effect – until the end of 1931, from which time onward, under modified closure conditions, the frequency jumped once more.[54] Medical students, on the other hand, multiplied enormously after 1925, and notably after 1928, with the result that by 1932, the climax of the Depression, doctors young or old were veritably petrified. Indeed, from 1925 to the end of the Republic, German students of medicine grew more than 13 times as fast in number as did their accomplished elders.[55]

It is enlightening to make the comparison between physicians and medical students from yet another angle by viewing the figures with the aid of coefficients indicating ratios between those social groupings and the general population. This possesses the advantage of compatibility with indices published for the doctors by contemporary social scientists, even though similar data for the students are conspicuously absent. In the years before the First World War, a ratio of approximately 5 physicians per 10 000 Reich inhabitants had been considered healthy and maintainable in terms of university leavers and annual *Jungarzt* recruitment, notwithstanding occasional grumblings and warnings of an impending oversupply of doctors.[56] After the war, the index figure rose to 5.5 in 1919, 7.7 in 1925, and 8.2 in 1932 (see Figure 3.1), while the experts kept insisting that German society could not accommodate more than 7 doctors per 10 000 people, at the very most.[57] In the large centres like Berlin and Hamburg, the ratio value chronically surpassed 10, giving rise to fears of a particular overcrowding of doctors in densely settled urban environments.[58] Figure 3.1 illustrates that a critical point in the development of the German medical profession was reached at about the same time in 1923 when the emergency closure began to take hold; but in spite of it, the benchmark figure of 7 was being exceeded beyond the mark of 8 as the Republic drew to its close. By the same token, the index number for the medical students appeared to signify no hazards until 1928, at which time it rose very swiftly in pursuit of the physicians' index value (see Figure 3.1). Overall, it is clear that the two trends marked by the curves in Figure 3.1 developed asynchronously during the last half of the

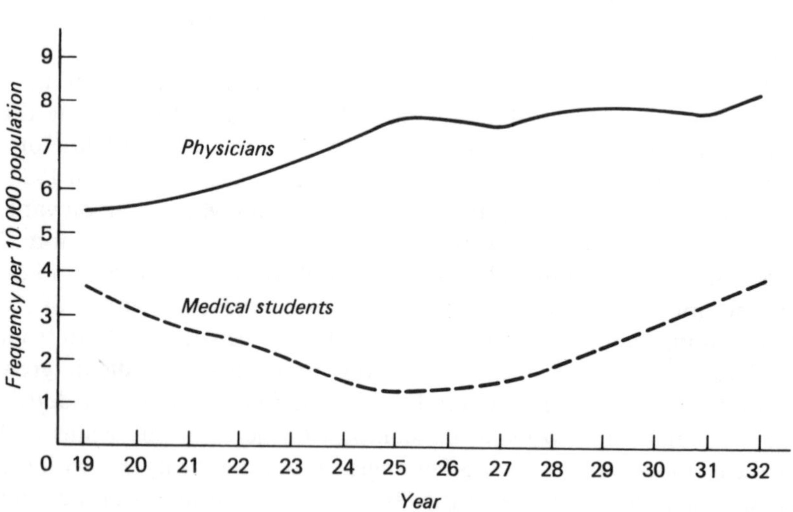

Figure 3.1 Students, physicians, 1919–32

Republic, nearing crisis dimensions in the phase of the Depression, as the students' curve threatened to approach the physicians' one until both would converge or cross. As can be gleaned from Figure 3.1, this would have meant the compounding of the problem of doctors' overrepresentation in the populace, serious enough in itself, through the pressure exerted by aspiring medical professionals who were themselves largely redundant. What should have existed is a perfect negative relationship between the ratio of physicians and that of medical students: As physicians went up in number, students should have gone down, as well as the converse. (This ideal mechanism seems to have been operative during the first half of the Republic merely until 1925, as indicated by the two diverging lines in Figure 3.1.)

The actual dysfunctionality in the two, ideally complementary processes of students' matriculation and doctors' recruitment may be expressed, for the over-all scenario in the Weimar Republic, by a correlation coefficient (product-moment Pearson's R) after regression analysis of the two trends. This coefficient turned out to be −0.236, which for our purposes may be read to mean that there was almost no meaningful relationship between the two factors: doctors on the one hand, and medical students on the other. The minus sign is an indication of the, however weak, negative relationship between the values for doctors and students; the size of the coefficient, not even a quarter of −1.00, denotes this weakness.

Throughout the Republic, and especially toward its demise, several normative figures kept being bandied about as a warning to students, if not to *Jungärzte*, referring to the maximum possible increment of newcomers to the medical profession in any given year. The ceiling of about 1500 new doctors annually, arrived at after complicated arithmetic by Professor Meerwarth of Leipzig at the end of the 1920s, was soon called the result of optimistic fantasising by more sceptical demographers such as Professor Müller of Mannheim, who held against it his own figure of 1200.[59] All this notwithstanding, young German medical students just would not be deterred. The reasons for their seemingly irrational behaviour were complex. Many were encouraged by the slump in medical-student numbers after 1919 when the first large post-war wave subsided. By the time alarms were sounded within the medical establishment many interpreted those as veiled signals of the relative prosperity of all doctors. To be sure, in the face of the ups and downs of a changing job market, the average earnings of German doctors were still regarded as quite acceptable. Moreover, the atypical examples of a few private specialty physicians with astronomical incomes and some well-grounded sickness fund doctors who valued the tricks of a trade more than the ethics of a calling inspired many in the wrong way. Even in adversity, a graduate would hope for a practice in some out-of-the-way location. And there were always those who placed medicine near the top of the social scale, particularly if they were self-recruited, with fathers, uncles and grandfathers as physicians. In a proclaimed era of emancipation, the Weimar Republic encouraged female students to realise themselves more fully by becoming doctors; hence the young women's share in this development was appreciably large. And lastly, medicine was not the only discipline the warners were crying about; similar calls were issued in regard to law, for instance.[60]

If certain students were inspired by rumours about physicians' incomes, one might do well to ascertain their nature. What actually were the earnings of medical doctors during the Weimar Republic, and how did the Depression affect them? In the period of post-war economic turbulence physicians did badly even in comparison with other less-well paid academic professionals, such as lawyers, and many higher (university-educated) civil servants. This had to do, on the one hand, with the rather abrupt lifting of the health insurance ceiling which reduced the, previously large, affluent circle of privileged private patients.[61] On the other hand, those private patients who remained – usually one-fifth to one-quarter of one's entire patient clientele – tended to lag behind with their payments so as to render them worthless in the course of the galloping inflation.[62] After financial stabilisation in 1924, the average income of all physicians improved noticeably, as was in keeping with the general rise of prosperity in the Reich. Thus in 1924, the insurance funds paid 205 million marks to their contractual physician partners (between 80 and 95 per cent of *all* physicians),[63] and they shelled out 433 million in 1926, and 476 million in 1929.[64] The average gross income in that period of about 12 000 marks annually was considered by many observers as adequate, if not profligate.[65] But it was also conceded that despite normalisation in 1924, the buying power of the mark was steadily corroding, doctors were still trailing some other academic peers, and there were precipitous extremes in the medical pay scale.[66]

And indeed, as the Depression entrenched itself in Germany, doctors were once again doing less well. Their mean gross income, by 1930, dropped to the vicinity of 10 000 marks, but figures of 8000 and 7000 were also mentioned as averages.[67] In early 1932, as the new ratio had been set at one doctor per 600 health-insured patients,[68] total earnings were expected to fall even lower because of the absorption of scores of *Jungärzte*.[69]

In order to be fully understood, these developments must be evaluated by the differentiating criteria of income polarity, overhead costs, and extraneous social phenomena. Throughout the Republic, and especially at its extremes, there were a lot of penurious physicians, always beyond any possibility of improving themselves, whose collective plight, nevertheless, tended to blow the over-all picture out of proportion because of constant publicity by the physicians' associations and some public media. There could be no question that during the post-war inflationary phase a larger share of physicians was practising medicine below or near the existential minimum than ever before, and that many lost their savings in the stock market or banks. Reports abounded about doctors accepting side jobs as bar musicians or night watchmen, and some were said to have committed suicide in order to escape starvation. In all, the percentage of totally indigent doctors rose substantially, from 8.3 in 1913 to 37.6 in early 1924.[70] At the height of the inflation many stirring testimonies about poor doctors' misery were printed in the press. Thus, in spring 1923, a story was circulating about a Bavarian practitioner, his wife and child, who were wanting in shelter, clothes and basic furniture to the point where the father was badly neglecting his professional appearance and the child was missing school because of undernourishment and exhaustion.[71]

During the so-called 'Golden Years' from 1924 to 1930 the number of destitute doctors clearly decreased in size, commensurate with the increase of the healthy middle core, but reports persisted of doctors of all ages requesting financial aid from the *Hartmannbund*.[72] Physicians continued to be seen peddling sausage snacks at Berlin's main train station,[73] and the Brunswick sociologist Theodor Geiger, after a scrupulous examination of the relevant statistics, coined the now classic phrase, 'proletaroid doctors'.[74]

The paupers among Germany's practising physicians became even more visible during the Depression. As the suicide rate shot up,[75] many of those who persevered ran deeply into debt. One doctor, who openly asked his more prosperous colleagues for help, wrote that his insurance fund income had been compounded for the next 18 months, that he was financially beholden to the medicinal instrument companies and that he was falling behind with his house calls, as he could not afford a car.[76] So great was the misery among the Reich's deficient doctors that, as early as June 1930, the *Hartmannbund* decided to collect from its regular members a one-time contribution of 100 marks in aid of the needy colleagues.[77]

By the same token, however, there always was a small but securely placed upper layer of physicians who, throughout the republican era, never ceased to earn excessively high incomes. These could be private physicians, often specialists with a professorial title who found it profitable to practise entirely beyond the funds, and clever fund physicians, the so-called 'fund lions' (*Kassenlöwen*), who had devised a system by which to multiply their daily patients' office calls. While it was generally expected that the privately practising specialist would earn, on average, up to twice as much as a fund-dependent general practitioner,[78] this formula was deceptive, for not all specialists were beyond the funds, and most fund-based generalists were treating private patients on the side. Altogether, however, there were only 600 000 private patients left by 1930[79] and merely a small handful of renowned specialists could dare charge them astronomical fees. It was rumoured that Professor August Bier, the famous Berlin surgeon, demanded and received 180 000 marks from tycoon Hugo Stinnes's widow after the (fatal) operation in 1924,[80] and the capital was notorious for its plastic surgeons who would take as much as 10 000 marks after a minor cosmetic correction.[81]

'Fund lions' had made the best of the lump payment system according to which insurance-registered doctors were entitled to recompense from the various sickness funds. With compensation being based either on the frequency of patients or of individual treatments, it became the object of a greedy doctor to cram as many warm bodies into his waiting room as the day was long. This might have filled those doctors' pockets, but it also led to rapid assembly-line routines, to mistakes in diagnosis and therapy and, inevitably, to the discrediting of the German medical insurance system, if not the entire medical profession. This may be illustrated with the uniquely horrible example of a physician who 'rationalised' his treatments by dealing with patients in bulk. First he would call in all those with a cough, and then those with the haemorrhoids. Each group was handed pre-written prescriptions without examination, and after surrendering their insurance forms, they were all dismissed. When one of the haemorrhoidic patients turned out to suffer from intestinal cancer, the physician lost his insurance fund registration, but no more.[82]

Without a doubt, there existed veritable capitalists among the doctors of the Weimar Republic, yet, as one contemporary critic has aptly put it, they were about as typical of the entire profession as stars of the stage for the whole of show business.[83] Only between 6 and 8 per cent of all physicians, 'fund lions' or private practitioners, exceeded the national average at all times, but the practice of those who did tended to see them through good and bad times consistently in style, as they were equipped to weather the storms of even the worst economic adversity.[84]

One factor which was often overlooked in the contemporary assessment of the doctors' situation was that of overhead and incidental expenses complicating the self-employed physicians' existence. Roughly one-third of a doctor's gross income had to be spent on an office, on instruments and specialised literature, on insurance (including a private old-age pension), and sometimes on a medical assistant or (in the case of country doctors) on a car. During the Depression, these costs actually escalated to reach well over 40 per cent of total compensation.[85] Such problems were compounded, toward the end of the Republic, by business taxes. To be sure, in certain regions of Germany such levies had been payable since the revolution of 1918 as decreed by the state legislatures, over the vigorous protests of the doctors' associations. However, in the early 1930s the central government, bent on raising revenue on any account, ruled all medical offices, regardless of their abode, subject to commercial taxation by emergency act.[86] While this stifled the ordinary practitioners, it smothered the proprietors of private clinics, who admittedly conducted their establishments according to the rules of capitalism, but now increasingly in futile competition with the public and charitable hospitals that were exempt from tax.[87] Because they were lacking patients and weighed down by the huge operating costs, private clinics and sanatoriums found it difficult to extend the contracts of their staff physicians even more than public institutions, to say nothing of hiring new ones.[88]

Hence, during the Depression, things did take a considerable turn for the worse for any but the most securely anchored and affluent physicians. The central government's emergency legislation was as much to blame for this as the protracted joblessness which it was meant to cure, for, ironically, both altered the traditional relationship between doctors and their patients significantly, let alone that between patients and insurance funds and funds and doctors. For the physicians, bad times were ushered in with a vengeance when by the act of July 1930 a nominal patient's fee of 50 pfennigs was introduced, to be solicited from each patient upon treatment by his doctor. This contribution was intended for the funds, and it had been clearly designed towards a reduction of the huge deficits threatening the fiscal administration of the Berlin government as unemployment payments were mounting. But because in the course of Brüning's deflationary policies wages in the Reich were falling and the unemployed multiplied much faster than expected, fewer and fewer patients were inclined to pay this fee, with the result that their ailments went untreated and the doctors' clientele began to dwindle. Although the surcharge was somewhat scaled down by December, the damage had been done, as far as the doctors and the trade union officials were concerned.[89]

But this was not yet everything. Registered fund doctors were known to have contended with a deep-rooted malpractice until the onset of the Depression, in that many patients came to consult them with the sole objective of receiving a false aegrotat, so that these in reality quite healthy people could shirk work and stay at home. Many doctors were angered by this not only for ethical reasons but also because it preoccupied them needlessly, as it diverted valuable time from important work. The real crux was that hardly a fund physician dared to oppose such 'patients' because he knew that he would forgo his lump payments, while the patients went to the competition. Unconscionable clients, especially in the industrialised cities, were very fond of this custom because it would relieve them of dreaded physical labour at unreduced wages; in some cases patients are said to have maimed themselves in order to reap a permanent welfare benefit. In addition, there were the genuinely jobless who hoped for all manner of financial insurance pay-offs by producing a doctor's sickness certificate.[90]

After 1929 this problem transformed itself characteristically, without leading to an improvement in the doctors' cause. The number of unemployed now became so large that no one who might run the risk of joblessness dared to jeopardise his post by applying for an aegrotat. Hence the doctors went begging for patients on that account alone. Furthermore, those masses who were out of work stood to lose substantial privileges tied to their insurance status while still employed, with the result that they could reach a stage at which the insurance funds would stop paying for the physicians of their choice. Instead, these patients would be treated by doctors in the employ and trust of the sickness funds (*Vertrauensärzte*), with a concomitant loss of earnings to the average free-wheeling fund physician. Lastly, as the insurance funds themselves became bereft of members as a consequence of massive unemployment, their services for the remaining patrons were cut short to the same degree as their emoluments for the less-occupied doctors were shrinking. It was a vicious circle which, by the end of 1932, had left physicians, insurance funds and patients in a social dilemma of major proportions out of which no one could point the way, least of all the totally unsympathetic cabinets of Chancellors von Papen and von Schleicher.[91]

In the context of this analysis, two kinds of physicians still deserve somewhat closer scrutiny: the family doctor in the countryside and a certain type of specialist. After the First World War it was an open secret among medical graduates that the fastest road to a well-secured insurance fund practice would be via the countryside. The reasons for this were the peculiarly adverse circumstances in which the country doctor had to live and work; he required a hardy disposition and the proper frame of mind not possessed by everyone. *Jungärzte* who experienced a sense of calling and who liked a challenge now recognised their opportunity. They settled and often did well in the country, as long as fund practices were available there.[92] When this ceased to be the case, just before the actual Depression struck, the malaise of the German country doctors added a special touch to the over-all conundrums of the medical profession.

Country doctors had to have a good physical constitution in order to withstand the vicissitudes of a rough life often spent outdoors. Many, especially those in eastern Germany, had to undertake house calls which might see them on the road for up to a 100 miles a day, and often during nights. Those who could afford it travelled by car, but bicycles were not uncommon. Cars were expensive to maintain, and so it became one of the eternal planks in the platform of country doctors to have the federal car tax removed, a goal the Republic never realised. If decent housing could be found, it was often discovered to be more expensive than comparable dwellings in the city. Schooling for the children became a major hurdle because upper schools were generally not available, and an urban boarding school was very dear. To boot, there was the lack of cultural stimulation for the doctor and his wife, the vastly higher expenses incurred in attempts at continuing medical education, and the nature of the work itself which, invariably, included strenuous obstetrical services and risky emergency surgery.[93]

Even before country practices became scarce, doctors starting out found it well-nigh impossible to cope with the growing lack of proper accommodation and with the exceptionally high cost of the medical instrumentarium, needed because hospitals and laboratories often were day-journeys away.[94] But when by 1927 the agricultural disaster was poised to strike, the economic infrastructure of the already thinly settled countryside was acutely endangered, with dire consequences for patients and doctors alike. Long-standing or potential patients tended to leave for the city where they might join the army of the unemployed, and in this way contribute to the festering Depression in the urban centres. Those rural residents who stayed, like the rest of the population in the Reich, showed a marked proclivity after 1929 not to appear for treatment of diseases, with resultant lower earnings for young and old physicians alike. In 1930 one doctor in East Germany was seeing no more than ten patients daily in his office, and perhaps one or two on house calls! By that time, entire formerly flourishing country practices in Pomerania and East Prussia were being shut down because diminutive financial returns had made them quite superfluous.[95]

Certain of the medical specialists, all of whom were usually city or small-town practitioners, found themselves in a somewhat different sort of quandary, although money matters were once again at the heart of the problem. At the dusk of the Republic, medical statistics demonstrated an unexpected rise in pediatricians, chest experts and dermatologists. This threatened to create an imbalance within the supply-and-demand mechanism that could not immediately be redressed. While the pundits saw little danger ahead for the pediatricians (indeed, the Third Reich would welcome them with open arms), the situation of the chest specialists was becoming critical because sanatoriums for tuberculosis patients were habitually strained, and near bankruptcy after the introduction of the commercial surcharge. The question was what to do with all those idle, highly qualified doctors.[96] Worst off were the dermatologists. After the war, when venereal disease was rampant, many a medical assistant in a hospital had acquired a competency to treat syphilis and gonorrhea. But with a new network of social-minded governments at every level, those scourges had been banished relatively quickly, so that by the middle of the 1920s there was a surplus of German dermatologists. These doctors tried to get by as best they could; but in as far as they were fund physicians they came to suffer from the inequitable manner in which they were remunerated. Their treatments per patient were long and complicated, necessitating frequent in-between visits that were not individually honoured under the insurance lump-sum system. During the Depression, even more patients stayed away than normally because the severity of their venereal disorders was often not immediately manifest, and they tried to cure themselves at home. The hapless specialists could not compensate for this loss of earnings like their colleagues in obstetrics or in ophthalmology, who would schedule fee-demanding operations of their own, because surgery was not part of the dermatologist's requisite expertise.[97]

At the end of the Weimar Republic, physicians in Germany looked back on their careers to the time of the revolution, and many of them sensed bitterness. As intensely as they disliked the Weimar regime, they resented the fund system that they were still beholden to, a system which had been pushed and supported with ideological fervour by the political leftists who also created Weimar. In marked contrast, the doctors had always been nationalistic, and to a very large extent they remained squarely on the political right. If they voiced opposition to Weimar, it was because both Weimar and the insurance funds spelled the danger of socialised politics generally, and socialised medicine in particular.

Nothing could be more anathema to the physicians. If they did not flaunt their capitalism, they surely conceived of themselves as independent professionals with the freedom to search out their own clientele or to let themselves be chosen, and with the right to proper compensation. For decades, going back well before the First World War, the funds had threatened to disrupt this, the ideal relationship between doctors and patients. The war had not healed the rift between the funds and the physicians, as many hoped might be the case in 1918–19. As the 'Berlin Agreement' of 1913 which had established some pre-war and intra-war tranquillity was about to expire in 1923, both parties were so much at loggerheads again that the Berlin government decided to step in and impose its own solution to the feuds in October of that year.[98] But, of course, even then the doctors remained dependent on the funds, as, for example, in the matter of medical prescriptions, where a certain price limit was posted which no doctor could exceed.[99] This thorny issue alone would lead to renewed physicians' strikes until the spring of 1924,[100] and those in turn caused the birth of the hated ambulatory clinics by the funds.[101] The incessant ambulant unit incursions into what was considered by the fund physicians as their solemn right to practice resulted in another wave of strikes by 1927–8. It was at this time, when the funds were not only dispensing medicare, but were also manufacturing medicine and setting up dental clinics that the disillusioned doctors feared socialised medicine had come to stay at last.[102] Throughout all this, doctors and fund officials were quarreling on the regional boards over how many new physicians to admit.[103] The contractual situation, in legal terms, was at best precarious for the doctors, in that separate agreements existed between each doctor and each of the hundreds of funds, and all on different terms.[104] Matters came to a head on the edge of the Depression when the funds' resources started to get low. The fact that the fund officials now singled out the private clinics for experiments in fiscal restraint created acrimonious resentment within the physicians' ranks,[105] and it did not help any when the network of stoolpigeon doctors on the payroll of the funds (*Vertrauensärzte*) was intensified and cemented by the ordinance of July 1930.[106] Once again a spending limit was imposed on medications and supplies that was sharply rejected by all practitioners.[107]

A relief of sorts came in December 1931 with the promulgation of another emergency act that led, in 1932, to ways of eliminating the economic dependence of the registered practitioners on the fund bureaucracy. While the funds themselves remained in existence (in particular to deal with the insured), the consignment of the diverse honoraria to the doctors was henceforth assumed by the newly-created *Kassenärztliche Vereinigungen*, a semi-detached, regionally deployed administrative system that acted as a mediator between insurance funds and *Hartmannbund*.[108] This fundamental reform of the national medical system amounted to a quasi-corporatist solution on the Fascist model, because it anticipated the neutralisation of friction customarily dividing both partners in a social contract, consecrated by the laws governing pluralistic democracy. Such a process of diluting the antagonistic quality inherent in voluntary, albeit tenuous, agreements was to be further encouraged, even enforced, after the Nazis had assumed power. The doctors who, at the end of the Weimar era, considered themselves momentarily liberated from the funds had no way of knowing whether their cause would be served more felicitously under a National Socialist dictatorship than under a Republic, even though many of them had already committed their allegiance to Adolf Hitler.

Notes

1. *Inter alia*, see *Ärztliche Mitteilungen*, 31, 1930, p. 158; B. Noltenius, 'Die Aussichten des ärztlichen Berufes', *Die Schwarzburg* (May 1927), pp. 131–2; Konrad H. Jarausch, *Students, Society and Politics in Imperial Germany: The Rise of Academic Illiberalism* (Princeton, 1982) pp. 62–3; Claudia Huerkamp and Reinhard Spree, 'Arbeitsmarktstrategien der deutschen Ärzteschaft im späten 19. und frühen 20. Jahrhundert: Zur Entwicklung des Marktes für professionelle ärztliche Dienstleistungen', in Toni Pierenkemper and Richard Tilly (eds), *Historische Arbeitsmarktforschung: Entstehung, Entwicklung und Probleme der Vermarktung von Arbeitskraft* (Göttingen, 1982) p. 95.
2. Background in Michael H. Kater, *Studentenschaft und Rechtsradikalismus in Deutschland 1918–1933: Eine sozialgeschichtliche Studie zur Bildungskrise in der Weimarer Republik* (Hamburg, 1975) p. 70.
3. Otto Baumgarten, *Die Not der akademischen Berufe nach dem Friedensschluss* (Tübingen, 1919) p. 24; *Burschenschaftliche Blätter* (August–September 1925) p. 245; Ludwig Preller, *Sozialpolitik in der Weimarer Republik* (Stuttgart, 1949) p. 234.
4. *Die Schwarzburg* (February/March 1921) p. 11; Anton Graf, *Die Stellung des Arztes im Staate* (Munich, 1935) p. 77; Wilhelm Ackermann, 'Der ärztliche Nachwuchs zwischen Weltkrieg und nationalsozialistischer Erhebung', MD dissertation (Cologne, 1940) p. 10.
5. Ackermann, 'Der ärztliche Nachwuchs', pp. 12–15; Julius Hadrich (ed.), *Wirtschaftstaschenbuch für wissenschaftliche Assistenten*, (Leipzig, 1925) pp. 297–302, 507–08; Martha Eva Prochownik, *Die wirtschaftliche Lage der geistigen Arbeiter Deutschlands: Erhebungen der Deutschen Gesellschaft zur Bekämpfung der Arbeitslosigkeit* (Berlin, 1925) pp. 33–4; Graf, *Die Stellung*, p. 77.
6. Ackermann, 'Der ärztliche Nachwuchs', pp. 19, 27; *Ärztliche Mitteilungen*, 30, 1929, pp. 544, 561; J. Diel, 'Aussichten der akademischen Berufe', *Academia* (15 April 1929) p. 328.
7. *Ärztliche Mitteilungen*, 30, 1929, p. 605.
8. F. Okrass, 'Zur gegenwärtigen Lage der Arztfrage', *Deutsche Krankenkasse*, 17, 1930, p. 525.
9. See *Ärztliche Mitteilungen*, 31, 1930, pp. 731, 824, 1046.
10. In general, see Reinhold Schairer, *Die akademische Berufsnot: Tatsachen und Auswege* (Jena, [1932]); and Kater, *Studentenschaft*, pp. 56–109. The *Jungarzt* lobby, *Reichsnotgemeinschaft*, was formed in 1926. On it, see Ackermann, 'Der ärztliche Nachwuchs', pp. 23, 27, 49; *Ärztliche Mitteilungen*, 30, 1929, p. 605.
11. See *Ärztliche Mitteilungen*, 30, 1929, pp. 605, 760–61, 833–4; ibid., 31, 1930, pp. 99–100, 613; Carl Haedenkamp, 'Zur Organisierung des ärztlichen Standes', *Ärztliche Mitteilungen*, 31, 1930, p. 553. On the phenomenon of generational conflict in the Weimar Republic, see Michael H. Kater, 'Generationskonflikt als Entwicklungsfaktor in der NS-Bewegung vor 1933', *Geschichte und Gesellschaft*, 11, 1985, pp. 217–43.
12. *Ärztliche Mitteilungen*, 31, 1930, p. 1046; Ackermann, 'Der ärztliche Nachwuchs', p. 68; Florian Tennstedt, 'Sozialgeschichte der Sozialversi-

cherung', in Maria Blohmke *et al.* (eds), *Handbuch der Sozialmedizin, III: Sozialmedizin in der Praxis* (Stuttgart, 1976) p. 401.

13. See Erwin Liek, 'Die Aufgaben der künftigen deutschen Ärzte', *Ärztliche Rundschau*, 41, 1931, p. 15; Friedrich Maetzel, 'Doktoren ohne Brot: Studierende Proletarier', *Die Tat*, 23, 1932, p. 1005.
14. *Ärztliche Mitteilungen*, 33, 1932, p. 772; *Internationale Zeitschrift für Sozialversicherung*, 8, no. 1 (January 1932) p. 7; Graf, *Die Stellung*, p. 37; Preller, *Sozialpolitik in der Weimarer Republik*, p. 473; Hans Schadewaldt, *75 Jahre Hartmannbund: Ein Kapitel deutscher Sozialpolitik* (Bonn-Bad Godesberg, 1975) pp. 124, 127.
15. See *Ärztliche Mitteilungen*, 33, 1932, p. 696; and Ackermann, 'Der ärztliche Nachwuchs', pp. 115–16.
16. For persuasive contemporary arguments, see Leonhard Achner, 'Der Arbeitsmarkt der geistigen Berufe', *Allgemeines Statistisches Archiv*, 21, 1931, pp. 481–2, 492; *Ärztliche Mitteilungen*, 31, 1930, p. 731. Also see the modern analysis in Huerkamp and Spree, 'Arbeitsmarktstrategien', pp. 77–9.
17. Achner, 'Der Arbeitsmarkt', p. 492. For 1932, a figure of 70 000 jobless academics was mentioned (Maetzel, 'Doktoren ohne Brot', p. 1005). A somewhat lower estimate is in Carl Haedenkamp, 'Die Berufsaussichten des Arztes', *Ärztliche Mitteilungen*, 33, 1932, p. 123.
18. See Müller's argument in *Ärztliche Mitteilungen*, 31, 1930, p. 731.
19. Georg Ried, 'CVer und soziale Frage', *Academia* (15 October 1924) p. 79.
20. B. Noltenius, 'Die Aussichten des ärztlichen Berufes', *Die Schwarzburg* (May 1927), p. 131.
21. Example in *Ärztliche Mitteilungen*, 31, 1930, p. 1039. Also see note 11.
22. Kurt Opitz (ed), *Bestallungsordnung für Ärzte und Prüfungsordnung für Zahnärzte*, 4th edn (Berlin, 1936) pp. 5–6, 35–7.
23. Noltenius, 'Die Aussichten', p. 129; Dr Hermann Radetzky's testimony in Günter Albrecht and Wolfgang Hartwig (eds), *Ärzte: Erinnerungen, Erlebnisse, Bekenntnisse*, 3rd edn (Berlin [East], 1973) p. 210; Werner Forssmann, *Selbstversuch: Erinnerungen eines Chirurgen* (Düsseldorf, 1972) p. 80; Ferdinand Hoff, *Erlebnis und Besinnung: Erinnerungen eines Arztes*, 4th edn (Frankfurt & Berlin, 1972) p. 228; Kurt Blome, *Arzt im Kampf: Erlebnisse und Gedanken* (Leipzig, 1942) p. 119. Also see the telling advertisements in *Ärztliche Mitteilungen*, 33, no. 12, 1932, p. X. The inadequacy of hospital board is detailed in *Gewerkschafts-Zeitung*, 34, 1924, p. 47.
24. Graf, *Die Stellung*, p. 38; Rudolf Neubert, *Mein Arztleben: Erinnerungen* (Rudolstadt, 1974) p. 33; Forssmann, *Selbstversuch*, pp. 84, 131; Peter F. Bischoff, 'Über 30 Jahre Arzt', in *Therapie der Gegenwart*, 104, 1965, p. 816; Radetzky in Albrecht and Hartwig, *Ärzte: Erinnerungen ...*, p. 210.
25. Neubert, *Mein Arztleben*, p. 50. For the pay range, see Ferdinand Fried, *Das Ende des Kapitalismus* (Jena, 1931) p. 107.
26. For the republican end phase, see the advertisements in *Ärztliche Mitteilungen*, 33, no. 12, 1932, p. X and ibid., 30, 1929, pp. 559–61; Hans Sikorski, 'Bemerkungen zur Entwicklung des Hochschulstudiums', *Studentenwerk*, 4, 1930, p. 283; Eva Jungermann-Travers, 'Das Medizinstudium im Spiegel der Statistik', *Ärztliche Mitteilungen*, 31, 1930, p. 654.

27. See Noltenius, 'Die Aussichten', p. 130; Otto Oertel, 'Der Arzt (Voraussetzungen, Studium und Berufskreis)', in Hans Sikorski (ed.), *Wohin: Ein Ratgeber zur Berufswahl des Abiturienten*, 2nd edn (Berlin, 1930) p. 89; Graf, *Die Stellung*, p. 33; Rudolf Nissen, *Helle Blätter – dunkle Blätter: Erinnerungen eines Chirurgen* (Stuttgart, 1969) p. 57.
28. Julius Hadrich, 'Die Zahl der Allgemeinpraktiker und Fachärzte in den deutschen Gross- und Mittelstädten im Jahre 1929', *Ärztliche Mitteilungen*, 30, 1929, pp. 542–4; Julius Hadrich, 'Die Zahl der Allgemeinpraktiker und Fachärzte in den deutschen Gross- und Mittelstädten im Jahre 1930', *Ärztliche Mitteilungen*, 32, 1931, pp. 386–8.
29. Cf. only the example of the surgeon Rudolf Nissen, who was fortunate enough to advance to the position of Ferdinand Sauerbruch's favourite assistant, and, later, *Privatdozent* in Berlin – Nissen, *Helle Blätter*, pp. 62–3 and *passim*.
30. Erwin Liek, *Der Arzt und seine Sendung: Gedanken eines Ketzers*, 4th edn (Munich, 1927) p. 88.
31. The physicians' organisations went to bat for some of these unfortunate doctors with the assistance of the courts – see Clemens Bewer, 'Der Fall Mannheim: Assistenzärzte an städtischen Krankenanstalten und Gemeindesatzungen', *Arzt, Hochschule, Krankenhaus*, 3, 1933, pp. 21–8, 28–9, 39–44; protocol, Baden Labour Court Mannheim, 'Urteil in Sachen der Assistenzärzte . . . Enger [*et al.*] gegen die Stadt Mannheim', 2 February 1932, Unterlagen der Kassenärztlichen Vereinigung Deutschlands Berlin (UKVDB)/190. Statutary rights of assistant physicians are outlined in Hadrich, *Wirtschaftstaschenbuch*, pp. 494–6; also see Noltenius, 'Die Aussichten', p. 129.
32. Forssmann, *Selbstversuch*, pp. 84–5, 131; Hoff, *Erlebnis und Besinnung*, p. 229; Neubert, *Mein Arztleben*, pp. 37, 46; Kurt Kuhn, 'Deutsche Mediziner im Kampf gegen den Faschismus – dargestellt an Lebensbildern antifaschistischer Ärzte', in Kurt Kuhn (ed), *Ärzte an der Seite der Arbeiterklasse: Beiträge zur Geschichte des Bündnisses der deutschen Arbeiterklasse mit der medizinischen Intelligenz* (Berlin [East], 1973) p. 234. Also see the advertisements in *Ärztliche Mitteilungen*, 33, no. 12, 1932, p. X.
33. Hermann Berger, *Kleiner Kulturspiegel des heutigen Arzttums nach Zeitschriftenstimmen des letzten Jahrzehnts* (Jena, 1940) p. 124.
34. Roscher to Hartmannbund, Buxtehude, 17 February 1931, UKVDB/97.
35. Cf. Graf, *Die Stellung*, p. 78.
36. Blome, *Arzt im Kampf*, pp. 180–81; Noltenius, 'Die Aussichten', p. 131.
37. Fried, *Das Ende*, p. 106.
38. Cf. Blome, *Arzt im Kampf*, pp. 180–82, whose experience as a specialist was not typical: His earnings were above average.
39. Ackermann, 'Der ärztliche Nachwuchs', pp. 22–3.
40. See the example of Peter Bamm, alias Dr Curt Emmrich, *Eines Menschen Zeit: Memoiren eines überheblichen* (Munich & Zurich, 1980) pp. 50–93.
41. With a view to jurists in the state bureaucracy see Kater, *Studentenschaft*, pp. 68–9. Also see Oertel, 'Der Arzt (Voraussetzungen)' p. 89; Noltenius, 'Die Aussichten', p. 132.
42. Carl Haedenkamp, 'Notverordnung!', *Ärztliche Mitteilungen*, 31, 1930, p. 663.

43. See Huss to Arbeitsgericht Berlin, Berlin, 19 March 1935, UKVDB/207; Prochownik, *Die wirtschaftliche Lage*, p. 32. Notwithstanding any legal arguments, the ambulant units did a lot of good for the working populace, especially in the large cities. See Eckhard Hansen *et al.*, *Seit über einem Jahrhundert . . .: Verschüttete Alternativen in der Sozialpolitik: Sozialer Fortschritt, organisierte Dienstleistermacht und nationalsozialistische Machtergreifung: Der Fall der Ambulatorien in den Unterweserstädten und Berlin* (Cologne, 1981) pp. 199–298, 413–59; Tennstedt, 'Sozialgeschichte', p. 398; Preller, *Sozialpolitik in der Weimarer Republik*, pp. 327, 382–3; Ariane Hesse, *Ärztliche Vereine und Standesorganisationen in Freiburg i.Br.: Entwicklung und Struktur* (Freiburg i.Br., 1978), pp. 141–2.
44. *Inter alia*, see Georg Kuhns, *Fünfundzwanzig Jahre Verband der Ärzte Deutschlands (Hartmannbund)* (Leipzig, 1925) *passim*; Huerkamp and Spree, 'Arbeitsmarktstrategien', p. 101.
45. Ackermann, 'Der ärztliche Nachwuchs', p. 35; *Ärztliche Mitteilungen*, 32, 1931, p. 983; Julius Hadrich, 'Der Hartmannbund im Kampf gegen die Überfüllung der Hochschulen', *Ärztliche Mitteilungen*, 32, 1931, p. 485; ibid., 33, 1932, pp. 696, 772.
46. Carl Haedenkamp, '"Arzttum in Not"', *Ärztliche Mitteilungen*, 31, 1930, p. 40; Jürgen Nachtigal, 'Der Deutsche Medizinische Fakultätentag 1913 bis 1972', MD dissertation (Erlangen-Nuremberg, 1974) pp. 36–7.
47. These and the following student frequencies are according to Table 3 in Michael H. Kater, 'Krisis des Frauenstudiums in der Weimarer Republik', *Vierteljahrschrift für Sozial- und Wirtschaftsgeschichte*, 59, 1972, p. 214. A reprint of this and other tables copied from my article without due mention of credit is in Kristine von Soden and Gaby Zipfel (eds), *70 Jahre Frauenstudium: Frauen in der Wissenschaft* (Cologne, 1979) pp. 39–42.
48. Technically speaking, the low point was reached during winter semester 1925/26, with 7674. See Walter Wienert, 'Die Berufslage der deutschen Akademiker', *Die Tat*, 20, 1928, p. 631.
49. Schairer, *Die akademische Berufsnot*, p. 32.
50. Frequencies for physicians, 1913–32, are according to Hans Tobis, 'Das Mittelstandsproblem der Nachkriegszeit und seine statistische Erfassung', PhD dissertation (Frankfurt, 1930) p. 80; Tennstedt, 'Sozialgeschichte', p. 403; Graf, *Die Stellung*, p. 61; Wilhelm Schlink and Hans Sikorski, 'Die Berufsaussichten der Akademiker', in Michael Doeberl (ed) *Das akademische Deutschland*, II (Berlin, 1931) p. 187; Gertrud Bäumer, *Schulaufbau, Berufsauslese, Berechtigungswesen* (Berlin: 1930) p. 12; *Ärztliche Mitteilungen*, 31, 1930, p. 612.
51. From 1919 to 1925 the physicians experienced positive growth (compound annual average growth rate of 6.28 per cent) while the students experienced extremely negative growth (−15.99 per cent). Growth rate calculations according to the formula in Roderick Floud, *An Introduction to Quantitative Methods for Historians* (London, 1974) p. 91.
52. Baumgarten, *Die Not der akademischen Berufe*, p. 23; Ackermann, 'Der ärztliche Nachwuchs', pp. 9–10.

53. Baumgarten, *Die Not der akademischen Berufe*, p. 23; Georg Schreiber, *Deutsches Reich und deutsche Medizin: Studien zur Medizinalpolitik des Reiches in der Nachkriegszeit (1918–1926)* (Leipzig, 1926) p. 82; *Die Schwarzburg*, 5, 1923, p. 13; Jungermann-Travers, 'Das Medizinstudium', p. 654.
54. The compound annual average rate of growth for physicians from 1925 to 1932 was 1.32 per cent, whereas from 1919 to 1932 it was 3.58 per cent. Calculations as indicated in note 51.
55. The compound annual average rate of growth for medical students from 1925 to 1932 was 17.76 per cent, compared with 0.76 per cent for the 1919–32 period. Calculations as indicated in note 51.
56. See Baumgarten, *Die Not der akademischen Berufe*, p. 22; Prochownik, *Die wirtschaftliche Lage*, pp. 30–1; *Burschenschaftliche Blätter* (August–September 1925), p. 245; Bäumer, *Schulaufbau*, p. 12; *Ärztliche Mitteilungen*, 33 (1932), p. 546; Graf, *Die Stellung* p. 61; Huerkamp and Spree, 'Arbeitsmarktstrategien', pp. 86–93.
57. The two curves in Figure 3.1 are based on data to be found in the sources listed in note 50 (for physicians), and on figures from *Statistische Jahrbücher für das Deutsche Reich* (1919–32) reproduced in Table 3 in my article, 'Krisis', p. 214 (for students). They were set in relation to figures for the general population based on the 1925 census. The census figures were adjusted for every year before and after 1925, in accordance with a formula stipulating an annual growth of 270 000. See Felix Burkhardt, 'Statistik der Berufsüberfüllung, mit besonderer Berücksichtigung der geistigen Berufe', *Allgemeines Statistisches Archiv*, 22, 1932, p. 488. For the maximum coefficient of 7, see Bäumer, *Schulaufbau*, p. 12; Schlink and Sikorski, 'Die Berufsaussichten der Akademiker', p. 187.
58. Hadrich, 'Zahl . . . 1929', p. 543; Tobis, 'Das Mittelstandsproblem', p. 81.
59. See Rudolf Meerwarth, *Bedarf und Nachwuchs an Ärzten* (Berlin, 1932); Schlink and Sikorski, 'Die Berufsaussichten' p. 187; Burkhardt, 'Statistik der Berufsüberfüllung' pp. 484, 491; Schairer, *Die akademische Berufsnot*, p. 31; *Ärztliche Mitteilungen*, 31, 1930, p. 824, 1070; ibid., 33, 1932, p. 547.
60. Liek, *Der Arzt . . . Sendung*, p. 58–9; Carl Jacobs, *Arzttum in Not: Betrachtungen über die Krisis im Ärztestand* (Leipzig, 1929), p. 18; Ackermann, 'Der ärztliche Nachwuchs' p. 40; Wilfried Cohn-Hülse, 'Ärztlicher Nachwuchs und Standesethik', *Ärztliche Mitteilungen*, 31, 1930, p. 174; Jungermann-Travers, 'Das Medizinstudium', p. 654; *Ärztliche Mitteilungen*, 31, 1930, p. 1071; Günter Keiser, 'Das Hochschulstudium in Deutschland im Sommer-Semester 1930 unter besonderer Berücksichtigung des Medizin-Studiums', *Ärztliche Mitteilungen*, 31, 1930, p. 1029; M. Breitinger, 'Warum so viele Medizinstudierende?', *Ärztliche Mitteilungen*, 32, 1931, pp. 1040–43; Kater, *Studentenschaft*, pp. 68–73. For a treatment of students and academic professions as parts of cyclical phenomena, see Hartmut Titze, 'Die zyklische Überproduktion von Akademikern im 19. und 20. Jahrhundert', *Geschichte und Gesellschaft*, 10, 1984, pp. 92–121.
61. See text near note 3, (p. 50).

62. Baumgarten, *Die Not der akademischen Berufe*, pp. 22, 24; *Die Schwarzburg* (February/March 1921): p. 11; Noltenius, 'Die Aussichten', p. 132; Siegmund Hadda, 'Als Arzt am Jüdischen Krankenhaus zu Breslau 1906–1943', *Jahrbuch der Schlesischen Friedrich-Wilhelms-Universität zu Breslau*, 17, 1972, p. 214; Schadewaldt, *75 Jahre*, p. 103. For physicians' reaction to this in rural Bavaria, see Gerald D. Feldman, 'Bayern und Sachsen in der Hyperinflation 1922/23', *Historische Zeitschrift*, 238, 1984, p. 598.
63. Franz Goldmann and Alfred Grotjahn, *Benefits of the German Sickness Insurance System from the Point of View of Social Hygiene* (Geneva, 1928) p. 18; Liek, 'Aufgaben', p. 31.
64. *Ärztliche Mitteilungen*, 31, 1930, p. 984.
65. The average gross income of doctors in 1928 was 12 616 marks. See Walter Wuttke, 'Die Herrschaft von Künstlern: Zur ärztlichen Methodenlehre', in Martin Doehlemann (ed), *Wem gehört die Universität? Untersuchungen zum Zusammenhang von Wissenschaft und Herrschaft anlässlich des 500jährigen Bestehens der Universität Tübingen* (Lahn-Giessen, 1977) p. 200, note 140. Also see the figures for single years of the mid-period in *Ärztliche Mitteilungen*, 31, 1930, p. 224; Carl Haedenkamp, 'Die Vorschläge der Ärzte für eine Reform der Krankenversicherung', *Ärztliche Mitteilungen*, 32, 1931, p. 688; Liek, 'Aufgaben', p. 30; and case of Eutin gynaecologist, Dr W. Saalfeldt, in Lawrence D. Stokes (ed), *Kleinstadt und Nationalsozialismus: Ausgewählte Dokumente zur Geschichte von Eutin 1918–1945* (Neumünster, 1984) p. 792, note 16. The figures indicated for Mainz, Munich, Stuttgart and Leipzig (1926) by Tobis, 'Das Mittelstandsproblem', pp. 83–4, appear much too low.
66. See Prochownik, *Die wirtschaftliche Lage*, p. 18; *Ärztliche Mitteilungen*, 30, 1929, p. 190; ibid., 31, 1930, p. 635. Lawyers were one academic profession earning palpably more than physicians: 18 428 marks as opposed to the latter's 12 616 marks in 1928. See Wuttke, 'Die Herrschaft', p. 200, note 140.
67. *Ärztliche Mitteilungen*, 31, 1930, p. 612; Ernst Mayer, 'Die Krise des Ärztestandes und die Sozialhygiene', *Ärztliche Mitteilungen*, 31, 1930, p. 154; Fried, *Das Ende*, p. 107; Stokes, *Kleinstadt*, p. 792, note 16. Also see J. F. Volrad Deneke and Richard E. Sperber, *Einhundert Jahre Deutsches Ärzteblatt – Ärztliche Mitteilungen* (Löwenich, 1973) p. 74. Comparative income figures are as follows: An unskilled worker in a shoe factory in March 1929 earned a weekly gross wage of approximately 30 marks (about 1500 marks annually. See *Statistisches Jahrbuch für das Deutsche Reich 1932*, p. 272). In Bavaria, a female milk vendor received 38 marks a month in 1930, a bank clerk received 170 marks net in 1932/33, and a police constable received 150 marks a month in 1932/33. These figures are according to Hartmut Mehringer, 'Die KPD in Bayern 1919–1945: Vorgeschichte, Verfolgung und Widerstand', in Mehringer *et al.* (eds), *Bayern in der NS-Zeit V* (Munich & Vienna: 1983) pp. 115–17.
68. See text near note 14, p. 53.
69. *Ärztliche Mitteilungen*, 33, 1932, p. 150.

70. Noltenius, 'Die Aussichten', p. 132. Also see Deneke and Sperber, *Einhundert Jahre*, pp. 66–8; Jacobs, p. 82; Hadda, p. 215.
71. *Münchener Neueste Nachrichten*, 13 March, 1923.
72. *Ärztliche Mitteilungen*, 31, 1930, p. 635.
73. Liek, *Sendung*, p. 165.
74. Geiger used Tobis's questionable figures for 1926 (see above n. 65) but modified them in accordance with his own data. Theodor Geiger, *Die soziale Schichtung des deutschen Volkes: Soziographischer Versuch auf statistischer Grundlage* (Stuttgart, 1967), first printing, 1932, pp. 43–4. Also see Ackermann, 'Der ärztliche Nachwuchs', p. 55.
75. See Graf, *Die Stellung*, p. 65.
76. Case (1932) is reported ibid., pp. 81–2. Also see case of Dr Hans Landauer (1931) in UKVDB/227.
77. Waldheim to Landgericht Leipzig, Leipzig, 7 December 1931, UKVDB/112. Also see Martin Kaehler, 'Die Berufsaussichten der Mediziner', *Die Schwarzburg* (February 1932) p. 56.
78. Noltenius, 'Die Aussichten', p. 130.
79. *Ärztliche Mitteilungen*, 31, 1930, p. 612.
80. Gerhard Jaeckel, *Die Charité: Die Geschichte des berühmtesten deutschen Krankenhauses* (Bayreuth, 1963) p. 336.
81. Martin Gumpert, *Hölle im Paradies: Selbstdarstellung eines Arztes* (Stockholm, 1939) pp. 200–01.
82. The case is reported in Paul Rosenstein, *Narben bleiben zurück: Die Lebenserinnerungen des grossen jüdischen Chirurgen* (Munich: 1954), p. 34. Also see Jacobs, *Arzttum in Not*, pp. 31–2; Blome, *Arzt im Kampf*, pp. 225–7; Liek, *Sendung*, p. 57; Liek, 'Aufgaben', p. 30; *Ärztliche Mitteilungen*, 31, 1930, p. 1082.
83. Baumgarten, *Die Not der akademischen Berufe*, p. 22.
84. Ibid., also Tobis, 'Das Mittelstandsproblem', pp. 83–4; T. Geiger, *Die soziale Schichtung des deutschen Volkes*, pp. 43–4; Kaehler, 'Die Berufsaussichten der Mediziner' p. 56.
85. Tobis, 'Das Mittelstandsproblem', pp. 83, 85; Liek, 'Aufgaben', p. 30; *Ärztliche Mitteilungen*, 31, 1930, p. 612; *Ärtzliche Mitteilungen*, 33, 1932, p. 150; Johann Peter Loewe, 'Die Entwicklung der wirtschaftlichen Verhältnisse des ärztlichen Berufes in Deutschland seit dem ersten Weltkrieg', MD dissertation (Freiburg i.Br., 1954) p. 12.
86. Schreiber, *Deutsches Reich*, p. 84; Clemens Bewer, 'Was bringt die Notverordnung vom 1. Dezember 1930 den Ärzten?', *Ärztliche Mitteilungen*, 31, 1930, pp. 1022, 1036, 1039, 1083.
87. See the letters in Kurt Klare, *Briefe von Gestern für Morgen: Gedanken eines Arztes zur Zeitenwende* (Stuttgart & Leipzig, 1934) pp. 69, 99–104; Bewer, 'Notverordnung', p. 1023; Sanatorium Dr Rosell to Verband der Ärzte Deutschlands, Ballenstedt/Harz, 4 October 1931, UKVDB/156.
88. Case of Professor Oscar David's dismissal, in Vorstand der Israelitischen Gemeinde to David, Frankfurt, 26 February 1931, UKVDB/146, vol. 2; Dr Steinmeyer to Verband der Ärzte Deutschlands, Görbersdorf/Schl., 28 July 1931, UKVDB/105.
89. In addition, there was, after July 1930, a similar user's fee towards

prescriptions. See Bewer, 'Notverordnung', p. 1020; *Ärztliche Mitteilungen*, 31, 1930, p. 1084; *Gewerkschafts-Zeitung*, 40, 1930, p. 422; Preller, *Sozialpolitik in der Weimarer Republik*, p. 472; Paul Peschke, *Geschichte der deutschen Sozialversicherung: Der Kampf der unterdrückten Klassen um soziale Sicherung* (Berlin [East], 1962) p. 394; Schadewaldt, *75 Jahre*, p. 123.

90. These problems, undeniable as they were, were much exaggerated by the medical right-wing critics at the end of the Republic. See Liek, *Sendung*, p. 57; Liek, 'Aufgaben', p. 30; Jacobs, *Arzttum in Not*, pp. 27–8, 33; Graf, *Die Stellung*, p. 76; in restrospect Blome, *Arzt im Kampf*, p. 224. Critically, from a trade union point of view, *Gewerkschafts-Zeitung*, 40, 1930, p. 435.

91. *Gewerkschafts-Zeitung*, 40, 1930, pp. 481–2; Haedenkamp, 'Vorschläge', p. 687; Verband der Ärzte Deutschlands to Betz, Munich, 4 April 1932, UKVDB/146; Ackermann, 'Der ärztliche Nachwuchs', p. 109; Georg Benjamin, in Irina Winter (ed), *Georg Benjamin: Arzt und Kommunist* (Berlin [East], 1962), pp. 85–6; Tennstedt, 'Sozialgeschichte', pp. 401–05.

92. Prochownik, *Die wirtschaftliche Lage*, p. 31; Breitinger, 'Warum so viele Medizinstudierende?', p. 1041; Jungermann-Travers, 'Das Medizinstudium', p. 654; Jacobs, *Arzttum in Not*, p. 47; Burkhardt, 'Statistik der Berufsüberfüllung', p. 488.

93. See Baumgarten, *Die Not der akademische Berufe*, p. 22; *Ärztliche Mitteilungen*, 30, 1929, pp. 831–2; ibid., 31, 1930, p. 548; ibid., 32, 1931, p. 1005; Schadewaldt, *75 Jahre*, p. 93.

94. Prochownik, *Die wirtschaftliche Lage*, p. 31; Ackermann, 'Der ärztliche Nachwuchs', p. 15.

95. *Ärztliche Mitteilungen*, 31, 1930, pp. 157–8, 548–50, 1083; ibid., 32, 1931, p. 1005; Haedenkamp, 'Vorschläge', p. 687.

96. Julius Hadrich, 'Altersgliederung und Verteilung der deutschen Fachärzte im Jahre 1929', *Ärztliche Mitteilungen*, 30, 1929, p. 672, note 87 above.

97. *Ärztliche Mitteilungen*, 30, 1929, p. 438; ibid., 33, 1932, p. 34; K. Schmitz, 'Die ungenügende Bewertung ärztlicher Leistungen', *Ärztliche Mitteilungen*, 31, 1930, p. 236.

98. Carl Haedenkamp, 'Die Zukunft des Kassenarztes', *Ärztliche Mitteilungen*, 31, 1930, p. 697; Tennstedt, 'Sozialgeschichte', p. 397.

99. Tennstedt, Sozialgeschichte, pp. 397–98; Peschke, *Geschichte*, p. 377.

100. Tennstedt, 'Sozialgeschichte', p. 398; Schadewaldt, *75 Jahre*, p. 93; Ackermann, 'Der ärztliche Nachwuchs', p. 11.

101. Tennstedt, 'Sozialgeschichte', p. 398; and the evidence in note 43.

102. Preller, *Sozialpolitik in der Weimarer Republik*, pp. 327, 382–83; Peschke, *Geschichte*, p. 377.

103. See text at note 5 (p. 51).

104. Schadewaldt, *75 Jahre*, p. 108; Hesse, *Ärztliche Vereine*, p. 143. On the multiplicity of funds see Peschke, *Geschichte*, pp. 377–8.

105. Schadewaldt, *75 Jahre*, p. 122.

106. Ibid.; Tennstedt, 'Sozialgeschichte', p. 401; Haedenkamp, 'Notverordnung!', pp. 662–3.

107. Schadewaldt, *75 Jahre*, p. 122. For a scathing contemporary comment on this limit, see Liek, 'Aufgaben', pp. 30–31.
108. The *Vereinigungen* consisted of regional representatives of the *Hartmannbund*, the physicians' 'union', who dealt with the funds over the finances collectively in place of the individually contracted physicians and then apportioned the money to them. Physicians' contracts with the various funds now were transferred to the *Vereinigungen*, and henceforth consolidated. See Tennstedt, 'Sozialgeschichte', p. 401; Schadewaldt, *75 Jahre*, pp. 123–7.

4 Unemployment also Hits Women: The New and The Old Woman on the Dark Side of the Golden Twenties in Germany*

Karin Hausen

Three passages from contemporary discussions can throw light on our theme:[1]

> Through so-called rationalisation, more women are working; in very many cases today, the unskilled woman worker is taking over the job of a skilled male worker; men – fathers of families – are being sacked and very young girls are being engaged in their place: these are things that every worker sees nowadays, and which bring suffering to thousands. Quite understandably, the feeling against this low woman competitor is more bitter than ever these days . . .

> The woman of the family struck by unemployment must confront an enormous task which is growing, and has a significance not yet recognised everywhere: she must, with all of her womanly and motherly strength, uphold the self-respect of the man, and maintain the respect of the children for him. Her understanding for his undeserved helplessness in the face of the family's poverty and want, is the prerequisite for family unity and a fruitful family life. The woman must use all her ingenuity to help him keep occupied, giving him the feeling that he is making good use of his time, and that this work is of value to the family.

> In many cases, the daughters of well-off parents are earning money to pay for such things as sports and travel. These facts are common

*I am most grateful to Jan Lambertz for translating this article into English. K.H.

> knowledge, and it therefore causes bitterness if ladies often queue up for the dole, when one knows that they are not really dependent on this support ... Double earning by some people, such as spouses, also cannot be justified – in many cases, at least – by financial troubles. Particularly in cases where a part of the family income or the income of the spouses is absolutely secure, double earning does not merely serve to put the household on a sure footing, but is often used to make life more comfortable. One can no longer excuse the fact that wives of civil servants hold civil service posts, when there are men and women, in every respect sufficiently trained and qualified, who are outside waiting for work. One tries to defend this employment using the constitution. There is absolutely no understanding for such a constitutional provision among the people.

Although our understanding has increased, we still know very little about the historical development of the sex-segregated labour market in Germany.[2] Furthermore, we know virtually nothing about the burdens and survival strategies existing in times of widespread high unemployment, and their different meaning for men and women.[3] Studies of the Weimar Republic still concentrate mainly on men when they neutralise gender in the available data on women and men, and produce accounts of 'people.' The occasionally inserted sentences about women as a 'special species' are insufficient prompting for thinking beyond the simple equation, people minus women equals men.[4] The more I looked about in the abundant research on Weimar, the more difficult it became – in the face of prevailing approaches – to present women and unemployment in a very broad context, rather than to discuss the subject exclusively in terms of a specific women's problem. In order to outline the broad range of issues which must be considered in such a historical investigation of the labour market position and unemployment of women and men, I am making a detour through current economic and political discussions.

The labour market mediates between people who supply their labour, and those who demand labour. This generally formulated, basic model of the labour market proves of little value as soon as one focuses on a special group within those who offer their labour. Can the special group simply be placed outside the model group? Can the structure of the model group be used as a norm or a yardstick for describing and measuring the differences of the special group? Does recognition of the 'special' not demand a new formulation of the abstract 'general', or even demand abandoning the latter entirely?

Today these questions are broadly discussed in labour market research, and they are a special preoccupation of feminist research, which criticises the considerable male bias in 'general' labour market research and labour market policy. More recent studies and attempts to develop theories about the segregated, segmented, or dualistic labour market and the problem of the marginalisation of labour are first steps toward a new conceptualisation of these problems.[5]

Women's recent deliberations over the occupational situation of females have opened the way toward an even more thoroughgoing revision of previous conceptions.[6] Up to now, labour market research and policy have normally left their accounts bare of the fact that – to a decisive degree – the very existence and capacity for work of the people moving within the bounds of the market have been, and are dependent upon, the unpaid work of women in private family households. An exclusive focus on wage work is a serious limitation in particular for our understanding of the situation of women. Such an approach completely sidesteps the importance of examining the structural tension existing between family work and wage work. In the course of the physical separation of home and wage work, as well as through the granting of equal rights (at least in principle) to women, this tension has played a decisive role in the life plans and patterns of ever increasing numbers of women. In the labour market, women come off much worse than men. Their disadvantages in wage work are manifested in lower wages, worse jobs, jobs with less security, more and longer intervals of unemployment. Taken exclusively from an occupational standpoint, these disadvantages appear as the inevitable result of less formal education and occupational training, less time spent in an occupation, less mobility and readiness to work, and an 'underdeveloped' career orientation. Using such a perspective, we inevitably arrive at the conclusion that women are deficient; in the final analysis, we gravitate toward a form of victim-blaming with this type of assessment.[7]

In a number of publications, Elisabeth Beck-Gernsheim and Ilona Ostner have shown what an occupational study might look like if it proceeds from the context of female lives. In contrast to the usual 'women should be changed, occupations should not . . .', they argue:[8]

> The disadvantages operating against women in wage work are not only those suffered by a minority group, encountering prejudice or being forced to carry specific burdens. These disadvantages are at the same time, and fundamentally also, the widespread undervaluing and negation of, discrimination against, but also the sanctioning of,

a different form of work – work not attached to occupation – and a different form of living.

With their at once oppositional and complementary qualities, occupation and family are firmly embedded in the social arrangement of modern industrial societies. The task of striking a balance in the difficult relationship between family and work has fallen on, and continues to fall on, women – primarily in their role as wives, mothers, and housewives – but often in their role as wage earners as well. Women in Germany were only granted formal equal opportunity in the labour market at the beginning of this century. Yet running alongside this development, the job and achievements of the housewife and mother were promoted all the more vigorously. Securing the highest prestige for the housewife-mother, and placing this identity firmly at the centre of women's future plans, could ensure that women, caught between the competing pulls of occupation and family, would not fully opt for occupation, as men already had.

The positions which women can and do occupy under these conditions mean that men essentially receive better opportunities in the labour market. In times of widespread high unemployment, women face the added difficulty that public opinion as well as political measures give primacy to the right of male family breadwinners to jobs. Married women – apart from those who directly work in family enterprises – no longer count as legitimate wage earners. In the current phase of high unemployment, pushing the 'reserve back into the home' can succeed without provoking a great uproar, merely through the quiet pressures of economic structure and institutionalised regulations put into force by state administration of labour and labour market policies.[9]

In contrast, during the Weimar Republic, not silent forces but an ardent public discussion pushed for discrimination against women in the labour market. In periods of economic crisis, vehement controversy raged precisely because increasing numbers of young women and even married women were taking up wage work outside the home, and because the freshly proclaimed constitutional principle of equal rights for women and men was a provocation. In the years of generally scarce job opportunities, women's wage work elicited vigorous defences of the apparently self-evident male priority in the right to a job. It is apparent in unemployment that the relation between family and occupation, and the many ties between women and men bound up in this relation, also operate, and these will be scrutinised. Therefore, the question of how unemployment affected women is far more complex than is evident at first. To avoid becoming completely entangled in the complex variety of questions thrown up by these considerations, I will select only a few aspects of the problem here to build up my argument.

I will take up women's unemployment, as measured in statistics, only in the final section of my discussion. The pivot on which my quantitative analysis turns will be the problem of 'invisible' unemployment; moving in this direction is prompted by the considerable bluntness of Weimar statistical instruments, a problem already acknowledged by contemporaries. These instruments were particularly imprecise where they measured women, and taking this into account alters any tendency to paint women simply as the 'winners' of rationalisation and the crisis in the labour market. I will lead up to this final section with a more precise analysis of labour market policy, which was institutionalised in the Weimar Republic as a coherent system of labour market analysis, employment referral programmes, and state aid for the unemployed. My interest concerns the question of whether this new branch of state social policy, built up during a time of economic instability and flagging prosperity, discriminated in a positive way for or in a negative way against women. In order to depict broadly the state interventionary practices surfacing here, I will dispense with a description of the features characterising the 'normality' of the sex-segregated labour market between 1919 and 1933, which lay on the other side of cyclical, structural and seasonal unemployment. Instead, I begin by sketching out how nonwage-earning women were affected by unemployment.

Few attempts have been made to understand and describe prolonged unemployment as an individual and collective experience in the daily lives of women and men, threading through different stages in their lives. These attempts have concentrated predominantly on those who offer their labour in the market without success.[10] However, their unemployment always touches on other people as well: marital partners, children, parents, the family. To begin writing the social history of families suffering the strain of unemployment would demand examining the growing burden of housework on women at length, and describing the place occupied by housewives and mothers. This history remains to be written, and here I can only direct some attention to this neglected reality, which ought to be kept in mind in the more labour market-oriented analysis which follows later.

Marie Jahoda, Paul F. Lazarsfeld and Hans Zeisel's study of Marienthal remains one of the most impressive accounts of living conditions in times of unemployment.[11] In Marienthal, an industrial village in

Austria, the textile factory had shut down operations. As a result, when the research team arrived on the scene for its 1931–2 'sociographical' study, nearly all of the women and men in the village's 478 families had already been unemployed for over a year. The team's richly detailed observations make all too obvious that – while both women and men had been employed, and both became unemployed – the differences between their daily lives during unemployment were enormous. This held true, even where both men and women could hardly aspire to more than physical and psychological survival for themselves and their children. The observers concluded succinctly: 'Time in Marienthal runs on a dual course: it is different for men and women'. For men, 'Doing nothing rules the day'. In contrast, the unemployed women's day was still 'filled with work: They cook and scrub, they mend and take care of the children. They plan and make decisions, and have very little leisure after doing the housework, which is twice as difficult in this period when housekeeping money is so limited'.

In the economics of poverty, it is first and foremost women who are responsible for preventing the complete collapse of family resources. Where the family 'provider' fails to obtain a wage, his power as the 'protector' also shrinks. It is women who must mobilise against growing poverty and against the family sliding into destitution. This task falls so heavily on them, for they are the ones – as housewives and mothers, and evidently often as daughters – who must manage to stretch ever smaller material resources with a corresponding increase in thriftiness. The task of satisfying the most pressing needs in terms of food, clothing, heat, cleanliness and creating a living space falls on them, time and again. Furthermore, the more exclusively dependent the household was on cash income before being ensnared in unemployment, the more difficult these tasks become, and the more they become relegated to women alone.

Only clues remain about the implications of these daily struggles. It was evidently rare for women in Germany to give up in the face of these unending tasks. For most of them the 'education' for economic crisis as a permanent state had already begun during the First World War; up through the later Depression, fleeting prosperity provided no real opportunity to forget these lessons. Women who were locked into family responsibilities seem to have typically strained all their reserves of strength and energy rather than giving up, becoming resigned. Resorting to the dangerous and bitter expedient of abortion was more prevalent than in financially better times.[12] Avoiding the drain of additional young children in bad times was a mutual goal of married couples; yet, often enough, accomplishing this became a burden resting solely on women. Accounts describing the work of advice centres for mothers provide us with some details on the emaciated women who appeared asking for help. No longer able to nurse their babies, they none the less wanted and felt compelled to continue doing so, to save on expenses. Mothers also appeared as clients in health welfare centres. Hoping to get access to the 'material advantages' which these centres made available for children, mothers decided to expose themselves to this new type of social control and assistance. Interestingly, while children were becoming perceptibly more ragged in appearance, doctors working for the welfare services actually recognised that mothers were making desperate efforts to present children in a clean state, in decent clothing. Even in the years of the Depression, during which the incidence of skin diseases stemming from dirt noticeably increased, these doctors – surprisingly – did not make allegations that mothers neglected their children; instead, they fixed blame on the general shortages of clothing, soap, warm water, and their lack of time. Visits to welfare centres to request material help such as clothing, food, shopping vouchers and fuel, to a large extent do not appear to have been the task of families' unemployed fathers.[13]

What happened to a home when the rent could no longer be scraped together? Local authorities helped with rent supplements, if housing conditions proved bad enough. Otherwise, moving became imminent. Often this would have entailed the loss of vital ties to neighbourhood survival networks, which could provide help such as food, credit at shops, or small sums of cash, borrowed for short periods to cover pressing hire purchase debts. Establishing and maintaining ties with these networks – and, if necessary, depending on them for help – probably fell much more on women than on men. Whether or not a family was forced to move because of unemployment, the fact that unemployment drastically altered the lifestyle of the man in the household (and perhaps also that of one or more children expected to earn wages), meant that strains on the relations within a family were inevitably created. During daytime hours, the unemployed would be around the family much more than usual, and already in this respect they interfered with the daily routine.

The father and husband who could no longer structure his life around his job also posed an additional strain on his children and wife if he came to perceive himself as a failure, the cause of his family's difficulties. No longer bringing home a wage, he could no longer function as provider and family protector. The obviously infrequent attempts by unemployed men to engage in household and family work more likely damaged their 'manliness' than helped to raise their self-esteem. Irritation, nervousness, and explosive struggles over authority characterised the climate in these homes. Accounts by students enrolled in vocational training schools in the period suggested how alcohol could hasten the material and emotional destruction of 'unemployed families'.[14] The long hours of unemployment corroded every form of security for the man, the husband and father, including his usual ostentatious and convincing self-confidence, which the family had for so long simply taken for granted. He became transformed into the unpredictable, the suffering one.

Accounts describing the women in families hit by unemployment ring quite differently. Even children saw them as the active, competent, central figures in their families. Paradoxically, their authority appeared to grow along with visible signs that their strength and resources had been taxed to the limit. Finally, if the wife of the worker or white-collar employee contributed more money to the household budget than her unemployed husband, then tensions mounted. Maintaining the 'stability of the family' in this situation (and stability appeared to be more in evidence than the oft-referred to 'crisis of the family') demanded enormous energies to smooth out tensions. Apparently, the 'stronger sex' profited far more from this 'tension management' than he invested in it.[15]

We can uncover statistics on unemployment in the general occupational census conducted on 16 June 1933. The peak of the Depression had already been passed, and these figures were also collected in a phase of optimal seasonal employment. Unemployment was directly hitting 11 400 000 people in the German Reich at that point, if one counts the unemployed together with members of their immediate family. This represented 17.4 per cent of the entire population, and 31.6 per cent of all those in manual and white-collar workers' families.[16]

Looking outwards from the perspective of this family situation, the problems of high unemployment and the spread of short-time work in the Weimar Republic appear in a new light. The insufficient number of jobs available, and the inadequate levels of income, provoked clashes not only between labour and capital, but also between women and men. Held up against pre-war experiences and the dreams of the 'good old days' and an even brighter future, the promise embodied by social democracy apparently remained indiscernible – and did so despite a considerable expansion of social benefits and of money invested for the social good.

The desperate and spiteful polemics arising particularly in the early 1930s against 'double earner' (dual income) families, cannot simply be written off as campaigns of inveterate male chauvinists.[17] These hostile slogans were also an expression of a society bearing the structural problem that the means to a livelihood and the interests of family households were effectively put into profound conflict with broad social organisation. Because it is primarily women whose place in society has been defined by the conflicting pulls of family and occupation, they have been the favourite target of complaints, and bitter disappointment has been projected onto them when an increase of social justice at one level has been experienced as an increase of injustice at another level. This projected disappointment on women has manifested itself in the view that they are both culprits and victims. Benefits falling to the wage-earning woman appeared to exist at the cost of the family breadwinner and his dependent wife. Characteristically, this prevailing perception also obscured the fact that it would have lain in the direct interests of precisely these families if their daughters had been accorded equal opportunities with sons in the labour market, or if discrimination had been exercised not only against married women, but also against single men.

I wish to illustrate these observations with a closer analysis of the labour market policies emerging in the Weimar period.[18] From their inception, these labour market policies were in some regards formulated as family policy. State assistance for the unemployed, or compulsory insurance against the risk of unemployment was, among other things, designed to provide security for women in their 'natural vocations' as housewives and mothers, for children, and for the family as a whole in cases where the 'provider' no longer had an income. The intentions underlying these policies and how they functioned deserve a separate study. However, the dilemma intrinsic to such policy development should at least be mentioned: if the comprehensive policies attached to the labour market would have to deal only with people of the male sex – with women existing only as unpaid home and family workers – the administrative machinery could have been cast in one uniform mould. In practice, however, these policies were forced to deal with women situated in the labour market. With their low wages, 'pin money' and – in the post-war period – their by no means unusual family 'breadwinner' function, these women cropped up, then, as irritations to the administrative machinery which was being established.

In this realm of labour market policy as well as in other areas of state social policy, it is clear that women could not gain as much as men by the creation of social security systems. Across the board, the systems of social security gave the support of men priority, even where women's need for social assistance was indisputably greater. This scale of priorities resulted from a mechanism set into motion by the contradictory valuing of women's work in the market system of wage work and in the social system as a whole. At its inception, and for a long time thereafter, social policy was principally not designed to guarantee the subsistence minimum operating at any given time. Such a guarantee would have interfered with the pressure to engage in wage work. Consequently, it would have disturbed the regulation of labour costs according to supply and demand deemed essential for the establishment of wage rates. The dominant wage systems of the Weimar Republic, however, were structured so that a woman could not have attained an income level sufficient for more than a quite meagre existence, had she wished for lifelong autonomy in an independent household.[19] The combination of these features of the prevailing wage system and social policy meant that discrimination against wage-earning women in a sense doubled within the system of social insurance. This discrimination affected in particular those women who needed, or rather, demanded, a subsistence and existence which were not derived from a man. Social policy measures were not only intended, but also structured to secure and stabilise the means of men who functioned as 'providers'. On the tails of this, they also operated to secure single men's means and to hinder women's ability to gain economic autonomy. Thereby, women found themselves pressured to take up the 'socially desirable' role of wife and mother, whose maintenance was derived from a husband.

The way in which unemployment insurance and the so-called 'productive unemployment assistance' programme functioned in the early phase of German labour market policy can show with unusual clarity how these systematically-described components of social measures worked in practice.[20]

On 11 November 1918, an ordinance was issued prolonging the wartime financial assistance to the unemployed for the period of demobilisation. All people who were 'able-bodied and available for work' who had lost jobs as a result of the war received assistance, if 'need' was proven. At first this ruling applied to all persons aged 14 years and above; as of February 1923, it applied to all those aged 16 years and over; and during more favourable employment conditions, only those aged 18 and over remained eligible. Up to 6 May 1920, the unemployed in need of assistance were covered for the entire duration of their unemployment, but thereafter, ordinarily for only the first 26 weeks. In exceptional cases, this was also extended to 39 or even 52 weeks. On 15 October 1923 and 13 February 1924, these regulations concerning unemployment assistance were fundamentally altered in the course of stabilisation of the German currency. As of those dates, employers and all employees who were subject to compulsory health insurance had to pay unemployment insurance contributions. Eligibility for benefits then entailed having been employed and having paid insurance contributions for at least 13 weeks within the 12 months preceding unemployment. None the less, making such insurance payments did not automatically mean the right to these benefits: benefits continued to depend on proving a lack of means. This form of the regulation remained in effect until 30 September 1927. On 1 October 1927, AVAVG, the Act on Labour Exchanges and Unemployment Insurance, came into force. From that point on, the AVAVG linked compulsory contributions to unemployment insurance and the right to benefits in the event of unemployment, irrespective of other means of support. However, the law stipulated that claimants had to meet the qualification of paying in 26 weeks of contributions in the preceding twelve months. The maximum duration of the benefit was set at 26 weeks, and 39 weeks in exceptional cases. Those qualified to draw benefits could also be granted a further 26 and possibly also 39 weeks of 'emergency assistance', which had already been established in November 1926. Yet the privilege of obtaining an emergency provision again at any rate only belonged to those who could furnish evidence of their lack of means.

Here we will steer around the story of how the unemployment insurance financially collapsed under the pressures of the Depression and was destroyed through a long series of amendments. Concretely, the ever increasing number of unemployed faced an ever more stringent means test, to get at ever less sufficient amounts of assistance money. With these developments as a backdrop, we will turn in a somewhat different direction instead. How were women dealt with in these early social measures against unemployment? Were they treated neutrally as labour, without reference to gender, and given the same opportunities for insurance and assistance as men? Here I will leave the situation of non-wage-earning wives out of my answer; these, along with children, were issued allowances as dependants through their families' main recipient of assistance.

In fact, evidence for the 'negative discrimination' facing unemployed wage-earning women in these developments appeared in three distinct ways:[21] first, evidence in the determination of whether a woman was able-bodied and available for work; second, in means testing, in so far as any assistance depended on it; and finally, in determining the amount of financial assistance issued to women. We begin with an analysis of the financial assistance for the unemployed.

On 15 January 1919 an ordinance laid down that state assistance money going to the unemployed would thereafter only be paid out in the framework of a system in which maximum assistance rates would be graded according to the classifications of localities, familial status and gender. In the period that followed, these authorised maximum assistance rates were repeatedly adjusted to inflation and wage trends, and the rate classifications were also changed. Yet this system as a whole was in force up to 1 October 1927. Only the classification according to gender was dropped earlier, on 9 February 1925. Up to that point, however, the amount of money deemed adequate for a subsistence level had been set distinctly lower for single women than for single men (see Table 4.1).

This unequal treatment did not go unchallenged. In the Reichstag, the Communists (KPD) and the Independent Social Democrats

Table 4.1 Maximum level of assistance for single women, as percentage of the corresponding rate for single men (based on the highest district and local rate authorised)[22]

	Aged 21 and above		*Under 21*
	Living in separate household (%)	*Living in household of another*[23] (%)	(%)
15 Jan. 1919	58.3	58.3	58.8
15 Jan. 1920	83.3	70.8	70.6
7 May 1920	75.0	71.4	60.0
4 August 1921	83.3	72.5	65.5
8 Feb. 1922	81.0	66.7	80.0
18 Nov. 1922	78.6	65.0	80.0
24 Apr. 1923	87.5	83.3	89.7
10 Dec. 1923	79.5	79.5	76.6
25 April 1924	78.9	78.9	75.9
9 Aug. 1924	90.9	90.9	90.9
8 Dec. 1924	89.6	89.6	90.6
9 Feb. 1925	100.0	100.0	100.0

(USPD) were the first and most persistent in demanding that women get the same benefits as men. An early debate over this issue took place on 5 August 1920. The Minister of Labour justified the difference between the rates by claiming that women required less calories for subsistence, that they had an easier time locating jobs, and generally received lower wages. Clara Zetkin responded with the sharpest rebuttal:[24]

> It is obvious that – for instance – a washerwoman needs to eat more than a delicate man who spends the whole of the day sitting behind an office desk . . . A man looking for a job has far greater freedom to move about than the woman who is tied to her family and local area . . . Male workers very often received clothing when they came back from the war to their jobs; but I tell you frankly: considering today's prices, there are thousands and ten thousands of women workers who have worn their meagre wardrobes down to the last shred and have no inkling of how they can replace them . . . If you do not make adequate provisions for the unemployed women workers, you are committing the sin of pushing many women down into vice. This fact has to be taken into consideration in calculating the assistance to the woman, whom you otherwise like to portray as so weak and in need of solicitude.

Not before 25 July 1924 did a Reichstag majority agree to equal treatment of women and men in unemployment assistance. The grounds given for this decision were that inasmuch as unemployment assistance in general only guaranteed an extremely tight minimum, reducing it again for women amounted to pushing them tacitly into prostitution. In her report over how the decision was reached in the Reichstag Committee for Social Policy, Louise Schroeder (SPD) summarised the prevailing opinion:[25]

> The Minister of Labour has argued that in most cases the woman is an additional earner, that the man, in contrast, is a sole earner, and furthermore, the possibility exists for the unemployed female to go into households needing hired help. In objecting to this opinion, all of the women on the Committee for Social Policy emphasised that what perhaps held true before the war, no longer applies today. Millions of women, of war widows, wives of men who were severely disabled in the war, not only have to provide for themselves, but are also the sole support of their children. Furthermore, through the

impoverishment of old people, many unmarried women are forced to care for their poor, elderly parents. And besides this, the time is long past when households were in the position to take up unemployed women; rather, there are many unemployed girls today who are perfectly willing to take up a domestic situation, but no longer can find one.

The Reichstag decision on 25 July 1924 to place unemployed women and men on the same footing in claiming assistance did not spring from an essential acceptance of the principle of equal opportunities for women, which in any case could have been corrected in the means test. Granting the same subsistence minimum to women that men got esentially expressed the fear of driving women to prostitution on the one hand, and acceptance of the 'breadwinner' function of more and more single women on the other. Opposition of the Ministry of Labour, even after the Reichstag decision had been made, proved effective to the extent that equal rates were only authorised on 9 February 1925.

Up to that point, the Ministry of Labour had successfully managed to advance labour market policy considerations over those of public welfare, and it did so with even greater efforts thereafter.[26] Thus the entire system of graded rates in unemployment assistance was adjusted according to the concurrent, prevailing wage standards. Yet despite this, the income needed by a family was in fact calculated along with the individual wage to determine assistance rates. The disregarding of actual welfare needs under unemployment assistance mainly affected single women, whom men otherwise viewed as weak and in need of protection. Nevertheless, officials in the newly-established Labour Administration did not feel compelled to call into question the principles operating in the labour market, in the name of sex equality. On the contrary: in this case it appears that the precedence given to labour market priorities was made easier by the fact that it was women who were kept below a minimum subsistence level required by a person living alone. Labour market policy was clearly more interested in consolidating than in altering gender divisions in the labour market and the clustering of women on the lowest level of the wages pyramid.[27] The second, no less disturbing part of the history of unemployment assistance shows this objective.

Table 4.2 depicts the development of unemployment assistance, which was thought to constitute a danger to labour market policies.[28]

After the level of women's assistance was upgraded to the level that men received, the discussion changed course. For women, securing a

Table 4.2 Highest rate of unemployment assistance paid to main recipients in relation to their normal gross income before unemployment, figures taken from 2 July 1926

Insurance amounts to percentage of normal gross income (%)	*For percentage of main recipient of assistance*	
	Women (%)	*Men (%)*
up to 10	0.0	0.1
over 10–20	0.9	8.5
20–30	9.1	28.5
30–40	21.8	27.9
40–50	25.8	17.7
50–60	16.5	8.8
60–70	9.8	4.0
70–80	5.6	2.0
80–90	2.7	0.9
90–100	2.4	0.6
over 100	5.4	1.0
Total	100.0	100.0

Women n = 317 981
Men n = 1 276 319

subsistence level meant that assistance actually came very close to the low level of women's wages. Of course, designers of the assistance system had not intended to use social benefits to push wages up.[29] The AVAVG provided the safeguard against this 'danger' to labour market policy. All those paying contributions were from that point on no longer subject to the means test, which had proven particularly strict with women. Thus, unemployed women's chances of claiming assistance certainly increased. None the less, most of them had to pay for this significant step toward equal opportunities with a severe cut in the amount of benefit that they could claim. The money 'saved' from these cuts in women's benefits at least partially financed the now distinctly higher benefit levels of most men. In contrast to the earlier system of unemployment assistance, this new system of unemployment insurance bore the outward appearance of unobjectionable, gender-neutral 'fairness'. Like every man, every woman could now claim unemployment benefits, providing that contributions had been paid for at least 26 weeks in the preceding 12 months. However, the benefits given, as well as the contributions paid, were now set according to a person's wage position in one of the 11 wage grades as created by the AVAVG.

For almost a year before AVAVG came into force, the same rates of unemployment assistance applied to women and men. The rates were graded according to three economic regions, each containing four divisions by locality, and to two age groups. For unemployed single people aged 21 and over, the highest benefit reached 13.20 marks per week, and the lowest, 7.38 marks; for the unemployed under 21 years, respectively, 8.70 marks and 4.68 marks. Table 4.3 shows how thoroughly this was restructured by the system of wage grades under the AVAVG (allowances for family dependants are not shown here).

Table 4.3 Benefits under the AVAVG (Paras 105–107)[30]

Wage grade	*Weekly wage marks*	*Wage assumed for calculation of benefit marks*	*Unemployment benefit marks*	*Unemployment benefit per cent of assumed wage*
I	0–10	8	6.00	75.0
II	10–14	12	7.80	65.0
III	14–18	16	8.80	55.0
IV	18–24	21	9.87	47.0
V	24–30	27	10.80	40.0
VI	30–36	33	13.20	40.0
VII	36–42	39	14.63	37.5
VIII	42–48	45	15.75	35.0
IX	48–54	51	17.85	35.0
X	54–60	57	19.95	35.0
XI	over 60	63	22.10	35.0

Under AVAVG, even in the lowest wage grade, 1, a benefit of only 75 per cent was given for an assumed 8 mark wage. Using the AVAVG classification as a standard to measure assistance under the earlier system, we can show that in 1926 (see Table 4.2), at least 10.5 per cent of all women receiving assistance – but only 2.5 per cent of the men – had been given 'excessively high' payments. At the other end of the scale, at least 37.1 per cent of the men, but only 10 per cent of the women came away 'badly' because their assistance lay even below 35 per cent of the normal wage level. At the end of 1927, the 'upside down world' of 1925 to 1927 ended up being fundamentally reordered to fit the labour market. Table 4.4 shows two actual distributions of people receiving unemployment benefit, according to their wage grade, and one distribution reconstructed using the AVAVG classification for a pre-AVAVG year.

Table 4.4 Distribution of main recipient of benefits in the wage grades established by the AVAVG of 22 July 1927[31]

	Main recipient of benefits					
	of unemployment assistance		*of unemployment insurance*			
Wage grade	*on 2 July 1926* women (%)	men (%)	*on 15 Nov. 1929* women (%)	men (%)	*on 15 Oct. 1930* women (%)	men (%)
I	7.7	1.4	4.3	0.8	4.1	1.2
II	12.5	1.5	7.0	1.1	8.3	1.5
III	20.7	3.6	11.5	2.0	11.5	2.3
IV	32.6	9.5	23.0	5.1	23.9	5.5
V	17.9	16.4	23.2	8.4	23.1	8.3
VI	5.6	20.2	16.3	12.9	15.3	13.6
VII	1.6	17.4	7.9	15.7	7.2	15.0
VIII	0.8	14.7	3.5	15.7	3.1	15.1
IX	0.3	7.5	1.6	13.3	1.5	13.1
X	0.2	4.3	0.8	10.7	0.9	10.4
XI	0.1	3.5	0.9	14.3	1.0	14.0
Total	100.0	100.0	100.0	100.0	100.0	100.0
	n = 317 981	n = 1 276 319	n = 207 799	n = 807 794	n = 296 716	n = 1 194 333

Among other things, the Table shows that 1929 was a year with a comparatively favourable wage situation. More relevant to our analysis is the observation that the three lowest income grades were very clearly reserved for women, and the three highest grades for men. In 1929, only 15 per cent of the women had earned more than 36 marks per week, in contrast to 70 per cent of the men. Using other data, we can calculate that around half of all women who were classified into AVAVG wage grades I and II, would have in part received much more than 6.00 or 7.80 marks under the unemployment assistance system operating in 1926. Even in wage grade III, the insurance benefits level got worse for at least a third of the unemployed women.[32]

The second way in which women may have encountered 'negative discrimination' lay in the means test. As already noted, until 1927 receipt of unemployment assistance depended on proving a lack of means, while under the AVAVG inadequate means were taken into consideration only when the 26 weeks of benefits under unemployment insurance had ended. During the Depression years people were subjected to the means test ever earlier as one way of cutting benefits, until finally, it was again attached to unemployment insurance itself in June 1931.[33] The interesting question here is whether the means test operated to make the chances of receiving assistance different for women and men.

First, it must be stressed that men, exclusively, made decisions on formal applications for support. These decisions rested with the chairman of the local labour exchange. As of February 1924, the executive of the local authority could also give him binding instructions concerning the assistance. Beyond that, an administrative committee was established alongside the labour exchange, in which employees and employers worked together; it could make general decisions about the type, rate and length of assistance, establish compulsory work programmes, and recruit unemployed young people into further education courses. However, as of 1924, this committee no longer had the power to suspend decisions made by the chairman alone.[34]

Yet even before decision-making operated in this way, the first ordinance concerning assistance for the unemployed, proclaimed on 13 November 1918, explicitly, and to a large extent, had denied women's claims to support. Paragraph 7 tersely stipulated:[35] 'Female persons are only to be given support if they are dependent upon employment. Persons whose former breadwinners return able-bodied, receive no unemployment assistance'. According to the state, the breadwinner had to be a man. This harsh definition only disappeared in January 1920.[36] What remained was a decision which defined eligibility or need in vague terms:[37]

> A situation of need is . . . only to be assumed in so far as the income of the person requiring support, inclusive of those family members living in the household, is so limited that the person is not in the position therewith to meet the necessary maintenance costs, and is in need in so far as it is not possible to make claims upon family members for support, which could cover necessary maintenance costs.

For married women, proving need was next to hopeless if a 'provider' was earning. In the reverse situation, however, a husband could expect less difficulty proving his case of need, for the earnings of a wife were more often regarded as an insufficient basis for a household's maintenance. Children who lived in their parents' household, these more usually daughters than sons, also did not count as being in need. However, even adult single women who no longer lived with their parents were possibly also treated less generously than men. This suggestion appears to be present in the statement made by Centre Party deputy, Andre, on 5 August 1920 in the Reichstag:[38]

> Unmarried women workers should and can draw no unemployment assistance, as long as domestic servants are in demand in cities and on farms, and as long as there are enough open positions on offer for laundresses, charwomen, dishwashers, etc.

The retort of deputy Kaiser (SPD) may have revealed even more about the practices involving the means test:

> Personally, I am entirely of the opinion that it does no woman worker any harm if she works in a household for a short or even longer time. She will very well be able to use the experience in later life. Nevertheless, simply to demand that an unmarried woman worker should in no case be given assistance when service positions are open – that's going decidedly too far! We must also keep in mind those cases where unmarried women workers must provide for their father who is ill, their mother who is ill, or for their young brothers and sisters.

We now turn to the third way discrimination may have operated against women in unemployment assistance. Is it possible that women in general had greater difficulties proving themselves available and able to work to the labour exchanges than men? In times of especially high unemployment, social policy discussion as well as state intervention in the labour market rated the right of men to employment, generally and irrespective of their family situation, as much more important than that of women.[39] If a woman who was formerly employed was neither recognised nor registered as unemployed or seeking work, then it appears that this could aid in efforts to oust women from the labour market as well as serve the assistance fund.

Displacement of women from the labour market during the period of economic demobilisation took a blatant form, particularly in 1919 and 1920.[40] Ranging from the demobilisation ordinances, to decisions by lower-level authorities, and to the co-operation of works councils, the attempts to dismiss women from their wartime workplaces and to free these for the men returning from the front occurred very openly and bluntly. 'Need of employment' claims by the wives of working men were generally denied. Many of these women probably gave up searching for a new post, in view of the high unemployment all around them. The ruling that 'persons who during the war moved in order to undertake work in another locality . . . may not draw assistance in this locality for longer than four weeks' pointed in the same direction.[41] The ruling affected chiefly unmarried and newly-married females; they were expected to return to the parental home, and above all, return to agricultural work, and through this to facilitate the authorities' rejection of their claims for work or assistance.

Already at the beginning of the Weimar Republic, female wage-earners found themselves in an extremely precarious position in terms of state labour market policy. On the one hand, the Weimar Constitution of 11 August 1919 laid down the right to work (Article 163, paragraph 2), and this could be read in conjunction with the equal rights clause (Article 109). On the other hand, neither stipulation had an effect on the demobilisation ordinances, which explicitly entailed discriminatory treatment of and against women. The equal right to work also remained problematic in the years that followed, at least for married women.

The violations of the constitutional provisions became most striking where the state, as an employer, had the largest opportunity to put its labour market policy objectives into practice.[42] The Weimar Constitution had expressly laid down: 'All special status accorded to female civil servants is removed' (Article 128, para. 2). This constitutional stipulation was openly disregarded. As staff reductions in the Reich's administration began in the context of the reorganisation of the Reich finances, paragraph 14 of the staff reduction ordinance decreed that married women civil servants, who already had been hired as permanent employees, could be dismissed without compensation, 'in so far as the economic security of the female civil servant appears to be established in the judgement of the duly qualified authority'. The general staff reduction went out of operation on 4 August 1925. However, the possibility of dismissing further women civil servants remained up until 31 March 1929, albeit in conjunction with a compensation payment. On 30 May 1932, mass unemployment again brought the Reichstag to require 'celibacy' from (a marriage bar for) women civil servants, and this time imposed it for an unlimited period. Barbara Greven-Aschoff rightly judges this decision as a very pointed expression of discrimination emerging under the banner of the campaign against 'double earners': This could no longer be 'a sensible measure in terms of finance policy', for, 'considering that 6.5 million people were unemployed, the dismissal of approximately 800–900 women civil servants was wholly without effect'.[43] To be sure, this policy of the Reich as an employer affected only a small group of women in public service. An exact study of how far the individual states and local authorities followed the example of the Reich still needs to be done. However, regardless of the quantitative impact of the Reich-level decision, its ideological meaning cannot be overestimated: this discrimination against the married woman civil servant was implemented by the highest layers of Parliament and Reich officials, and not even the women's or the workers' movements responded with a thoroughgoing critique. When the state singled out the woman civil servant for special treatment and withdrew her former right to life-time employment only because she married, it strengthened the older norm of the incompatibility of wage work and marriage for women.

During the demobilisation period, when the fear that the free play of forces on the labour market would work against men was not unfounded, social policy intervention was used to counteract this trend, and therefore worked to the disadvantage of women. If a woman retained the right to a job at all, she was not to find one in the male occupations. Women in the labour market were given to understand that they belonged in domestic positions, agricultural work and the pre-war women's industries.[44] The displacement of women from the labour market in general, or out of occupations which also interested men, remains difficult to map out statistically, not only for the demobilisation phase, but also for the Great Depression.[45] Obviously, the interest of business in cheap women workers was running against politicians' intent to push women out of jobs. But on the whole, state labour market intervention could not have been completely ineffective. This is suggested by scattered information coming from the Central Office of Labour Administration. Official observations record that in 1928–9, 3 per cent of unemployed women, but only 2.1 per cent of the men receiving assistance, temporarily had payments cut off because they had rejected a job referral without acceptable grounds. Moreover, 12 per cent of women, but just under 5 per cent of male applicants, failed to prove insufficient means in order to get the special assistance grant for the seasonally unemployed.[46] Also, a memorandum from the Reich Labour Office on 4 May 1929[47] made hints in a similar direction, with its decision that 'a woman whose household duties demand her attention over most of the working day is in general not available for work in the labour market'. Along these same lines, a complaint was also expressed in the Reichstag on 30 September 1929, over the 'misuses' and 'abuses' resulting from the 1927 AVAVG: 'large numbers of wives whose men are working, for example, are also out working, then become unemployed, and although they are fully occupied with their households, they still draw benefits'.[48] Shutting married women out of insurance protection was again discussed in all seriousness – as in the period from 1924 to 1927 – even if they had earned a right to unemployment benefits by paying contributions like everyone else. Of course, simultaneously abolishing compulsory insurance contributions for these same women was never considered.

The 'productive unemployment assistance' programme very clearly expressed the efforts of the public Labour Administration Office to push unemployed women totally out of the labour market or to steer them toward unattractive positions in urban and rural households. This type of assistance measure made its appearance in Labour Administration schemes beginning in October 1919.[49] Primarily men benefited from job-creation measures and occupational training schemes. As the Stuttgart Labour Office explained in 1927,[50] 'Courses for the female unemployed have in general not been supported on such a large scale as the courses for the male unemployed, because unemployment among females was comparatively less and, moreover, the female unemployed could find useful things to do in their own households'. Nevertheless, even the few activities specifically assigned to women under the productive unemployment assistance programme are revealing.

The Centre Party deputy, Andre, provoked no controversy when he declared in the Reichstag on 5 August 1920:[51]

> The task of productive unemployment assistance is to provide instruction for this female labour through courses in sewing, mending, and housekeeping of every kind, so that they will be ushered into domestic work, and then can also go into households, into individual families, as useful members ... This kind of productive unemployment assistance has yet a further advantage: that these women workers are also being prepared for their own households. One of the great problems of today is that our women are not capable of keeping house in the manner in which it is desirable and necessary for the interests of the families of workers and the salaried classes ... If the period of unemployment is used toward this end, and women workers are given the opportunity to master these housekeeping skills, then this effort is not only an advantage for the

individual, but also an advantage for the worker's family and for the state and society.

Very much in keeping with these attitudes, a decree of the Prussian Ministry for Welfare recommended on 15 February 1924,[52] that occupational, technical and further education schools should be set up, and job opportunities be created to keep unemployed youth 'from idleness, and to bring them up to be responsible adults'. Women and men with 'practical' skills and experience were supposed to be recruited to help in this effort.

> For the education of girls, apart from professional women of all levels, housewives and mothers shall also be taken into consideration, because girls' preparation for their future duties as housewives and mothers is absolutely imperative. We must strive to steer growing girls more in the direction of domestic occupations again, and to fight the great aversion exhibited toward these vocations, an aversion especially evident in the industrial areas.

Where courses actually did exist for unemployed women – which they could attend voluntarily, or were forced to attend in order to be granted unemployment assistance – then at least up to 1928, these courses in fact first and foremost offered instruction in housekeeping, sewing, and hygiene.[53] It almost seems that both the funding made available through the state labour administration, and the fact that girl school-leavers had poor chances of finding a job, gave fresh impetus to all those who had pressed for obligatory home economy lessons for girls of the lower classes since the end of the nineteenth century.[54] I will present one example. The Stuttgart adult education school set up special classes for unemployed women in January 1926, in which a total of 3418 women enrolled during that year.[55] Of these participants, 40.5 per cent took sewing classes, 15.2 the classes, 'Medical Problems of Women, Health Care, Nursing and Infant Care', 9.9 per cent enrolled in gymnastics courses, 8.2 per cent in cooking, and a further 5.4 per cent were distributed among courses in gardening, about 'The Woman and Her Household', childrearing, handicrafts, activities for children, and making children's toys. In contrast, courses not centred around family and household attracted only a total of 20.8 per cent of the women: general adult education courses (7.1 per cent), stenography (6.8 per cent), courses on political, occupational and existential problems, on further education in general commercial affairs, German courses, public reading and speaking (a total of 6.9 per cent). Thus, it appears that what had begun in the demobilisation phase as a kind of compulsory education of unemployed women for family duties, was continued in Stuttgart through the funds of the city's labour administration office. Until April 1921 an educational centre existed in the city's Labour Office which organised courses in home economics and hygiene; these courses became compulsory as of 12 April 1919 for unemployed women up to age 21, and as of 1 April 1920, even for women up to age 35.

The 'natural' division of work along gender lines even prevailed when work for the 'common good' was assigned to the unemployed. Beginning on 15 October 1923, the unemployed could be forced into these assignments for a period ranging from 8 to 24 hours per week. The spectrum of typical jobs that were created appears in the following, contrasting lists:[56]

> For men:
> Snow removal, street cleaning, levelling tracts of land, melioration work, river regulation, dredging of community ponds, peat-bog work, road and ditch work, chopping down trees, chopping up wood, unloading of potatoes and distribution of coal and wood to the needy, maintaining order and providing first aid at offices where unemployment is paid, mass distribution of food, etc., distribution of goods, running errands, shoe and clothing repair work for recipients of unemployment assistance and poor relief, coffin-making for the poor by unemployed joiners, brick-making in brickyards made available to the community by the owners, production of slag stones for buildings for the common good, gardening and cemetery work, office work in the labour exchange, filing, keeping lists, giving instruction to unemployed youth.
>
> For women:
> Sewing and repair work for welfare institutions, cleaning work in buildings used for welfare work, in schools, and other public buildings, help in soup kitchens, children's homes, and other welfare establishments.

This policy of giving gender-specific work assignments continued in the voluntary labour service, which was scheduled for expansion in the summer of 1931, and which was first and foremost intended for the benefit of young men.[57] Intensified thinking about how to incorporate women into the labour service led to a special order from the Reich Commissioner for Voluntary Labour Service.[58] According to this directive, female youth were to be placed in domestic and agricultural work, and particularly in:

1. Laundry and clothing care for the male voluntary labour camps;
2. kitchen service for the non-residential labour camps;
3. cultivation of crops destined for the common good on uncultivated lands;
4. creation of small garden allotments;
5. service groups for women welfare workers in settlement programmes, and
6. workshop tasks for the winter relief action.

The productive unemployment assistance, financed by the Labour Administration, did not even structure its education programmes to give unemployed women skills relevant to the labour market.[59] Yet the training offered to young women for their own future households probably found wide endorsement, just as the fact that women were concurrently gaining ground in the sphere of wage work outside the home triggered suspicion, as always, and was viewed as dangerous by men facing potential unemployment. Young women may well have mistrusted and reacted defensively against the compulsory work which their Labour Exchanges thought up for them, for these jobs far too closely paralleled their situation in parental households. Daughters were not only subject to parental control much longer and more intensely than their brothers, and had to turn over a greater portion of the money they earned; in contrast to their brothers' situation, they also had far less free time, because housework still awaited them when they came home from their jobs.[60] If young women, through wage work and before marrying, attempted to be as independent as possible from parents and from male assistance, then long-term unemployment undermined these efforts; they were pushed back into some kind of domestic service, whether in the parental home, in other private households, or in public welfare institutions, situations perhaps not all that different from one another in the eyes of young women.

We still need to examine how the system of unemployment assistance and insurance actually functioned. How many unemployed women even received financial support, and how large was the group of women receiving it in relation to the entire group of unemployed women? No conclusions of any kind can be deduced from published statistics for

1919. In the years that followed, households' main recipients of assistance/benefits – and those were unemployed people who received unemployment assistance/benefits or emergency relief/assistance – were at first registered on a monthly basis, and then every fortnight (see Table 4.5).

These figures show distinct seasonal shifts. In the winter months, the largest number, and in the summer months, the least number of women received support. The degree to which the observable fluctuations of the absolute number of recipients from year to year also followed the cyclical and structural movements of the labour market can only be determined if the number of these recipients is compared to the number of all unemployed women. Unfortunately we lack reliable statistics for making this comparison. Labour market statistics continuously improved in quality during the Weimar years (which reduces their ability to be compared from year to year), to the point where they could register changes in the labour market with some sensitivity. Nevertheless, they lacked a data base for ultimately capturing the absolute number of unemployed, and the specific unemployment quota with any certainty. The statistical data available to us may be particularly unreliable in depicting women's unemployment.[61]

Table 4.5 Women as main recipients of assistance/benefits (in 1000s)[62]

	Unemployment assistance/ unemployment benefit		*Emergency relief/ emergency assistance*	
	Highest number	*Lowest number*	*Highest number*	*Lowest number*
1920	109 Aug.	62 June		
1921	81 May	35 Dec.		
1922	33 Jan.	4 Sept.		
1923*	283 Dec.	14 Jan.		
1924*	260 Jan.	27 June	only from	
1925	93 Dec.	22 Aug.	autumn, 1926	
1926	335 July	162 Jan.	7 Dec.	4 Oct.
1927	283 Jan.	65 Oct.	44 May	23 Oct.
1928	310 Dec.	147 May	37 Jan.	13 Aug.
1929	341 Jan.	182 Oct.	41 June	23 Jan.
1930	426 Dec.	297 Oct.	103 Dec.	44 Jan.
1931	537 Feb.	251 Oct.	197 Dec.	112 Jan.
1932	444 Feb.	136 Nov.	246 June	180 Nov.

*Figures apply only to the unoccupied territories during the Ruhr Occupation.

The extent to which women in the 'silent reserve' were regarded as employable depended, in times of high unemployment, not only on women's own attitudes toward wage work, but also on labour market policy decisions. Women also remained invisible in the 'informal' labour market, with pay by the hour or day, and with its jobs located in private households, in small business enterprises, and in seasonal or other temporary workplaces; here too, opportunities for wage work decreased with an increasing number of job seekers during times of economic crisis and high unemployment. Even within the 'regular' labour market, however, the female sector eludes capture in a statistical form more than the male sector. The statistics directly collected from the labour exchanges and from lists of recipients of assistance/benefits necessarily led to a less complete record of unemployed women. This was inevitable as long as on the one hand, only people who received assistance/benefits were obliged to register as unemployed and getting assistance/benefits was attached to a proven lack of means, and on the other hand, labour exchanges showed little inclination to refer positions to married women who were regarded as 'less employable' or as 'provided for'. Earlier information about the relation between jobs on offer and applications for work are of no use for our analysis. Figures on the numbers of 'job seekers at the labour exchanges' only become available from 1926, and in the beginning these were at first collected incompletely, and sometimes flawed by counting people twice; only from 1929 were the more reliable 'number of unemployed at labour exchanges' available. We can make at least some use of the figures, if working under the assumption that the registration flaws in them did not affect women any differently than men. Table 4.6 pulls together various aspects of the available data.

One interesting feature revealed by this data is the striking fluctuation in the relation of female as compared to male main recipients (Table 4.6, Column 3). The series of January figures show throughout, the seasonally-determined, clearly higher portion of male recipients. Therefore, we will only analyse the July series more closely here. In the years 1920 to 1922, against expectation, the women did better than in other years, making up a quarter to a third of all recipients. However, the women's portion then dropped back drastically from the summer of 1924 to the summer of 1925. Economic reasons doubtlessly did not lie behind the reduction of the portion of women receiving assistance. It seems much more likely that they had to face a far harsher means test from the spring onwards, and possibly up to the beginning of 1926.[64] We must remember that, from February 1925, those women who had

Table 4.6[63] Data available on unemployment (1920–32) of men and women

	Main recipients (women)								*Unemployed women*				*Women*		*Men*	
	(no. of 1000s)				*(% of all main recipients)*				*(no. in 1000s)*		*(% of all unemployed)*		*(main recip. as % of unemployed women)*		*(main recip. as % of unemployed men)*	
	un-emp. assis.	*un-emp. ben.*	*emer-gency assistance*													
	31/1-1/2	31/7-1/8	31/1-1/2	31/7-1/8	31/1-1/2 (with)	31/1-1/2 (w/o)	31/7-1/8 (with)	31/7-1/8 (w/o)	end of Jan.	end of July	end of Jan.	end of July	end of Jan.	end of July	end of Jan.	end of July
1920	107	109			24.8		27.0									
1921	75	63			17.7		23.6									
1922	31	5	*(figures for 1/8/23*		15.3		33.3									
1923	21	28	*and 1/2/24 only*		14.0		20.1									
1924	181	51	*the unoccupied*		12.6		9.7									
1925	41	22	*territory)*		6.9		11.2									
1926	257	324	*(only from autumn, 1926)*		12.7		19.6		411	485	16.5	21.5	62.5	66.8	85.1	75.2
					(with	w/o) *(emergency assistance)*	(with	w/o)								
1927	268	95	23	37	14.7	14.8	21.0	20.9	445	240	17.5	23.1	65.4	55.0	80.1	62.7
1928	178	166	35	15	13.3	13.8	29.4	28.0	342	308	17.0	26.7	62.3	58.8	80.0	79.5
1929	338	207	24	32	14.8	14.9	29.1	27.7	489	343	17.2	27.4	74.0	69.7	87.7	68.8
1930	391	330	48	74	17.5	17.7	22.0	21.3	619	585	19.2	21.2	70.9	69.1	78.6	68.7
1931	535	268	121	134	20.9	19.5	22.2	18.0	993	772	20.3	19.3	66.1	52.1	69.6	56.8
1932	439	211	212	212	23.3	18.7	27.9	20.0	1198	1093	19.8	20.2	54.3	38.7	58.4	39.3

proven a lack of means received the same assistance rates as men. The figures for 1928 and 1929 are interesting, for these were the only two years before the Depression in which the unemployed had a legal claim to unemployment benefits without the means test. The portion reached by the women in these years, 30 per cent, was very clearly an effect of equal treatment under the AVAVG. The somewhat lower portion of women drawing emergency assistance can presumably again be explained by the reintroduction of the means criterion, rather than by the possibility that women were less subject to long-term unemployment. This also holds true for developments in the years 1930–1932, where the portion of women receiving benefits again decreased. Perhaps mass unemployment actually did affect women less than it affected men; however, presumably the means criterion ultimately reduced the chances of unemployed women to obtain benefits.

According to unemployment statistics,[65] the portion of women among all those unemployed as of 1930 lay at about 20 per cent (see Table 4.6, Column 5); this would basically correspond to the portion shown to be receiving benefits in that year. This impression is also confirmed if we compare the respective portions of female benefits recipients at the end of July with the portion of male recipients (see Table 4.6, Columns 6 and 7). The generally worsening chances of getting sufficient support before falling dependent on welfare relief affected women and men to nearly the same degree in the course of long-term unemployment. In the summer of the years 1926 to 1929 – and these were the years with less reliable unemployment statistics – only about 55 to 70 per cent of those women registered as unemployed received benefits/assistance, whereas 60 to 80 per cent of the men did. If only a registration error lay behind these differences (and this explanation may have some basis), then women must have been 'double counted' much more often than men; or more women than men must have been seeking work in the labour market for the first time (that is, not yet eligible for any assistance/benefits). The other explanation remaining for this is that unemployed women's chances for receiving payments were simply much smaller than men's chances.

Comparing the unemployment quotas of women and men is of interest. Yet, for making such a comparison, knowledge of the period's general occupational developments is essential. The compulsory health insurance statistics from the 1920s, which the Reich Labour Office used to help derive a picture of contemporary employment, are not very exact. The number of female wage earners may have been particularly underestimated because all those people voluntarily enrolled in compulsory insurance – and these were mainly women – were simply left out of the account. Nevertheless, it is by no means clear whether all these women were exclusively housewives, rather than to a large degree part-time wage workers. On the basis of these health insurance statistics, it is possible to calculate – using the total number recorded each August – what portion of all people employed in wage-based jobs and subject to compulsory health insurance were women.[66] Using these figures, women stood at around 34–36 per cent of all workers and white-collar employees with low incomes and in jobs for which unemployment was a threat. Inasmuch as they only represented around 20 per cent of the unemployed, the risk of unemployment for women wage workers has been deceptively estimated as lower than for men.

The trade union statistics, and above all those constructed by the statistician of the ADGB (General Federation of German Trade Unions), Wladimar Woytinsky, can provide further information pertinent to these questions. In general, the statistics concerning unemployment among trade union members are the earliest and most reliable on unemployment. But even these may have depicted women's occupational situation less accurately than men's: the extent of organisation, fluctuation in membership, and occupational positioning differed markedly between the sexes. It is entirely possible that unionised women fell victim to unemployment far less often than unorganised women workers (see Table 4.7).

Until the Great Depression, unemployment (recorded at the end of July) hit women somewhat more often than men; yet among the January unemployed – with the exception of the demobilisation years of 1919 and 1920, as well as 1923 – the incidence of jobless men was higher. This statistic again confirms our assumption that the widely fluctuating portion of women who cropped up as main recipients in the years before 1928 cannot be explained by varying vulnerability of women to unemployment.

For the Free Trade Unions' membership, Woytinsky drew even more information out of these highly aggregated statistics by differentiating between the cyclical and seasonal groups of workers in the unions.[68] Virtually no women (1928 = 1.7 per cent) were organised in the seasonal group (gardeners, builders' union, carpenters, painters, roofers, stone workers, and the division for 'coarse ceramics' workers in the factory workers' union). In contrast, unions categorised in the cyclical group counted women as 20.3 per cent of their members in the same year. This differentiation no doubt captures women's occupational situation with a fair amount of accuracy. It shows that women became unemployed as often as – or even slightly more often – than men, not only in 1926, a cyclically bad year, but also in the 'favourable' years of 1927 and 1928. Even extreme unemployment becomes visible if one scrutinises five particular unions closely, five which included 22 per cent of the ADGB's women members, but only 5 per cent of its men in 1928. In December 1928, around 23 per cent of the men and 25 per cent of the women in these five unions were unemployed.[69] Taking this result into account, a study of women's unemployment needs to examine the development of the typical 'women's trades' very closely. At least 65 per cent of the unemployed women registered by the Reich Labour Office during the years 1930 to 1932 had come from the occupational sectors of clothing, textiles, wage work of various kinds, domestic service, and sales personnel.[70]

'Partial' unemployment, which Woytinsky emphasised, must also be taken into consideration. Short-time work was widely instituted during the Weimar Republic as a labour market policy and business strategy in response to economic crisis. With the exception of the period between April 1924 and the end of February 1926, it was flanked by a short-time workers' assistance measure, which was tied to a means test. During all the Weimar years, considerably more women were always forced into short-time work than men (see Table 4.7).[71]

Table 4.7 Unemployment and short-time work as per cent of trade union members (all figures representing end of month)[67]

	Unemployment				*Short-time work*	
	Women		*Men*		*Women*	*Men*
	(*January*)	(*July*)	(*January*)	(*July*)	(*July*)	(*July*)
1919	7.9%	4.2%	6.2%	2.8%	–	–
1920	3.6	10.0	3.3	5.0	–	–
1921	3.7	2.8	4.7	2.5	6.5%	4.7%
1922	1.7	0.8	3.8	0.5	1.4	0.6
1923	5.3	4.7	3.9	3.1	19.8	12.4
1924	17.1	11.3	29.4	12.9	35.2	25.7
1925	4.7	4.2	9.0	3.5	9.1	4.7
1926	17.6	18.5	23.8	17.5	28.7	13.7
1927	11.3	5.6	17.6	5.5	4.6	2.1
1928	6.4	8.1	12.3	5.9	15.5	4.6
1929	11.4	10.6	21.1	8.2	15.6	5.1
1930	14.6	16.5	23.5	21.2	24.8	11.8
1931	27.0	22.4	35.6	32.6	29.9	17.1
1932	32.0	34.6	45.7	45.5	33.3	21.2

Looking at the available statistics from several different angles tends to confirm, rather than weaken, the probability that more women were unemployed during the Weimar Republic than the statistical picture suggests, and that, furthermore, women's chances for obtaining financial support during unemployment appear too rosy in this picture. This dawned on labour market statisticians in the summer of 1932, as they were forced to acknowledge the existence of an army of some 1.5 to 2.5 million 'invisible' unemployed missing from the figures. Nothing else could have explained the fact that for months both the number of the unemployed and the employed had sunk. In 1935, using a sophsticated calculation, Hemmer came to the conclusion that the highest number of 'invisible unemployed' existed in the middle of 1932, with 1.5 million. In the months that followed, the number dropped to 500 000, with a simultaneous increase in the share of women.[72]

Contemporaries most typically concluded from available data that women were less affected by unemployment than men throughout the Weimar Republic, and especially during the Great Depression period. Unemployment figures emerging from the 16 June 1933 occupational census, appear to support this interpretation fully. 4.7 million men reported themselves to be unemployed, in contrast to only 1.1 million women. Among white-collar workers, 23.3 per cent of the men were recorded as unemployed, but only 16.9 of the women, and among manual workers, 36 per cent of the men as compared to only 19.5 of the women. The Reich Office for Statistics reasoned that women were doing better than men because of the lower number of women in occupations which were channelled through the labour market, and asserted, above all, that women far more frequently worked in those economic and occupational sectors (textiles, clothing, white-collar jobs) which had contracted least during the Depression. The possibility that their low wages gave women more job security was mentioned, but left an open question.[73]

Regardless of such reasoning, the 'women displace men' slogan, already a favourite during the rationalisation phase, achieved great popularity in the 1930s: 'the cheap female hands were pushed out of the production process less vigorously than expensive male hands, and were often even put in men's positions'.[74] What was, indeed, never questioned in this plausible interpretation, was how reliable was the statistical picture presented by the occupational census. However, why should married women have listed their occupations as 'unemployed' rather than as 'housewife' during the June 1933 census, given that months had passed without prospects of a further regular job, and given the ever more vehement campaign against 'double earners'?[75] The solution to the riddle of why women's occupations seemed so 'crisis-resistant'[76] could in part rest with their according first place to this alternative, 'occupation: housewife'.

This leads me back to my introductory comments. The fair weather conditions of full employment defuse and cover up the tense competition existing between women and men in the labour market. However, in times of high unemployment, this competition is experienced more intensely as the delimitation between men's and women's wage work becomes less sharp, as male dominance so long assured in the hierarchy of income and jobs appears to be more and more threatened, and as the male-breadwinner and woman-mother-housewife roles are socially prescribed as mutually exclusive. In the Weimar Republic, the potential for conflict may have become more and more explosive. The years of tenacious high, and finally extreme, mass unemployment, were simultaneously years in which the old systems of clearly segregated male and female occupations appeared to become destabilised. Economic mobilisation for the war, diverse rationalisation measures, and the rapid expansion of white-collar occupations, opened up additional and more secure job opportunities for women outside the home. In this context, women's lesser occupational qualifications, as well as lower wages, boosted the social prestige of men further; yet at the same time, and for exactly these reasons, women came to be regarded as dangerous and unfair competitors. The constitutional guarantees of equal rights also may have contributed to male insecurities, alongside the first visible occupational results of higher education for women, which had only become available in the last years before the war.

Never before had so many women earned their living through occupations outside of their families and outside private households. The newly-emerging job opportunities enabled women to deal with new economic pressures.[77] The world war had taken 2.4 million German men to their deaths and buried many women's prospect of having a male family breadwinner. The pressure to find wage work also reached new groups of single and married women, when the pensions of disabled veterans proved insufficient for family maintenance, when unemployment struck the homes of ever more manual and white-collar workers, when war, inflation, and the Depression also brought poverty to the middle class. The daily experience of seeing many more women than before earning money and spending money they had earned themselves led to heated debates.

At the centre of conflict was not the 36 per cent of all employed women who in 1925 were listed as 'helping dependants' (occupied in family enterprises), nor the 7.8 per cent of employed women who strove to be self-supporting mainly in very small enterprises in agriculture, the retail trade, tailoring, and through laundries, boarding and guest-houses, and restaurants. Instead, complaints arose because only 11.4 per cent of employed women remained in household service, and only 9.2 per cent in agricultural work, proof that women were increasingly shunning the typical 'female' corners of the labour market. The large number of homeworkers, listed as 1.6 per cent of all wage-earning women, also caused concern, albeit for other reasons. Fears over possible competition with men were essentially fixed onto the remaining 33.8 per cent of all employed females. These women were dependent on and channelled through the formal labour market. They retained their earlier positions as manual and white-collar workers, and much less often as civil servants in industry and craftwork, commerce and transport, administration, the independent professions, and public health, and occupied new jobs in the course of the restructuring and expansion of enterprises and business. According to the occupational census of 1925, these represented altogether 3 879 584 women.[78]

The campaign against the double earner grew out of feelings of helplessness, but was none the less extremely vicious, and proved troublesome for wage-earning women. It came into currency in the demobilisation period, and was revived again and again in the years that followed. Reappearing in full force during the despair of 1930 to 1934, it became the most salient expression of anxieties about labour market competition, and of the diffuse hope that the 'natural' order could be restored, in which the male breadwinner, again secure in his rights, duties and power, could provide protection and maintenance for his wife.[79] To be sure, cries of 'double earner' did not only apply to wives: they also underlined that men should be prevented from procuring a 'double' income. Despite this, the most forceful attacks of the campaign were mobilised against wives who earned wages but allegedly did not need them. This discrimination had a tradition. Married women had not only been carrying the excessive burden of wage work outside the home, on top of performing services for their families; they had also been forced to ward off the social stigma that they neglected their families and stole work from men. Unlike during the demobilisation phase, at the end of the Weimar Republic, convincing proof was furnished that forbidding married women's wage work would have had absolutely no positive effect on the employment opportunities of married and single men. Married women wished to have a job as a 'luxury' in only the most exceptional cases. A husband's unemployment or disability, or his insufficient income and the family's consequent struggle for mere subsistence drove wives into employment, and in fact, mostly into the worst jobs available. In 1927, the factory and workshop inspectorate for Hamburg reported:[80]

> Married women are particularly to be found in those workshops in which work takes place under disagreeable circumstances, such as great heat, the issuing of dust and steam, dampness, dirt . . . The single women, with their greater freedom of movement, stay clear of these workshops; the married ones are often forced out of sheer necessity to be less selective.

It was an absurd expectation that an appreciable number of attractive workplaces would open up, if only married women disappeared from the labour market. Already in 1930, the Social Democrat Anna Geyer dismantled this demagogic parole through a careful examination of all employment sectors; she concluded that out of the 3.7 million married women in the labour market, 200 000 at the very most held jobs that might also have interested men.[81] All contemporary politicians actually knew this. Thus, in renewing the celibacy requirement for women civil servants in 1932, it seems they were exclusively aiming at 'obtaining a psychological effect' through such a forceful reaffirmation of the 'natural' order.[82]

It remains unclear what insecurities the revived attacks on the 'double earner' may have stirred up among those women who retained their jobs, or those who were only beginning to work toward occupational qualifications.[83] Presumably, the vehement anti-feminist polemics emerging in the public realm made women more acutely see and feel the dilemma central to their life choices: that they were pulled back and forth between occupation and family. Possibly the general calling into question of women's orientation around wage work, in so far as the social legitimation of their employment outside the home was only conceded in cases of extreme hardship, may have increased women's inclination to resolve the dilemma by more decisively opting for a family orientation. Women were often reproached for their lack of job orientation.[84] The social production of this 'deficiency' was only occasionally recognised. Writing in the *Sozialistische Monatshefte* in 1928, Anna Siemsen captured the central problem operating in this dilemma:[85]

> Those women who find themselves facing harsh economic competition, who suffer under men's rebuffs, and have poor job prospects, naturally look for a way out through marriage. But that is not what is unhealthy in this situation – that a woman wishes to marry: rather, that she seeks security and an improvement of her lot, which she does not get through her job, in marriage.

Apart from this, however, how could wives have expected to improve their situation through employment, having experienced the demobilisation dismissals of married women from 1919 to 1923, having witnessed the staff reductions of women civil servants, and even having been told by socialist trade unions during the Depression:[86]

> We must demand the removal of married women from the production process where their husbands have a sufficient income or hold a steady salaried post which is affected neither by unemployment nor short-time work, or where other favourable conditions are present, such as childlessness or good pecuniary circumstances, etc.

The period of high unemployment in Weimar was a poor time for convincing working men, and even comrades, that women deserved equal access to employment. The 'new woman' had to expect more hostility than support if she attempted to make use of increased training and job opportunities. She was expected to step back into the place of the 'old woman' and behind the family provider as soon as she married. Yet at the same time the years of high unemployment taught the lesson that married women, confronted with family poverty and need, were pressed harder than ever to take up wage work, and that they had few reserves of strength left over to resist drifting into the worst possible jobs.

Notes

1. Isa Strasser, *Frauenarbeit und Rationalisierung* (Moscow, 1927) p. 5; Ruth Weiland, *Die Kinder der Arbeitslosen* (Berlin, 1933), p. 46; M.P. of the 'Bayrische Volkspartei' on 14 March 1931 in the Reichstag, *Stenographische Berichte der Verhandlungen des Deutschen Reichstages* (RT), vol. 445, p. 1548.
2. Cf. among others, Stefan Bajohr, *Die Hälfte der Fabrik. Geschichte der Frauenarbeit in Deutschland 1914 bis 1945* (Marburg, 1979); Barbara Duden and Karin Hausen, 'Gesellschaftliche Arbeit – Geschlechtsspezi-

fische Arbeitsteilung', in Annette Kuhn and Gerhard Schneider (eds), *Frauen in der Geschichte*, vol. 1 (Düsseldorf, 1979) pp. 11–13; Ulla Knapp, *Frauenarbeit in Deutschland* (2 vols, Munich, 1984); Jürgen Kuczynski, *Die Geschichte der Lage der Arbeiterinnen unter dem Kapitalismus* (Berlin, 1963); Walter Müller, Angelika Willms and Johann Handl, *Strukturwandel der Frauenarbeit 1880–1980* (Frankfurt, 1983); Jürgen Reulecke, 'Veränderungen des Arbeitskräftepotentials im Deutschen Reich 1900–1933', in Hans Mommsen, Dietmar Petzina and Bernd Weisbrod (eds), *Industrielles System und politische Entwicklung in der Weimarer Republik* (Düsseldorf, 1974) pp. 84–95; Angelika Willms, 'Modernisierung durch Frauenarbeit? Zum Zusammenhang von wirtschaftlichem Strukturwandel und weiblicher Arbeitsmarktlage in Deutschland 1882–1939', in Toni Pierenkemper and Richard Tilly (eds), *Historische Arbeitsmarktforschung* (Göttingen, 1982) pp. 37–76; and Dörte Winkler, *Frauenarbeit im 'Dritten Reich'* (Hamburg; 1977).

3. This aspect is of interest neither to Manfred Lohr, 'Langfristige Entwicklungstendenzen der Arbeitslosigkeit in Deutschland', in Ernst Wiegand and Wolfgang Zapf (eds), *Wandel der Lebensbedingungen in Deutschland* (Frankfurt, 1982) pp. 237–334, nor to Frank Niess, *Geschichte der Arbeitslosigkeit. Ökonomische Ursachen und politische Kämpfe. Ein Kapitel deutscher Sozialgeschichte*, 2nd edn (Frankfurt, 1982).
4. For studies of the history of gender relations, see Renate Bridenthal, Atina Grossmann, and Marion Kaplan (eds), *When Biology Became Destiny. Women in Weimar and Nazi Germany* (New York, 1984).
5. Cf., for example, Dieter Freiburghaus, *Dynamik der Arbeitslosigkeit. Umschlagprozeß und Dauerverteilung der Arbeitslosigkeit in der Bundesrepublik Deutschland von 1966 bis 1977* (Meisenheim/Glan, 1978); Brigitte Nauhaus, *Probleme der Frauenarbeitslosigkeit in der gegenwärtigen Krise* (Köln, 1979); Ingrid Peikert, 'Frauenarbeit – Proletarisierung auf Widerruf?' in Claus Offe (ed.), *Opfer des Arbeitsmarktes. Zur Theorie der strukturierten Arbeitslosigkeit* (Neuwied/Darmstadt, 1977) pp. 63–92; and Günther Schmidt, *Strukturierte Arbeitslosigkeit und Arbeitsmarktpolitik* (Königstein/Ts, 1980).
6. See, for example, Elisabeth Beck-Gernsheim, *Der geschlechtsspezifische Arbeitsmarkt. Zur Ideologie und Realität von Frauenberufen* (Frankfurt, 1976); Regina Becker-Schmidt, Uta Brandes-Erlhoff, Mechthild Rumpf, and Beate Schmidt, *Arbeitsleben – Lebensarbeit. Konflikte und Erfahrungen von Fabrikarbeiterinnen* (Bonn, 1983); and Ilona Ostner, *Beruf und Hausarbeit.* Die Arbeit der Frau in unserer Gesellschaft (Frankfurt, 1978); and this approach is also used by Angelika Willms in Müller, Willms, and Handl, *Strukturwandel.*
7. This is the thesis of Peikert, 'Frauenarbeit'.
8. Title of their article (literally, 'Frauen verändern, Berufe nicht . . .') in *Soziale Welt*, 29 (1978), pp. 257–87; quotation, p. 279.
9. Herta Däubler-Gmelin, *Frauenarbeitslosigkeit oder, Reserve zurück an den Herd* (Reinbek, 1977).
10. See the general account by Ali Wacker, *Arbeitslosigkeit. Soziale und psychische Voraussetzungen und Folgen* (Frankfurt, 1976). The strain on

the family becomes clear in Fred S., *Ich wurde immer kleiner. Die Familie eines Arbeitslosen erzählt*, with the help of Karlheinz Schmidt-Lauzemis (Berlin, 1979).

11. Marie Jahoda, Paul F. Lazarsfeld, and Hans Zeisel, *Die Arbeitslosen von Marienthal. Ein soziographischer Versuch*, (reprinted Frankfurt, 1975) quotations from pp. 84, 88, 98.
12. Cf. Atina Grossmann, 'Abortion and Economic Crisis – The 1931 Campaign Against Paragraph 218', in Bridenthal, Grossmann, and Kaplan, *When Biology*, pp. 66–86; and Hauptverband deutscher Krankenkassen (ed.), *Jahrbuch der Krankenversicherung* (1928) pp. 285–90, contains the estimate of 500 000–800 000 abortions per year, and the assumption that a third of all pregnancies ended in abortion
13. Information of this type appears in Weiland, *Die Kinder*.
14. Remarks noted by Günter Krolzig, *Der Jugendliche in der Großstadtfamilie. Aufgrund von Niederschriften Berliner Berufsschüler und -schülerinnen* (Berlin, 1930) esp. pp. 40–41, 58.
15. Alice Salomon and Marie Baum, (eds), *Das Familienleben in der Gegenwart. Forschungen über Bestand und Erschütterung der Familie in der Gegenwart*, vol. 1 (Berlin, 1930); and Gertrud Bäumer, *Familienpolitik* (Berlin, 1933). The sociocritical novels of the period are revealing for these issues. The problems of women therefore no doubt lay less in the fact that they 'were especially hard hit by the loss of the outer beauty of life', as implied in the generally informative and provocative article by Rudolf Vierhaus, 'Auswirkungen der Krise um 1930 in Deutschland', in Werner Conze and Hans Raupach (eds), *Die Staats- und Wirtschaftskrise des Deutschen Reichs 1929/1933* (Stuttgart, 1967) pp. 155–75, quotation on p. 165.
16. *Statistik des Deutschen Reichs*, vol. 458 (Berlin, 1937) p. 78.
17. This is one of the explanations suggested in the complex interpretation developed by Tim Mason, 'Women in Nazi Germany, Part I', *History Workshop Journal*, no. 1 (1976), pp. 74–113, see p. 93.
18. Cf. Anselm Faust, 'Arbeitsmarktpolitik in Deutschland. Die Entstehung der öffentlichen Arbeitsvermittlung 1890–1927', in Pierenkemper and Tilly (eds), *Arbeitsmarktforschung*, pp. 37–71.
19. On the development of wages, cf. Bajohr, *Die Hälfte*, pp. 28–100. While women's standard wages and salaries were brought closer to those of men than before the world war, a gap of 20–40 per cent still remained, ibid., p. 46. On the wage policies of trade unions, cf. Gisela Losseff-Tillmanns, *Frauenemanzipation und Gewerkschaften* (Wuppertal, 1978) pp. 282–92.
20. Apart from the *Reichsgesetzblatt* (hereafter RGB1) and *Reichsarbeitsblatt* (hereafter RAB1), cf. esp. Ludwig Preller, *Sozialpolitik in der Weimarer Republik* (1949, reprinted Kronberg/Ts., 1978); and Michael T. Wermel and Roswitha Urban, *Arbeitslosenfürsorge und Arbeitslosenversicherung in Deutschland*, (3 parts, Munich, 1949).
21. Kuczynski, *Arbeiterinnen*, already emphasised this, pp. 231–2.
22. Maximum rates calculated from tables in RGB1 and as of 1921, in the 'Amtlicher Teil', RAB1.
23. The differentiation in household status for persons aged 21 and over was

introduced on 15 January 1920 for women, but only on 7 May 1920 for men.

24. RT, vol. 345, p. 728, the discussion on pp. 686 ff.
25. RT, vol. 381, p. 535, the debate from July 23–25, 1924.
26. This was stressed by Syrup, the first president of the Reich Office for Labour Exchanges and Unemployment Insurance ('Reichsanstalt für Arbeitsvermittlung und Arbeitslosenversicherung'). Cf. Friedrich Syrup and Otto Neuloh, *Hundert Jahre staatliche Sozialpolitik 1839–1939* (Stuttgart, 1957) pp. 328–9. When Dietrich Hertz-Eichenrode, *Wirtschaftskrise und Arbeitsbeschaffung* (Frankfurt, 1982) pp. 42–3, judges the equalisation of assistance rates as legitimate on 'social-ethical' grounds, but wrong in terms of 'economic policy', he is following the opinion of the Reich Labour Office.
27. See statements by the Communist Party M.P. Arendsee on 15 November 1926 in the Reichstag; and cf. RT, vol. 391, p. 7899.
28. Calculated using RT, vol. 413, no. 2885, 'Entwurf eines Gesetzes über Arbeitslosenversicherung', p. 65; the figures are based on an inquiry which involved 91.5 per cent of registered main assistance recipients on 1 July 1926. Their last employer had to provide information on their last 'normal gross wage', that is, the income not including additions for overtime, deductions stemming from short-time, illness, or holidays, nor deductions for taxes and social insurance contributions.
29. In his justification for the AVAVG plan, the Labour Minister emphasised that: 'The distress of the skilled workers whose unemployment assistance is already devoured by their fixed costs, constantly pushes for a further raising of the amount of general assistance; but each increase at the same time extends the circle of those whose assistance payment is moving too close to their wage levels'. RT, vol. 432, no. 2885, p. 64.
30. RGB1 (1927), I, pp. 199–200.
31. Calculated using RT, vol. 413, no. 2885, p. 158, and RT, vol. 452, no. 1423, 'Dritter Bericht der Reichsanstalt für Arbeitsvermittlung und Arbeitslosenversicherung für die Zeit vom 1. Januar 1930 bis zum 31.Dezember 1931', p. 45.
32. Calculated using RT, vol. 413, no. 2885, pp. 162–3.
33. The emergency decree of 26 July 1930 laid down that where the income of a spouse was more than 35 marks per week (as of 11 October 1930, over 20 marks/week), it would be taken into account for calculating the benefits given to a married unemployed person. The emergency decree of 5 June 1931 amended par. 107d AVAVG with: 'Married women will only be granted the unemployment benefits in so far as they lack sufficient means. The regulations of the emergency assistance apply to the means test for unemployment', cf. RGB1, I, p. 294; the *Jahrbuch 1931 des ADGB* (Berlin, 1932) pp. 133–4 commented: 'In general, married women today only receive that amount of money from the unemployment insurance fund which they would get from the welfare fund without paying contributions' (cited in Kuczynski, *Arbeiterinnen*, pp. 249–50).
34. Cf. Frieda Wunderlich, *Die Bekämpfung der Arbeitslosigkeit in Deutschland seit Beendigung des Krieges* (Jena, 1925) pp. 63–4.

35. RGBl (1918), I, p. 1305.
36. Ordinance of 15 January 1920, RGBl (1920), I, pp. 54–9.
37. Ordinance concerning unemployment relief, par. 7, section 1, RGBl (1924), I, p. 128; defined more precisely in RGBl (1927), I, p. 50.
38. RT, vol. 345, p. 705; Kaiser, p. 725.
39. For the Federal Republic in the 1970s, cf. Däubler-Gmelin, *Frauenarbeitslosigkeit*, pp. 97–8; and Nauhaus, *Probleme*, p. 115.
40. On demobilisation, cf. Bajohr, *Die Hälfte*, pp. 158–67; Richard Bessel, '"Eine nicht allzu große Beunruhigung des Arbeitsmarktes." Frauenarbeit und Demobilmachung in Deutschland nach dem Ersten Weltkrieg', *Geschichte und Gesellschaft*, 9 (1983), pp. 211–29; Losseff-Tillmanns, *Frauenemanzipation*, pp. 213–21, 231–45; and Werner Thönnessen, *Frauenemanzipation. Politik und Literatur der deutschen Sozialdemokratie zur Frauenbewegung 1863–1933*, 2nd edn (Frankfurt, 1976) pp. 101–08, 141.
41. This was para. 5, section 2, the ordinance concerning unemployment relief in the formulation of 15 January 1919, RGBl (1919), I, p. 82.
42. Cf. Bajohr, *Die Hälfte*, pp. 182–8; Barbara Greven-Aschoff, *Die bürgerliche Frauenbewegung in Deutschland 1894–1933* (Göttingen, 1981) pp. 172–80; and Claudia Hahn, 'Der öffentliche Dienst und die Frauen. Beamtinnen in der Weimarer Republik', in Frauengruppe Faschismusforschung, *Mutterkreuz und Arbeitsbuch. Zur Geschichte der Frauen in der Weimarer Republik und im Nationalsozialismus* (Frankfurt, 1981) pp. 49–78.
43. Greven-Aschoff, *Frauenbewegung*, p. 175. Ursula Büttner, in *Hamburg in der Staats- und Wirtschaftskrise* (Hamburg, 1982) p. 242 and p. 577 (notes 309 and 310), makes note of a political reaction. On 30 January 1930, the League of Hamburg Women's Organisations took a petition to the city's Senate, which referred to the fact that of a total of 38 000 women civil servants employed by the post office, 1000 were married, and of these, some 250 were essentially provided for by their husbands. The petition proceeded: 'It appears that more important than even these economic and social considerations is the necessity of defending the integrity of the state, in times such as today, when the notion of law and justice is precarious. The rights of the citizen may not be sacrificed only with regard to women. The state has the duty, especially as an employer, not only to observe its own laws, but at the same time to serve as a model for private business enterprises and other private employers'.
44. Pointed out by Bajohr, *Die Hälfte*, p. 206; Losseff-Tillmanns, *Frauenemanzipation*, pp. 252–5; and Bessel, '"Eine nicht",' pp. 222–3.
45. A quantitative picture of the displacement of women from the labour market, that is, from their wartime jobs, can probably only be reconstructed through case studies: Cf. Merith Niehuss, 'Arbeitslosigkeit in Augsburg und Linz A.D. 1914–1924', *Archiv für Sozialgeschichte*, 22 (1982), pp. 133–58.
46. RT, vol. 441, nr. 2006, 'Zweiter Bericht der Reichsanstalt für Arbeitsvermittlung und Arbeitslosenversicherung für die Zeit vom 1. Januar 1929 bis zum 31.Dezember 1929', pp. 46, 54.

47. Cf. RABl (1929), I, p. 94, 'Maßnahmen gegen ungerechtfertigte in Anspruchnahme der Arbeitslosenversicherung'.
48. RT, vol. 426, pp. 3137–8.
49. On 'productive unemployment assistance', cf. Preller, *Sozialpolitik*, p. 367; Wunderlich, *Bekämpfung*, pp. 38–54; and for a specific description of the crisis in 1926, Hertz-Eichenrode, *Wirtschaftskrise*, pp. 155–9.
50. Egon Petersen, *Arbeitsmarkt und Arbeitsamt in Stuttgart* (Stuttgart, 1927) p. 165.
51. RT, vol. 345, p. 705.
52. Quoted in Ernst Herrnstadt, *Die Lage der arbeitslosen Jugend in Deutschland* (Berlin, 1927) pp. 45–7.
53. In November 1930, the third report of the National Agency reports on the occupational training measures instituted for unemployed white-collar workers in Germany: RT, vol. 452, no. 1423, p. 24. 5281 women (43.6 per cent of all participants) took part in the 211 courses.
54. Cf. this with Gerda Tornieporth, *Studien zur Frauenbildung* (Weinheim, 1979).
55. Information in Petersen, *Arbeitsmarkt*, p. 168. Calculated using p. 265; cf. also pp. 165–6.
56. See Wunderlich, *Bekämpfung*, pp. 50–51.
57. Cf. Lore Kleiber, '"Wo ihr seid, da soll die Sonne scheinen!" Der Frauenarbeitsdienst am Ende der Weimarer Republik und im Nationalsozialismus', in Frauengruppe Faschismusforschung, *Mutterkreuz*, pp. 188–214; and Hennig Köhler, *Arbeitsdienst in Deutschland. Pläne und Verwirklichungsformen bis zur Einführung der Arbeitsdienstpflicht im Jahre 1935* (Berlin, 1967) esp. pp. 143–4.
58. Cf. RABl (1932), I, pp. 256–8.
59. See Wunderlich's assessment, *Bekämpfung*, p. 44, in 1924: 'The attempts implemented in many localities to retrain female factory workers for domestic service mostly fai..'. Similarly, Herrnstadt, *Die Lage*, p. 25, writing in 1927, concluded, 'If the many home economy courses only succeed in their retraining efforts to a limited degree, the significant accomplishment that remains is that young girls, who must often later manage households of their own, have been better prepared for this important duty upon which a large part of our national product rests'.
60. Cf. Robert Dinse, *Das Freizeitleben der Großstadjugend. 5000 Jungen und Mädchen berichten* (Berlin, 1932); Lisbeth Franzen-Hellersberg, *Die jugendliche Arbeiterin. Ihre Arbeitsweise und Lebensform* (Tübingen, 1932), esp. pp. 46–7; Krolzig, *Der Jugendliche*, *passim*; and also of interest, Johanna Ernst, 'Die wirtschaftliche und berufliche Lage der weiblichen Jugend im Winter 1931/32', *Beruf und Arbeit* 9 (1933), pp. 129–31, 149–52.
61. On unemployment statistics, cf. Lohr, 'Langfristige', pp. 237–84; Manuel Saitzew, (ed), *Die Arbeitslosigkeit der Gegenwart*, vol. 1 (3 vols, Munich, 1932–3) pp. 118–20; Wunderlich, *Bekämpfung*, pp. 7–17; and on women's unemployment, also Bajohr, *Die Hälfte*, pp. 170–77; Däubler-Gmelin, *Frauenarbeitslosigkeit*, pp. 72–3; and Nauhaus, *Probleme*, pp. 50–54.
62. Assembled out of *Statistisches Jahrbuch für das Deutsche Reich*, vol. 44 (Berlin, 1924/25), p. 299; vol. 45 (1926), p. 307; vol. 46 (1927), p. 339; vol.

47 (1928), p. 338; vol. 48 (1929), p. 281; vol. 49 (1930), p. 323; vol. 50 (1931), p. 308; vol. 51 (1932), p. 299; and vol. 52 (1933), p. 299. *Wohlfahrtserwerbslose* (the unemployed who were dependent on welfare) – in other words, those who were unemployed for more than 52 weeks – are not taken into account here.

63. Table assembled from *Statistisches Jahrbuch für das Deutsche Reich* (see note 61 above), with the additions of vol. 46 (1927), p. 331; vol. 47 (1928), p. 381; vol. 48 (1929), p. 274; vol. 49 (1930), p. 316; vol. 50 (1931), p. 301; vol. 51 (1932), p. 291; and vol. 52 (1933), p. 291.

64. That approximately 12–15 per cent of the unemployed were refused assistance because of a particularly strict means test was noted in *Jahrbuch des ADGB 1924* (Berlin, 1925) p. 43.

65. Part-time workers were hardly ever registered as unemployed. Under para. 79 of the AVAVG, they could apply to be exempted from compulsory insurance contributions. In 1929, a new para. 98a made it more difficult for part-time workers to fulfil the requirements entitling them to unemployment benefits. The emergency decree of 26 July 1930, freed minor forms of employment from compulsory insurance, that is, employment for less than 30 hours per week, or monthly earnings of less than 45 marks. Cf. RT, vol. 452, no. 1423, p. 48; ibid., p. 5, that 14 per cent of the unemployed who were not dependent on welfare relief received no assistance in 1930, on the grounds of not making enough payments for the qualifying period, of illness, short-term exclusion from benefits, and being an 'unemployed person of a special kind, as for example, married women, casual workers, holders of small pensions, and persons limited in their ability to pursue gainful employment'.

66. Assembled from *Statistisches Jahrbuch für das Deutsche Reich*, vol. 41 (1920) p. 239; vol. 42 (1921/22), p. 423; vol. 43 (1923), p. 405; vol. 44 (1924/25), p. 287; vol. 45 (1926), p. 294; vol. 46 (1927), p. 325; vol. 47 (1928), p. 376; vol. 48 (1929), p. 370; vol. 49 (1930), p. 270; vol. 50 (1931), p. 312; vol. 51 (1932), p. 300; and vol. 52 (1933), p. 290.

67. Assembled from *Statistisches Jahrbuch für das Deutsche Reich*, vol. 44 (1924/25), p. 296; vol. 47 (1928), p. 386; and vol. 52 (1933), p. 307.

68. Wladimir Woytinsky, *Der deutsche Arbeitsmarkt. Ergebnisse der gewerkschaftlichen Arbeitslosenstatistik 1919–1929*, part 1 (2 parts, Berlin, 1930), pp. 49–54, 72.

69. Ibid., p. 74.

70. Cf. *Statistisches Jahrbuch für das Deutsche Reich*, vol. 50 (1931), p. 301; vol. 51 (1932), p. 291; and vol. 52 (1933), p. 291.

71. Cf. also Wladimir Woytinsky, 'Arbeitslosigkeit und Kurzabeit', *Jahrbuch für Nationalökonomie und Statistik* 134 (1931), I, pp. 13–48.

72. Willi Hemmer, *Die 'unsichtbaren' Arbeitslosen. Statistische Methoden, soziale Tatsachen* (Zeulenroda, 1935).

73. *Statistik des Deutschen Reichs*, vol. 458 (1937), pp. 78–82.

74. See Angela Meister, *Die deutsche Industriearbeiterin. Ein Beitrag zum Problem der Frauenerwerbsarbeit* (Jena, 1939) p. 167, also p. 193; and similarly stated in Otto Michalke, 'Die Frauenarbeit', *Jahrbuch für Nationalökonomie und Statistik* 142 (1935), pp. 435–47.

75. Willms makes a comparable observation in Müller, Willms and Handl, *Strukturwandel*, p. 34, for the 1950 census in the Federal Republic.

76. Michalke, 'Frauenarbeit', p. 439.
77. On structural changes in women's wage work, cf. Renate Bridenthal and Claudia Koonz, 'Beyond Kinder, Küche, Kirche. Weimar Women in Politics and Work', Bridenthal, Grossmann and Kaplan (eds), *When Biology*, pp. 33–65; Bajohr, *Die Hälfte*; Reulecke, 'Veränderungen'; Willms, in Müller, Willms and Handl, *Strukturwandel*; and Willms, in Pierenkemper and Tilly, eds, 'Modernisierung'.
78. Cf. the occupational census of 1925 in *Statistik des Deutschen Reiches*, vol. 402 (Berlin, 1927), pp. 228–33.
79. Cf., for example, Adolf Damaschke, *Die Arbeitslosigkeit und ihre Überwindung. Briefe an einen jungen Staatsbürger* (Berlin, 1931); in his tenth letter he discusses '1. Settlement for additional income', '2. On the woman's question', and writes, p. 61: 'The settlement for additional income is also of consequence for the labour market in another way . . . It is the only way to save German family life. One cannot take seriously enough the devastation of health and morals in our family life and also in the education of our children entailed in the words, "German mothers in factories"', also cf. Bajohr, *Die Hälfte*, pp. 180–88, 219–21.
80. Cited in Louise Schroeder, *Die proletarische Frau als Hausfrau und Mutter*, in Anna Blos (ed.), *Die Frau im Lichte des Sozialismus* (Dresden, 1930) pp. 148–181, on p. 149. Results of a survey of industrial women workers by Anna Geyer, 'Die Frau im Beruf', in Blos (ed.), ibid., pp. 183–219, on pp. 190–95.
81. Geyer, 'Die Frau', pp. 210–13. The Gutachterkommission zur Arbeitslosenfrage, the Brauns-Kommission, published a report of experts on the unemployment question in a special issue of the *Reichsarbeitsblatt* (Berlin, 1931); in the first part of the report they looked very precisely at the possibility of fighting unemployment by eliminating 'double earning', drawing on a wide range of material, and largely deciding in the negative. Despite this, the Commission could not come to an agreement over whether a marriage bar for women civil servants should again be ordered or not.
82. See memorandum of the Hamburg mayor, Roß, issued on 29 December 1930, cited in Ursula Büttner, 'Hamburg in der Großen Depression', unpublished PhD Dissertation (University of Hamburg, 1979) p. 417, note 330.
83. In contrast to Winkler, *Frauenarbeit*, pp. 47–52, who found no significant displacement of women from jobs in 1933, Bajohr, *Die Hälfte*, pp. 220–27, emphasises the serious consequences of the campaign.
84. Cf. Losseff-Tillmanns, *Frauenemanzipation*, p. 298.
85. Cited in Thönnessen, *Frauenemanzipation*, p. 159.
86. Vorstand des Deutschen Metallarbeiterverbandes, (ed.), *Die Frauenarbeit in der Metallindustrie* (Stuttgart, 1930) p. 203, cited in Bajohr, *Die Hälfte*, p. 180; and on trade union policy, cf. esp. Losseff-Tillmanns, *Frauenemanzipation*, pp. 310–18. In contrast, the resolution made at the SPD Congress in Leipzig in 1931: 'The SPD fights vigorously to check the heated agitation mounted against working woman, regardless of whether she is single or married' (cited in Thönnessen, Frauenemanzipation, p. 143).

5 The Social and Implications of Unemployment i Weimar Germany 1929–1933*

Peter D. Stachura

Before the onset of the Depression at the end of the 1920s, periods of economic crisis during the earlier history of the Weimar Republic had clearly identified the younger generation as particularly vulnerable to the threat and reality of large-scale unemployment. This situation stood in stark contrast to the years of the First World War when, in the absence of adult manpower, working youth had enjoyed full employment and relatively high wage levels. During the phase of demobilisation immediately following the end of the war younger, especially unskilled, workers in industry, and to a lesser extent, in commerce and transport, became conspicuous early casualties of dismissal, short-term working and shrinking career opportunities.[1] Apprenticeships, which traditionally were taken up by a large majority of German youths, were at that time in comparatively short supply, allowing employers to pick and choose more or less as they wanted from the avalanche of job applications confronting them. The labour market in 1919–21 was so competitive that parents often sent in to prospective employers supplementary statements lending support to sons' and daughters' applications for an opening.[2]

The relative paucity of apprenticeships continued during the early and mid-1920s in many sectors of the economy as Germany struggled to secure a firm basis for recovery and development. In the hyperinflation crisis of 1923 young unskilled workers under 25 years of age,

*I am grateful to the Economic and Social Research Council for awarding me a grant that made possible my visits to West German archives as part of the research for a larger project of which this article is the first publication.

[illegible] ingle and without family responsibilities, were among [illegible] e made redundant.[3] By that time a pattern of high youth [illegible] yment during times of recession had been established. As the [illegible] ss of extensive and concentrated rationalisation in industry got [illegible] nder way in the mid-1920s, and as the economy showed itself susceptible to alarming fluctuation, the advent of mass unemployment claimed, in relative and absolute terms, a considerable proportion of younger workers.[4] The national census of June 1925 indicated that of a Reich population of 62 million, 9 million were aged 14–21 years; in Prussia's population of just over 38 million, 30 per cent were aged 14–25 years.[5] The first half of the following year saw a noteworthy increase in unemployment generally, with the youth sector badly hit. In January 1926, 40 303 under-18-year-olds were registered jobless, constituting 2.3 per cent of the total registered unemployed; the figure rose to 52 228 youths in March of that year, and to 272 137, or 2.7 per cent of all those out of work, in July 1926. More strikingly, when the 18–21 year old male unemployed in July 1926 are added, some 15.8 per cent of the total male jobless were aged 14–21 years of age.[6] From this experience it could have been reasonably anticipated that younger Germans would be even more dramatically affected by the massive, spiralling unemployment of the Depression years. There is ample statistical data to underpin this point, although it needs to be borne in mind that the precise extent of youth unemployment cannot be ascertained because only figures for the *registered* jobless, that is, those in receipt of unemployment or other insurance or relief benefit (*Hauptunterstützungsempfänger*) are available, and then only, of course, from the mid-1920s when systematic records first began to be kept.

At the moment of the Depression's initial impact the situation of the younger generation in the labour market was complicated by a number of conflicting demographic trends. While there were by 1929–30 more 18–25 year olds than ever before because of the heavy birth-rate in some pre-war years, notably in 1910, the 14–18 year old cohort declined in number, due to the low birth-rates of the war and early post-war period, from 4 068 000 in 1931 to 3 101 000 in 1933, a drop of 24 per cent.[7] Whatever way one looks at the statistics, however, the clear fact emerges that the size of the youth labour pool was already in 1929–30 far too large for the number of jobs available, thus causing some authorities to talk in December 1929 of the existence of 'an emergency situation', especially among 18–21 year olds.[8] In Germany as a whole there were, in March 1929, some 245 888 unemployed aged under 20 years (12 per cent of the total registered) with another 465 398 aged 20–

25 years (22.5 per cent of the total).[9] Even when a few months la unemployment figures showed a substantial decrease, the under-ᴢ year-olds constituted 14.2 per cent of the jobless.[10] Matters could only become worse as the Depression set in. At the beginning of 1930, 297 088 (of whom 58 590 were female) aged 14–21 years were officially out of work – most of them over 18 years of age – but at the end of that first full year of the Depression some 450 000 under-21-year-olds were unemployed: the half-million mark was reached in February 1931 when the total out of work in Germany was already over 4.5 million. By the spring, unemployment among the under-21-year-olds was 16.3 per cent of the total, meaning that a larger proportion of the younger employable population was jobless than the proportion of older workers – a trend which persisted and even intensified until the end of the Weimar period.[11] By September 1931, 650 000 youths aged under 21 years were without a job, and as the Depression entered its deepest trough in 1932 against a background of Brüning's severe deflationary policies the plight of the younger generation became more marked; when the jobless total edged over six million during the first half of that year, approximately one million, or one in six, were young men and women under the age of 25 years.[12] The entire younger generation, between the ages of 14 and 25 years, made up 24.1 per cent of the total male unemployed and 38.5 per cent of the total female unemployed in mid-1932.[13] In other words, by 1932 younger workers were a far larger percentage of the unemployed than had been the case in pre-Depression years: for example, the jobless aged 14–18 years constituted a mere 2.6 per cent of the unemployed on average in 1925–27.[14] Taking into acount those not registered because of non-entitlement to benefits – a situation which applied in particular to females out of work – youth unemployment may have been in reality almost double the officially recorded levels by the end of 1932.

Since about three-quarters of employable youths in Germany were classified as 'workers', with over 50 per cent of them in industrial occupations,[15] it is axiomatic that the working class, particularly if aged between 18 and 25 years and unskilled, bore the brunt of youth unemployment. Within that category the areas of highest job losses for males were in the construction and machine-making industries and the metal trades, and for females, in the clothing and textile industries. Unemployment among white-collar younger workers (*Angestellte*) was insignificant prior to the Depression, but rose thereafter, resulting, by mid-1931, in some 15–18 per cent of the 300 000 jobless employees being aged under 21 years.[16] One of the few areas of the economy

e economic crisis, there was a continuing demand for
s child labour was in agriculture and related industries.
tion for employers was obviously the cheapness of their
and the fact that they were able to maintain, especially in
provinces of Eastern Germany, feudalistic conditions of
official interference.[17]

d regional pattern of youth unemployment emerged quite clearly by early 1930 and did not basically alter over the next few years: Westphalia, parts of Hesse, and the Rhineland were identified as black spots, to be joined before long by Berlin – Brandenburg, Saxony and Silesia – in effect, the most heavily industrialised areas of the country. Consequently, the major cities of Berlin, Cologne, Düsseldorf, Essen, Breslau and others, became notorious for their large degree of youth unemployment. For instance, on the eve of the National Socialist assumption of power, 63 per cent of young males aged 14–25 years were out of work in Berlin. More surprisingly, perhaps, it is claimed that in 1930–31, and presumably in 1932 also, youth unemployment rates were higher in small towns of under 50 000 inhabitants than in medium-sized towns of under 100 000.[18]

The development of unemployment among young Germans in the early 1930s produced some novel and interesting characteristics, including most notably, a new group of long-term jobless of substantial dimensions. As early as November 1930 the youth welfare authorities in Hamburg recognised the arrival of this unprecedented phenomenon among the young unemployed,[19] and authorities in other cities soon reached the same conclusion: in Cologne it was estimated that a significant, though unspecified percentage of the 8869 jobless aged under 21 years in January 1931 had been in that predicament for a lengthy period of time.[20] A large number of the long-term jobless youth were apprentices who had been dismissed before completing their training during the years 1925–9 because of the pressures from rationalisation combined with adverse financial and economic influences. The fact that many apprentices did not have a written contract with their masters (*Lehrlingsvertrag*) facilitated their dismissal. Unable to secure re-engagement before the Depression struck, these apprentices faced the early 1930s with virtually no prospects of a position.[21] On the other hand, there were apprentices who on finishing their training satisfactorily were dismissed in any case. They were too expensive to employ on a regular basis and there was a growing tendency to employ unskilled labour. For them, suitable employment appeared only after 1933. The disillusionment and frustration experienced by these unwanted skilled young people was acute, leaving them with a feeling that their long years of arduous and underpaid training had been a waste of time.[22]

Besides apprentices, school-leavers formed another prominent component of the long-term youth unemployed during the Depression. Those leaving school in 1929–30 were particularly unfortunate, for not only were many of them unable to find a job, but they had also been born and brought up amidst the stringent conditions of wartime and the early 1920s. On leaving school at the age of 14 years a good number of them were physically weak and intellectually below average, thus adding to their already very difficult task of finding employment. Employers and other interested adults frequently complained that such youth were immature in various ways and simply ill-equipped to pursue a demanding job or period of training.[23] In the highly competitive labour market of 1930 when, for example, 793 000 school-leavers were chasing only 290 000 apprenticeships, or of 1931 when 717 000 were jostling for a mere 160 000 apprenticeships,[24] this cohort was bound to contain vast numbers of bitterly disappointed youths, destined for the very bottom of the economic and social ladder. Thus, the Depression threw up another new category of unemployed: a group of 14–18 year olds who had never worked.

While unemployment was a tragic intrusion into the lives of so many young Germans, it is worthwhile pointing out, from the need to establish a wider perspective, that the situation for those in employment was too often far from congenial. Notwithstanding the provision of protective legislation for working youth by the state, the supervisory machinery that was created proved to be more and more ineffectual as it was scaled down following cuts in public expenditure by the Brüning government and its successors. Abuses became more common throughout industry and other sectors of the economy, leaving young workers deprived of adequate safeguards and too frequently at the mercy of unfair employers.[25] The Left, in particular, had been complaining about the alleged exploitation of working-class youth for long before the Depression.[26] Working conditions were characterised by low rates of pay, unpaid or inadequately paid overtime, long hours, Saturday working, and few holidays.[27] There was no statutory holiday entitlement for young workers as there was, for instance, in Austria. In practice, therefore, many of them had less than a week's annual vacation, and without pay. Employers successfully resisted pressure from various concerned bodies such as the *Reichsausschuss der deutschen Jugendverbände* for legislation on the grounds that they could not afford to grant the two or three weeks' holiday being demanded, and argued further that the absence from work of the youths for that length of time would disrupt work schedules and production in factories.[28] Given the unequal balance of power between capital and labour in Germany during the Depression, employers faced little difficulty in imposing even these obviously spurious views. As it transpired, however, there were young workers and parents in the early 1930s who were so apprehensive of jobs being put at risk through periods off work in a tight labour market that they were not unduly concerned about the holiday issue: those employed in small or family businesses where unionisation was weak were especially nervous in this respect.[29] In these circumstances, it was felt, the advisable course of action was simply to put up with matters as they were. Indeed, the holiday issue was perhaps understandably not all that important in view of other realities in the workplace: the ever-present threat of industrial accident for one, and the widespread physical maltreatment, particularly of apprentices, for another.[30]

The working life of apprentices could be most depressing. Responsible authorities had long been aware of the necessity of providing protection for apprentices and a good deal of time and energy had been spent discussing their general conditions of employment, including the question of contracts between them and their masters.[31] But the resultant legislation, such as it was, was not enforced as strictly or as widely as it ought to have been. Complaints about masters' violations of their rights over their charges – *väterliche Züchtigungsrecht*, according to Paragraph 127 of the Commercial Code (*Gewerbeordnung*) of 1869 – grew in number year by year: brutality against apprentices increased in frequency and severity, and periodic public outcries had no lasting ameliorative influence.[32] The young female worker, however, was perhaps the most disadvantaged of all as regards both her working conditions in the factory or on the land, and at home. Many led a life of unremitting drudgery and gloom – a fate to which nearly everyone else, including the socialist and labour movements, were almost totally indifferent.[33]

Clearly, therefore, there were some harsh penalties for those who were young and in work. It was an unattractive, rather miserable existence in many respects, through on balance it was preferable to being on the dole, or jobless and not on the dole, as was often the case by 1932. That repugnant prospect, however, was constantly before the eyes of millions of young workers as the crisis bit harder and harder into Germany's economic infrastructure, making life even for those still in work progressively more insecure. The future meant no farther than the next day.

II

A society cursed with unprecedented levels of unemployment such as the Weimar Republic in the early 1930s might have been excused to some extent if it had not paid much attention to the plight of its younger members. After all, the social and political pressures emanating from the Depression immediately put the Republic's very existence at stake and ultimately resulted, unfortunately, in the destruction of the democratic system of government. But even if the Republic was unable at the end to offer meaningful assistance to youth, it could not simply close its eyes to the problems of the young jobless because of broader historical developments in Germany since the turn of the century.

For much of the nineteenth century German youth had been a submerged, if not subjected, social group with few rights of its own and with no settled profile or identity – thus broadly comparable to the lowly status of women. A highly authoritarian school and further educational system, tight and often heavy-handed supervision in employment, and the strict discipline of military conscription counted among the most important factors keeping the younger generation firmly in a subordinate position in a society informed by adult values and perceptions. The first crucial challenge from the ranks of youth to that rigid dominance came from the newly-created independent youth movement, the *Wandervogel*, in the early 1900s, with its emphasis on the individuality of youth and its need for self-determination. The *Wandervogel's* impact on society as a whole was rapid and considerable. While it proved attractive to growing numbers of middle-class youth in many Protestant areas of Northern and Central Germany, it encouraged the formation of a parallel organisation for working-class socialist youth.[34] More significantly, the awakening of youth that was epitomised by these groups virtually forced the Wilhelmine Reich into adopting a series of counter-measures, including the establishment of the state-sponsored paramilitary youth group, the *Jungdeutschlandbund*, and the repressive Law of Association in 1908, in an attempt to regain, and more fully assert, control over the younger generation. By 1914, however, the *Wandervogel*, in particular, had been so successful that the concept of a 'kingdom of youth', which had been proclaimed by its leading spokemen like Gustav Wyneken, was well and truly established. Youth had finally come of age in German society. One important manifestation of this achievement was the long overdue attention given by the state to the sphere of youth welfare provision.

The major Churches, the *Deutsche Zentrale für Jugendfürsorge*, and other private bodies, had been campaigning for some time for youth welfare legislation of one type or another without a great deal of success.[35] But as the attitudes of state officialdom began to take a positive turn in the 1900s in response to the increasing signs of restlessness among youth (health problems, rising criminality and so on) and the exertions of the youth movement, new legislation specifically directed at youth found its way into the statute books: protection was offered against alcohol abuse, trashy literature, and other perceived nefarious influences of modern industrial society, coupled with legislation outlawing night-time and Sunday working for children aged 9–12 years, reducing the working hours of juveniles and forbidding the employment of under-14 year-olds in factories.[36] The most decisive step came in January 1911, when a decree from the Prussian Ministry of Education (*Jugendpflegeerlass*) created the concept and practice of a state-fostered youth welfare system for the largest and most populous German province. The decree stated:

> The State government regards youth welfare (*Jugendpflege*) as one of the most important tasks of the present time because of its great significance for the future of our people.

And further:

> The task of youth welfare is to co-operate in the rearing of happy, physically able, morally sound and public-spirited young people, filled with the fear of God and love for their home and Fatherland. Its purpose is to support, supplement and continue the educative activities of the parents, school, Church, the master and the employer.[37]

The Prussian authorities publicly appealed to organisations and institutions throughout the province for their support in the new scheme, and youth welfare committees were set up on a local basis with government funding. Progress was inevitably interrupted, of course, by the war, and indeed, legal restrictions on youth's freedom of movement and the suspension of various protective measures in factories suggested a temporary reversal of prewar trends.[38] But, overall, the right direction had irrevocably been taken, and in view of the further maturation of the younger generation's contribution to the economy in the absence of male adults during the war, the end of hostilities was bound to witness a consolidation and extension of the state's concern for youth.

The campaign for a comprehensive and progressive juvenile welfare law immediately gathered momentum. Two particular influences had a vital bearing on the outcome: first, the youth movement, which grew dramatically in size after 1918 within organisations of many different social and political complexions, was able to keep the special problems of youth before the public eye and to act as a fairly effective lobby in politics.[39] It helped that many members of the independent sector of the youth movement in the 1920s – *Bündische* Youth – joined the social and caring professions, especially teaching and social work, and supplied a whole range of new ideas for the reform and modernisation of youth welfare practices.[40] Secondly, the central role played by the Social Democrats, the trade union movement and the Centre Party, in pushing for improvements in the welfare field generally during the early 1920s, ensured that the necessary political clout was added to the youth case. A series of measures culminated in the *Reichsjugendwohlfahrtsgesetz* (National Youth Welfare Act) of July 1922, representing on paper at least a major step forward.[41]

Its implementation having been delayed by the hyper-inflation crisis of 1922–3 the Act, when it finally took effect in April 1924, established within the Ministry of Public Welfare (*Ministerium für Volkswohlfahrt*) a string of youth welfare offices (*Jugendämter*) throughout the country, to operate as centralised co-ordinating and supervisory agencies of the many different existing branches of youth welfare, including those for abnormal, orphaned and delinquent youth aged 14–21 years.[42] The timing of this legislation was fortunately related, of course, to the modest revival of the Republic's economic and political standing following the traumatic events of late 1923, so that the funding of the Act by central and provincial government was not in the initial stages a serious problem.[43] And, conversely, in the Weimar Republic of the mid-1920s there was a great deal of welfare work for the younger generation to be accomplished, above all, in major cities. In Hamburg the authorities remarked on the considerable undernourishment of children from families afflicted by unemployment,[44] and the material conditions generally of young people in working-class areas of the city such as Hammerbrook were deplorable: their health standard was below average, and their schools were often badly-equipped, cold and dull.[45] Similarly disadvantageous conditions for working-class youth prevailed in Berlin.[46] In fact, there was widespread disquiet among welfare officials at the plight of that cohort of youths who had grown up amidst the often chronic deprivation of the war – and early post-war years.[47] The authorities' response varied from one part of the country to another, but in Hamburg and Cologne, for example, where the problems were acute, a clear-sighted and progressive programme of action was pursued. A noteworthy feature was the provision of holidays for deprived youngsters.[48] By 1927 the expenditure levels of Hamburg's youth welfare office lay above the national average, though its budget had to be defended against sharp competition from other public bodies in the city.[49]

The provision of welfare, educational and sporting facilities for youth was complemented to a degree by the greater attention given to improving the working environment and opportunities of young workers. Progress was patchy, however, and there were wide regional variations. Hence, vocational training was efficiently organised and widely available in Hamburg but not in Prussia as a whole.[50] In addition, legislation aimed at protecting youth from undesirable literature in 1926 and protecting them at places of amusement in 1927 completed the measures for youth from the state. It may be said that this legislation laid the foundations at least for a reasonably harmonious relationship between the Republic and substantial sections of youth, including working-class youth, who stood to gain most from advances in official thinking and action in the mid-1920s.

The growing matter of youth unemployment was a constant reminder, however, even during the so-called 'golden years' of the mid-1920s, of the complexity and extent of the welfare problem. Younger workers had not been sufficiently well looked after, in any case, by the embryonic unemployment relief scheme created after the war, while school-leavers unable to find a job were not entitled to any support at all.[51] The notion of providing the more extensive welfare for youth that the 1922 Act had enshrined resulted, on the other hand, in some remedies for youth unemployment being offered, particularly from about 1926 when the problem grew noticeably worse. Vocational and educational courses, day centres with recreational and catering facilities, and other measures were forthcoming, though the proposed *Berufsausbildungsgesetz* (Vocational Training Act) for the young unemployed took some time to materialise.[52] Indeed, the limitations of welfare provision were readily apparent even before the advent of the Depression. A clear pattern of response had emerged by the late 1920s: expenditure on youth welfare was substantially reduced when diminishing resources were required for the alleviation of other kinds of need and distress deemed more pressing by the authorities. However well-intentioned the Republic may have been in the mid-1920s towards the position of young Germans, it simply could not afford to honour all its pledges and promises to the full once economically stringent times appeared. Not unnaturally, that reality inevitably caused increasing disillusionment among the young of every social class, but none more so than working-class youth who were to be the hardest hit. The development of a widening credibility gap between the youthful proletariat and the Republic could not be avoided in these circumstances. The modest material gains they had generally experienced during the mid-1920s – for example, in respect of health standards[53] – were being eroded before 1929, so that they still constituted an extremely vulnerable and underprivileged section of Weimar society. Significant deficiences in their schooling and employment were not solved by the welfare net set up by the 1922 Act,[54] and the Depression exacerbated the situation, thus raising further questions about the relationship between the Republic and proletarian youth. Above all, when it became apparent that the state could offer little cushioning to the devastating effects of mass unemployment, large segments of working-class youth were decisively alienated from it.

The cornerstone of the Republic's welfare programme, the Unemployment Insurance Act of July 1927 (*Gesetz über Arbeitsvermittlung und Arbeitslosenversicherung* – AVAVG), had done relatively little to improve the lot of jobless youth. It failed to extend to them the same level of benefits, in proportion, as it did to adults: young workers had fewer rights, lower rates of relief and for shorter periods, and if aged under 16 years, had to perform, in theory at least, if not always in practice, compulsory labour (*Pflichtarbeit*) or, when aged 16–18 years, participate in some form of training in return for benefit.[55] The implementation and funding of the Act in general was fraught with difficulties before very long,[56] and the Depression then put it and the rest of the public welfare system under intolerable strain. As the system was drastically reduced in scope, particularly following a succession of emergency presidential decrees in October 1929, July 1930, June 1931 and June 1932, tens of thousands of unemployed youngsters found that the benefit due to them was woefully inadequate or that they were excluded altogether from the relief system and its supplementary forms (*Krisenfürsorge* or emergency relief, and poor relief), making them dependent on their families. In many instances, the latter were unable, or unwilling, to bear this burden, causing desperate hardship among the young and forcing a large number on to the streets. The much-reduced openings even for 'black' (unrecorded, non-taxed) work, a traditional recourse for the young working class in periods of unemployment, added to the misery.[57]

In view of the escalating plight of the young unemployed, some attempt had to be made by the state to activate and extend existing relief schemes and, if possible, to take new initiatives. Central government's intention of devoting additional funds to vocational training and other courses at further education centres was made clear in 1930 by Dr Syrup, President of the *Reichsanstalt für Arbeitsvermittlung und Arbeitslosenversicherung*,[58] but the commitment was not fully honoured, despite the stipulation in the Weimar constitution that on leaving primary school every youth was entitled to three years' further vocational instruction on a part-time basis. The state did take a leading role in setting up day centres where some work and recreational facilities were provided, but by late 1931 many of them had been forced to close due to lack of funding.[59] So-called 'Work Homes' (*Werkheime*) and special homes for the long-term jobless (*Erwerbslosenheime*) made an appearance, but again to very limited effect.[60] Emergency public works schemes were another favourite device of government which soon floundered, [61] and official attempts to structure the long idle hours of the young jobless through the creation of *Freizeitsheime* did not get far either.[62] These centrally-organised measures were designed to strengthen the youths' willingness to work, maintain morale and lay on the sort of training that would be useful to them when jobs once again became available. Certain government spokesmen earned a degree of notoriety for loudly proclaiming the merits of what had been done, but the government's own statistics on the numbers benefiting contradicted their statements. The stark reality was that the measures touched only a relatively small percentage of jobless youth, and then invariably for short periods only.[63]

Relief measures at the local and provincial level varied in scope and efficacy, as was only to be expected. With budgets being trimmed all the time, even enlightened Hamburg discovered the necessity of constantly scaling down its welfare support for the young and unemployed.[64] The city's *Arbeitsausschuss zur Fürsorge für jugendliche Erwerbslose*, which was created in 1931, was gravely hampered by inadequate financing – the budget for youth welfare having been reduced by 10 per cent for 1931/2 – and failed to make a significant impact on the problem, much to the disappointment of officials who were concerned at the moral dangers to the young jobless.[65] This feeling of frustration in the face of such overwhelming difficulties was shared by most other authorities, with the probably unique exception of Cologne, which somehow contrived, despite the odds, to maintain its customary high level of commitment to youth welfare.[66]

In the highly-charged political atmosphere of the early 1930s, certain approaches by central government to the vexed question of youth unemployment aroused bitter controversy, indicating that non-material constraints on action could be as important as the more obvious economic and financial factors involved in the situation. One of these was the proposal put forward by the Prussian government in 1931 for an extension of the compulsory period of attendance at school to a ninth year, not for positive educational reasons but rather for the purpose of giving short-term relief to the problem of unemployment among school-leavers. But this move, which formed part of a broader package deal addressed to the unemployment problem, ran into formidable opposition, especially from employers interested in preserving plentiful supplies of very cheap juvenile labour. Consequently, a much watered-down scheme, devoid of adequate financial support and only made voluntary, was introduced in Prussia in early 1931, to little effect.[67]

Even more contentious was the introduction in 1931 of voluntary labour service (FAD) by the Brüning government. Building on similar schemes devised by various right-wing organisations and youth groups in the 1920s, FAD immediately met vehement opposition from the extreme Left, which was not too surprising in view of the enthusiastic backing given to the initiative by a score of conservative and nationalist associations. It was alleged that FAD was essentially a form of state-sponsored political and economic repression of unemployed working-class youth who, if given the opportunity, were virtually coerced into joining the scheme by their poor material circumstances.[68] It was further claimed that FAD had been set up to divert, or bring under control, the growing political radicalism among the young unemployed which was causing alarm in government circles.[69] The scheme itself, which aimed to provide short-term, low-paid work and accommodation in spartan camps for the unemployed aged 18–25 years, was of modest dimensions, and in November 1932 had only 285 000 enrolled – a mere drop in the ocean of young out-of-work Germans.[70] For those youths willing, but unable, to join FAD, the Schleicher government established in December 1932 a '*Notwerk der deutschen Jugend*' which offered broadly the same activities.[71] The militarisation and politicisation of youth relief implicit in schemes such as FAD and the *Notwerk* were perhaps most vividly illustrated by the establishment by the Papen administration in September 1932 of the *Reichskuratorium für Jugendertüchtigung* (National Board for Youth Training) under the supervision of the Interior Ministry. The new body was led by General von

Stülpnagel and served to lay on voluntary short courses for youth in paramilitary training and military-styled sports (*Wehrsport*). The hostile reaction of working-class youth was predictable.[72]

Interested bodies such as the *Reichsausschuss der deutschen Jugendverbände*, and the trade unions, offered well-meaning, constructive but strictly limited proposals for tackling youth unemployment.[73] Individual youth organisations also joined in the debate. The Hitler Youth advanced in 1930 a comprehensive plan for a National Youth Law (*Reichsjugendgesetz*),[74] and the Communist youth association (KJVD) helped the Communist Party to draw up a *Gesetz zum Schutz der Jugend gegen soziale Verelendung* (Law for the Protection of Youth from Social Immiseration) which was defeated in the Reichstag in early 1931.[75] Pseudo-moralistic exhortations from certain Christian groups for youth to grin and bear their misery were unhelpful,[76] of course, while the Social Democratic response was noticeably belated and unremarkable: the establishment in summer 1932 of the *Sozialer Dienst – Hilfswerk der Arbeiterschaft für die erwerbslose Jugend* as a body to co-ordinate principally with the voluntary labour service (FAD).[77]

The inadequacy of government and private endeavours to combat youth unemployment was plain enough. That gulf only grew wider and more intense as resources continued to lag behind needs and as the political will of the Republic progressively weakened. There was no way of avoiding the manifold and disastrous social consequences of the tragedy.

III

The industrial proletariat suffered more than any other group in Germany during the Depression as a consequence of mass unemployment. Progressive and catatrophic immiseration made life a nightmare for them: lower incomes, lower consumption and lower morale were the hallmarks of their situation.[78] One sympathetic observer noted that as early as 1930 the condition of the working class was generally characterised by 'increasing misery, increasing bitterness, increasing despair. A world of poverty, hunger and exploitation'. To the more obvious signs of material deprivation, including shabby clothing, indebtedness and sub-standard housing, could be added the widespread breakup of marriages and families.[79] Somewhat less apparent, but just as damaging, was the mental and psychological anguish that was felt, in particular, by the long-term unemployed. In such circumstances, the young working class sustained immeasurable harm.

The dire straits of younger children of the working-class unemployed was graphically depicted by a number of contemporary commentators, but none more so than by Weiland.[80] Their living standards often fell below the poverty line, their education was retarded in badly-equipped schools, their chances of advancement to secondary schooling – never very high at the best of times – were all but eradicated,[81] their self-confidence and appreciation of moral values were destroyed, and their expectations for the future totally undermined. The inability of parents to cope was reflected in the higher incidence of cases of child neglect and the abandonment of children.[82] As for jobless working-class youth, their lot was hardly any better as an avalanche of often conflicting responses filled their daily lives: despair, desperation, bitterness, pessimism, hopelessness and frustration could link up with a sense of outrage and resentment against an economic and political system that was seemingly impotent to help, or even care, to produce an explosive mixture of emotions. The entire range of established authority – parents, the older generation, politicians, social workers, welfare and reform institutions – became targets for youth's hatred and rejection. On other occasions these emotions could lead merely to a mood of sullen resignation. Their disillusionment effectively removed many of these youths from the mainstream of Weimar society. They retreated to become outcasts and rebels on the periphery.[83] Such was the widely perceived alienation and demoralisation (*Jugendverwahrlosung*) that they were spoken of as 'a lost generation', destroyed by unemployment and its shattering socio-psychological repercussions. Even highly placed government officials, like Dr Gertrud Bäumer of the Reich Interior Ministry, shared this view. She told a meeting in Spring 1932 that 'never has the task of protecting and helping an endangered generation been so pressing as it is today . . . We are in danger of losing an entire generation of youth'.[84] The evidence for the alarming decline in the morale and over-all placement of the younger generation was overwhelming.

The savage reductions in youth welfare expenditure throughout most of the country after 1929–30 contributed to a decline in the health standards of young working-class people. In Hamburg, the authorities spoke of 'an important deterioration' in this regard, and rickets, a sure sign of inadequate and poor quality dieting, reappeared on a large scale.[85] In other areas the incidence of certain diseases, including tuberculosis, and nervous disorders rose. Many hard-up authorities had to savagely curtail provision of holidays for deprived children and youths.[86] Child vagrancy and street-begging, which had been a common sight in the early 1920s but had disappeared in better times, now re-emerged on an expanded scale. But authorities in large cities where the problem was most acute could do little to help. In 1930 there were no fewer than 19 185 vagrant youths in Berlin and over 11 000 in Frankfurt-am-Main,[87] while Hamburg, Nuremberg and Karlsruhe also had large numbers.[88] By late 1932, estimates of the total number of '*Wanderburschen*' varied from 200 000 to one million,[89] and with them came the additional problem of petty criminality.[90] If vagrant youth constituted one of the most striking manifestations of the disintegration of Germany's social fabric during the Depression, however, no less distressing was the marked increase in juvenile prostitution[91] and the soaring suicide rate among young people. Even for a country with traditionally one of the highest rates in the world, the figures were arresting, particularly in Berlin where, during 1932, there were an average of 10 or 11 suicide attempts by youths every day.[92] By way of sharp contrast, there were in the whole of Germany in 1924 some 104 suicides by under-15-year-olds.[93]

For many adult contemporaries, however, the most disquieting social consequence of mass youth unemployment in the early 1930s was the appreciable rise in juvenile criminality. A majority of those professionally active in the field – social workers, psychologists and criminologists – accepted that the connection between the two phenomena was neither as straightforward, nor as simplistic, as could appear at first sight, but remained convinced, none the less, that it was important, and they produced a substantial body of empirical evidence from different parts of the country in support of their case. In Hamburg in 1930, 35.7 per cent of juvenile criminals were jobless at the time of committing the offence, and in 1932 the figure had risen to 43.5 per cent.[94] Oberhausen, in the heart of the Rhenish-Westphalian industrial belt, told a similar story: in 1932, 43.3 per cent of its juvenile offenders were out of work.[95] For the Reich as a whole the figure in large towns and cities in 1932 averaged out at 36.6 per cent.[96] In Berlin, Cologne, Leipzig, Dortmund, Bochum and Duisburg/Hamborn the link was particularly clear and significant. In contrast, in years of relative economic stability and modest unemployment, as in 1927 and 1928, the association was low: in the former year only 9.4 per cent of juveniles convicted in large urban areas were unemployed, and in the latter year the figure was 11.7 per cent.[97] Of related interest, and rather revealing, is the fact that in these years the percentage of the 14–18 age group convicted of an offence was merely 0.47 and 0.54 respectively.[98] High crime figures during the Depresssion were not too unexpected when it is recalled that in periods of socio-economic and political instability, when the normal pattern of daily life is upset, as happened during the First World War and early 1920s, juvenile criminality in Germany considerably increased. And between 1930 and 1933 there was, after making allowance for the fewer numbers of youths as a result of low birth-rates during and immediately after the war, an unmistakable upward trend, even if the situation did not reach the cataclysmic proportions feared by some observers. Thus, although the number of juvenile convictions fell from 26 409 in 1930 to 21 529 in 1932, this represented an increase in real terms.[99] Furthermore, these figures are superficially misleading because they do not reflect the many offences which, because of their petty nature, went undetected or unreported, nor do they take account of the fact that in many instances prosecution was not followed through by the authorities for a variety of reasons: they were increasingly hard-pressed to cope not only with the wave of adult crime but also with the vast escalation of crime related to political violence. More to the point, the delinquency rate for juveniles rose from 566 per 10 000 in 1930 to 623 per 10 000 in 1932.[100] In addition to the quantitative increase there was also a disturbing qualitative aspect of juvenile crime at this time, namely the growing frequency of serious crime, including murder, manslaughter, assault and rape.[101] Petty theft, however, remained as before the Depression the most common juvenile crime by far, which was not surprising in a period of acute economic hardship, experienced in particular by the most criminally-involved section of society, the working class.

An unambiguous social, class and occupational profile of juvenile offenders emerged. A large preponderance, approximately 75 per cent on average across the country, fell into two categories: first, they were from unskilled manual working-class backgrounds, of limited education (up to primary school level only), and resident in large urban and industrial centres – indeed, often the poorest and most deprived neighbourhoods such as Hamburg's Hammerbrook, St Pauli, Emsbüttel and city centre, and Berlin's Wedding and Friedrichshain districts; and secondly, they were apprentices, especially those in industrial, commercial and skilled manual trades (*Handwerk*), also working-class and living in industrial cities. Males vastly outnumbered females in offenders' lists.[102] A large proportion of all delinquents came from homes broken up by divorce, separation, orphaning, or alcoholism, or were illegitimate. In Hamburg the figure was 39.5 per cent in 1930 and

32.5 per cent in 1932, in Oberhausen 20.7 per cent and 29.8 per cent respectively,[103] while there were comparable statistics for many other large cities. That kind of unsettled background may help explain one other tragic aspect of the rise in juvenile criminality: many offenders could no longer appreciate they had broken the law. The moral and ethical values of these young people had been so corrupted by deprivation that they simply could no longer distinguish between what was right and what was wrong.[104]

The administrative legal machinery for dealing with juvenile crime had been put on a much more realistic and constructive basis with the introduction in February 1923 of the *Reichsjugendgerichtsgesetz* (National Juvenile Courts Law).[105] It extended recognition to youth as a separate legal category entitled to its own rights, and gave substantive meaning to this status by reorganising the system of juvenile courts that had existed since pre-war days. The Act also established juvenile detention centres and independent wings in prisons for youth. Above all, the Act now placed the emphasis in handling juvenile offenders on educational and rehabilitative measures instead of the prevailing punitive and retribution approach (*Vergeltungstheorie*). As a further supplementary, but important progressive step, the Act raised the age of culpability from 12 to 14 years. Regretfully, however, the implementation of these modern reforms was not uniform, and in a large number of areas, notably east of the Elbe, the old practices and attitudes continued to inform officialdom's disposition towards young offenders.[106] This state of affairs was most vividly illustrated in the sphere of *Fürsorgeerziehung* (the care of abnormal, orphaned, and delinquent youth), and especially in the ideology and organisation of remand homes and other correctional institutions.

The entire system of care of wayward youth was in deep crisis by the early 1930s, as diminishing resources and poor staff morale failed to cope with the constantly more onerous demands imposed by the requirements of pupils (*Zöglinge*), numbering 77 846 in 1932 alone.[107] In the remand homes, which had enjoyed since the early 1920s a dubious reputation in Socialist quarters,[108] a growing number of incidents involving brutal maltreatment of youths by staff, inhuman discipline, poor food, exploitation and even suicide, produced a public outcry on several occasions. The squalid and punitive regimes that were exposed at the remand centres in Scheuen, Ricklingen, and Rastenburg came to epitomise in the public mind all that was wrong with the system, particularly after corrupt officials from these institutions were brought before the courts in 1931.[109] When it became clear that remand homes administered on the progressive pedagogical methods sanctified by the 1923 Act were in a minority, demands for a thoroughgoing reform of the system were forthcoming from a wide spectrum of opinion. Prominent among these were a small group of enlightened officials working within the system who were motivated by the care ethic of the *Bündische* youth movement, and a number of Socialist and Communist youth organisations as well as the Communist Party, which unsuccessfully presented a bill of reform in the Reichstag in January 1931.[110] For working-class youth, who formed almost exclusively the clientele of *Fürsorgeerziehung*,[111] the remand homes and the whole correctional system had come to represent further evidence of an unsympathetic, bullying, anti-working-class animus among officials of the state, and thus in the same category as the courts, police and labour offices. The considerable percentage of former inmates of the homes who found their way on release, or on the run, into the street gangs of Berlin and other major cities would appear to show that the homes exercised something far short of a reformative influence.

The gangs (*Cliquen*), whose genesis can be traced back to the First World War, constituted the 'rough and ready' end of the unofficial youth movement spectrum in the Weimar Republic. Comprehensively anti-authoritarian and anti-social in outlook, they recruited overwhelmingly from déclassé, unemployed male proletarian youths, many of them from broken homes, who were searching for some kind of identity and comradeship in the poverty-stricken districts of major town and cities. The gangs, of which there were about 100 in Berlin alone in 1930, adopted a few of the conventional activities and external forms of the organised Youth Movement, and added colourful, at times rather shocking names. During the Depression the gangs attained a reasonably high profile through their penchant for vandalism and rowdy behaviour and the small minority of them that were thoroughly criminal in character aroused a degree of public concern.[112] The very existence of the gangs and their ethos of aggressive masculinity and violence, however, was yet one more lucid example of the extent to which working-class youth, and particularly the vast numbers of unemployed in their ranks, had been pushed into a posture of rebellion and violent antagonism towards a society which had so resoundingly failed them.

The profound deterioration in the material, spiritual and psychological well-being of working-class youth during the Depression is undeniable. The evidence of mass unemployment, poor conditions of employment experienced by those in work, fewer vocational and educational opportunities, the virtual collapse of the welfare system, and increasing vagabondage, suicide and criminality admits of no other conclusion. Against this background of catastrophe the political radicalisation before 1933 of the young, both working-class and middle-class, is easier to understand. In particular, the rapid expansion of youthful support for the two major extremist parties, the NSDAP and KPD, constituted a major indictment of the feeble Weimar system. The Nazis, while attracting some younger working-class support, drew most heavily from the lower middle class, and to a lesser extent, from other sections of the middle and upper classes; the Communists, on the other hand, emerged as a party largely representative of the young working class unemployed in Germany's main urban and industrial centres. Notwithstanding the argument adduced by Jahoda *et al.* for the apathy and resignation of the working class in face of unemployment and its attendant problems,[113] there was undoubtedly in Germany during the early 1930s a very significant connection between social and economic blight and a proclivity to radical political activism, at least among the younger generation. What does not emerge with the same clarity and unambivalence, however, are answers to several leading questions: what were the longer-term social and political consequences of the desperate situation of the young working class? Did they remain as alienated from the Third Reich as they had become from the Weimar Republic? Alternatively, is there a case for saying that the disillusionment of young workers with the democratic state, with the Social Democratic Party and trade unions, and with the older generation as a whole somehow make them susceptible to the blandishments of Nazism after 1933? The controversial relationship between the German proletariat and the Third Reich has begun to attract more and more attention from scholars and much valuable ground has already been covered. But the response of the younger elements of the working class still awaits thorough, detailed investigation. That task lies outside the scope of this paper, of course, but hopefully this outline of the position of working-class youth during the final phase of the Weimar Republic provides a few useful pointers in the direction of answers to these larger and historically important problems.

Notes

1. Dick Geary, 'Jugend, Arbeitslosigkeit und politischer Radikalismus am Ende der Weimarer Republik', *Gewerkschaftliche Monatshefte*, May 1983, p. 307.

2. Rhenisch-Westfälisches Wirtschaftsarchiv zu Köln (RWWAK): Akten der Industrie – und Handelskammer Münster: 5/24/13, 14 and 16 for details.
3. Joachim Bartz and Dagmar Mor, 'Der Weg in die Jugendzwangsarbeit – Massnahmen gegen Jugendarbeitslosigkeit zwischen 1925 und 1935', in Gero Lenhardt (ed.), *Der hilflose Sozialstaat-Jugendarbeitslosigkeit und Politik* (Frankfurt, 1979) p. 28; Ernst Herrnstadt, *Die Lage der arbeitslosen Jugend in Deutschland* (Berlin, 1927) pp. 5f.
4. Eva C. Schöck, *Arbeitslosigkeit und Rationalisierung. Die Lage der Arbeiter und die kommunistische Gewerkschaftspolitik 1920–1928* (Frankfurt, 1977) pp. 151 ff, 171; Frank Niess, *Geschichte der Arbeitslosigkeit. Ökonomische Ursachen und politische Kämpfe. Ein Kapitel deutscher Sozialgeschichte* (Cologne, 1979) pp. 35 ff.
5. Bernhard Mewes, *Die Erwerbstätige Jugend. Eine statistische Untersuchung* (Berlin & Leipzig, 1929) p. 6; Erwin Niffka and Hertha Siemering, *Jugend in Wirtschaft und Beruf* (Berlin, 1930) p. 12.
6. Mewes, ibid., pp. 10 ff; Niffka and Siemering, ibid., pp. 61–3.
7. Justus Ehrhardt, 'Die Kriminalität der Jugendlichen in den Jahren 1932 und 1933', *Zeitschrift für die gesamte Strafrechtswissenschaften* (ZStW), 54, 1935, p. 669.
8. Staatsarchiv Hamburg (StAH), Sozialbehörde I: AWOO. 77. Letter of 4 December 1929 from Jugendamt Hamburg to Wohlfahrtsbehörde Hamburg.
9. Niffka and Siemering, *Jugend in Wirtschaft*, p. 67.
10. Bernhard Mewes, 'Die Arbeitslosigkeit der Jugendlichen', *Das Junge Deutschland*, 25, 1931, Heft 11, p. 554.
11. Mewes, ibid., pp. 553, 558; Niffka and Siemering, *Jugend in Wirtschaft*, p. 61.
12. Rudolf Wiedwald: 'Die Arbeitslosigkeit der Jugend in den Jahren 1932 bis 1934', *Zentralblatt für Jugendrecht und Jugendwohlfahrt*, XXVI, 1934, no. 8, p. 231, quoting 915 576 jobless youths in Spring 1932 out of a total of 5 575 492. The official figures for 30 July 1932 were: 15–18 year olds, 68 370: 18–21 year olds, 339 837: 21–25 year olds, 617 536, giving a total of 1 025 743 (*Reichsarbeitsblatt*, II, 25 September 1932, p. 383).
13. Wiedwald, ibid., p. 232.
14. Herrnstadt, Jugend in Deutschland, p. 7.
15. Niffka and Siemering, *Jugend in Wirtschaft*, pp. 43, 54.
16. Herbert Strauf, 'Die Berufslage der jungen Angestellten', *Der Zwiespruch*, 14 June 1932, p. 280.
17. Waltraut Forkel, 'Kinderarbeit auf dem Lande', *Zentralblatt für Jugendrecht und Jugendwohlfahrt*, XXV, 1933, no. 1., pp. 238–43; Helene Simon, *Landwirtschaftliche Kinderarbeit* (Berlin, 1925) *passim*.
18. Mewes, 'Die Arbeitslosigkeit der Jugendlichen', pp. 556–7: Walter Schönstedt, *Kämpfende Jugend – Roman der arbeitenden Jugend* (Berlin, 1932 – new ed, Berlin, 1971) p. 132.
19. StAH: Sozialbehörde I:AWOO. 77. Memorandum of 6 November 1930 from Jugendamt to Wohlfahrtsbehörde, Abteilung Arbeitsfürsorge.
20. Historische Archiv der Stadt Köln (HAK): Bestand 610, nr. 1. Letter of 20 January 1931 from Jugendamt to Dr Berndorff.

21. *Arbeiter-Jugend. Monatsschrift der Sozialistischen Arbeiter-Jugend*, 23, 1931, Heft 7, p. 150.
22. Ibid., 22, 1930, Heft 2, pp. 25–6, article 'Arbeitslose Jugend'; HAK: Bestand 1187/K38, brochure of *Nachrichtendienst*, XIII, 1932, no. 7, pp. 186 ff.
23. *Arbeiter-Jugend*, 22, 1930, Heft 2, pp. 25–6.
24. Hellmut Lessing and Manfred Liebel, 'Jungen vor dem Faschismus. Proletarische Jugendcliquen und Arbeitsdienst am Ende der Weimarer Republik', in Johannes Beck *et al.* (eds), *Terror und Hoffnung in Deutschland 1933–1945* (Reinbek, 1980) p. 392.
25. *Arbeiter-Jugend*, 23, 1931, Heft 11, p. 254, article entitled, 'Jugendschutzarbeit in der Praxis'.
26. HAK: Bestand 903/160, report in *Sozialistischen Republik zu Köln* of 14 February 1926.
27. Mewes, *Erwerbstätige Jugend*, pp. 30 f, 37 ff, 54 ff, 74 ff, for details.
28. StAH: Sozialbehörde I: GF 51.02. *Nachrichtendienst* report, nr. 6, June 1928.
29. Ibid., 'Niederschrift über die Oberfürsorgeinnensitzung,' Hamburg, 19 May 1932.
30. *Arbeiter-Jugend*, 25, 1933, Heft 3, pp. 75 f; P. F. Lazarsfeld, *Jugend und Beruf. Kritik und Material* (Jena, 1931) pp. 55f.
31. RWWAK: Akten der Industrie-und Handelskammer Duisburg: 20/574/16, memorandum of Deutscher Industrie-und Handelstag of 5 December 1919. For examples of apprentices' contracts see ibid., 20/588/7.
32. *Arbeiter-Jugend*, 24, 1932, Heft 3, pp. 69 ff, article emotively entitled, 'Lehrlinge, wehrt euch gegen Prügel'. The same theme is discussed in ibid., 22, 1930, Heft 9, pp. 194–5, article entitled, 'Lehrlings-misshandlungen und Jugendausbeutung'.
33. Lisbeth Franzen-Hellersberg, *Die jugendliche Arbeiterin. Ihre Arbeitsweise und Lebensform* (Tübingen, 1932) pp. 46 ff.
34. Walter Z. Laqueur, *Young Germany. A History of the German Youth Movement* (London, 1962) chapters 1 and 2; Erich Eberts, *Arbeiterjugend 1904–1945. Sozialistische Erziehungsgemeinschaft – Politische Organisation* (Frankfurt, 1980) pp. 33 ff.
35. Cf. Hertha Siemering (ed.), *Die Deutschen Jugendpflegeverbände. Ihre Ziele, Geschichte und Organisation. Ein Handbuch* (Berlin, 1918) esp. pp. 222–75, 377–438; Jürgen Reulecke, 'Bürgerliche Sozialreformer und Arbeiterjugend im Kaiserreich', *Archiv für Sozialgeschichte*, XXII, 1982, pp. 299–329.
36. Walter Friedländer and Earl D. Myers, *Child Welfare in Germany Before and After Nazism* (Chicago, 1940) pp. 166 ff; Rose Ahlheim *et al.*, *Gefesselte Jugend. Fürsorgeerziehung im Kapitalismus* (Frankfurt, 1978) p. 44.
37. Ahlheim, ibid., pp. 50–51; John W. Taylor, *Youth Welfare in Germany* (Nashville, Tenn., 1936) pp. 10 ff; Dr Becker and Regierungsdirektor Gildemeister, *Förderung der Jugendpflege durch Reich, Länder, Gemeinden und Gemeindeverbände* (Berlin – Eberswalde, 1932) pp. 4 ff. The

1911 decree applied to male youth only; a supplementary decree providing similar coverage for female youth was issued in April 1913.

38. Ludwig Preller, *Sozialpolitik in der Weimarer Republik* (Kronberg, Ts/Düsseldorf, 1978 edn) p. 55; John R. Gillis, *Youth and History* (New York, 1981) p. 162.
39. Justus Ehrhardt, 'Amtliche Jugendpflege und ihre Grenzen', *Das Junge Deutschland*, XXIII, 1930, no. 2, p. 97.
40. Werner Kindt (ed.), *Die deutsche Jugendbewegung, 1920 bis 1933. Die Bündische Zeit. Quellenschriften* (Düsseldorf, 1974) pp. 1477 ff.
41. The full text in Taylor, *Youth Welfare*, pp. 197 ff; E. Friedeberg, *Reichsjugendwohlfahrtsgesetz (Kommentar)* (Berlin, 1930), *passim*; Becker and Gildemeister, *Förderung der Jugendflege*, pp. 53 ff.
42. The small-scale welfare activities of the Churches and private bodies continued independently of the new mechanism, though contact with the State system was maintained.
43. *Arbeiter-Jugend*, 24, 1932, Heft 4, p. 99; Mewes, *Erwerbstätige Jugend*, pp. 104, 108, 120 ff, 134 ff.
44. StAH: Medizinalkollegium: 352–3: IK 6, Band 5: Jahresbericht der Distriktsärzte der Vororten Ritzebüttel und Bergedorfs 1925 (Dr Bulle).
45. StAH: Medizinalkollegium: 352–3: IK 27a, Band 3: Report by Dr Schall of 11 April 1927; Ibid., II S 3, Band 2: report in 'Hamburger Anzeiger', nr. 293, 16 December 1926.
46. StAH: Medizinalkollegium: 352–3: II S 7b, Bericht über die Jahresversammlung des deutschen Vereins für Schulgesundheitspflege, Bonn, 10–11 September 1925.
47. StAH: Sozialbehörde I: GF 51.02, letter of 3 March 1927 from the Hamburg Jugendamt to the Rechnungsamt.
48. StAH: Medizinalkollegium: 352–3: II S 4, Band 2, for details; also Ibid., Sozialbehörde I: GF 51.02, Richtlinien of 21 November 1927. For Cologne, see HAK: Bestand 610, nr. 1: Amtliches Stadtbericht, October 1928.
49. StAH: Jugendbehörde I: 98: Report of Jugendamt, 2 November 1927, and in 'Wohlfahrtswoche', nr. 40, 2 October 1927; and ibid., 99: Memorandum from Jugendamt to Senat, 28 January 1928.
50. StAH: Berufsschulbehörde I: 361–8^{I}: B 703, Jahresbericht für das Jahr 1927, dated 10 July 1928; Ibid., Medizinalkollegium: 352–3: II S 7b, Bericht über die Jahresversammlung des deutschen Vereins für Schulgesundheitspflege, Bonn, 10–11 September 1925.
51. Bartz and Mor, *Jugendzwangsarbeit*, pp. 29–30.
52. Niffka and Siemering, *Jugend in Wirtschaft*, pp. 84 ff., 1926 statement by the Reichsausschuss der deutschen Jugendverbände.
53. StAH: Sozialbehörde I: GF 51.05. Report of 27 January 1929 by Dr Erichsen.
54. StAH: Sozialbehörde I: AF 70.01. Memorandum 'Umbau – nicht Abbau', dated January 1932, issued by Reichsausschuss der deutschen Jugendverbände.
55. Walter Bogs, *Die Sozialversicherung in der Weimarer Demokratie*

(Munich, 1981) pp. 118 ff; Preller, *Sozialpolitik*, pp. 368, 373 ff; Bartz and Mor, *Jugendzwangsarbeit*, p. 30.

56. Bernd Weisbrod, 'The Crisis of German Unemployment Insurance in 1928/1929 and its Political Repercussions', in Wolfgang J. Mommsen (ed.), *The Emergence of the Welfare State in Britain and Germany* (London, 1981) pp. 188–204.
57. Bartz and Mor, *Jugendzwangsarbeit*, p. 30; Helmut Drüke *et al.*, *Spaltung der Arbeiterbewegung und Faschismus. Sozialgeschichte der Weimarer Republik* (Hamburg, 1980) pp. 91 ff, 97; Preller, *Sozialpolitik*, pp. 418–95.
58. Staatsarchiv Bremen (StAB): Bestandsgruppe 3: Senatsregistratur: 3-A. 18, nr. 145, statement of 20 December 1930 to Landesarbeitsämter.
59. *Der Zwiespruch*, nr. 45, 7 November 1931.
60. Cf. Erna Magnus, *Werkheime für erwerbslose Jugendliche* (Berlin, 1929).
61. Willi Gleitze, 'Fürsorge – und Arbeitsmarktpolitische Massnahmen für Erwerbslose Jugendliche', in Carl Mennicke (ed.), *Erfahrungen der Jungen* (Potsdam, 1930) pp. 17–40; Herrnstadt, *Jugend in Deutschland*, p. 18; Erwin Niffka, 'Berufsausbildung und Erwerbslosenschulung', *Arbeit und Beruf*, Ausgabe A, nr. 7, 10, 1931, pp. 100 ff; for the broader context see Michael Wolffsohn, 'The Creation of Employment as a Welfare Policy. The Final Phase of the Weimar Republic', in *Mommsen (ed.), Emergence of the Welfare State*, pp. 205–44.
62. Wilhelm Hertz, 'Freizeiten für Jugendliche Erwerbslose', *Zentralblatt für Jugendrecht und Jugendwohlfahrt*, XXIII, 1931, nr. 7, pp. 245 ff.
63. StAB: Bestandsgruppe 3: Senatsregistratur: 3-A. 18, nr. 145, report by Dr Syrup dated 15 July 1932; and report of 20 August 1931 from Syrup to the Reich Labour Minister.
64. StAH: Jugendbehörde I: 99. Statement of 23 May 1930 from the Finanzdeputation to Jugendbehörde, and statement of 12 May 1930 from the Rechnungsamt to Jugendbehörde, and reply of 2 August 1930. For a wider view of Hamburg, see Ursula Büttner, *Hamburg in der Staats – und Wirtschaftskrise 1928–1931*, (Hamburg, 1982.)
65. StAH: Sozialbehörde I: AF 70.01. Report of Jugendausschuss April 1929 – March 1932; Ibid., AW 00.77. Correspondence from Jugendamt to Wohlfahrtsbehörde of 4 December 1929, 6 November 1930; and from Jugendbehörde to Senator Neumann of 21 February 1931; also letter of 18 June 1930 from Jugendamt to Wohlfahrtsbehörde, and of 16 January 1930 to Senator Neumann.
66. HAK: Bestand 610: nr. 13, 'Nachrichten aus dem Städtischen Amt für Jugendpflege und Leibesübungen, Köln, 31.12.32'.
67. Ministerialrat Ziertmann, 'Zur Frage der Verlängerung der Schulpflicht', *Arbeit und Beruf*, Ausgabe A, nr. 5, 10, 1931, pp. 59 ff; Preller, *Sozialpolitik*, pp. 457–8; Bartz and Mor, *Jugendzwangsarbeit*, pp. 38 ff.
68. Lessing and Liebel, 'Jungen vor dem Faschismus', pp. 403 ff; Bartz and Mor, *Jugendzwangsarbeit*, pp. 53 ff, 60 ff, 67 ff, 77 ff; Bruno Klopfer, 'Die jungen Arbeitslosen und der freiwillige Arbeitsdienst', *Soziale Praxis*, XL, 1931, nr. 28.
69. StAB: Bestandsgruppe 3; Senatsregistratur: 3-A. 18, nr. 145, letter dated

22 December 1930 from Reich Labour Minister to Reichszentrale für Heimatdienst.

70. Cf. Henning Köhler, *Arbeitsdienst in Deutschland* (Berlin, 1967).

71. StAB: Bestand 4/65: 721/135, proclamation of 24 December 1932. See also Fritz Petrick, *Zur sozialen Lage der Arbeiterjugend in Deutschland 1933 bis 1939* (East Berlin, 1974) p. 7.

72. *Arbeiter-Jugend*, 25, 1933, Heft 1, pp. 8f.

73. StAH: Sozialbehörde I: AF 70.01. Document entitled 'Umbau – nicht Abbau', January 1932; for the trade union contribution see, for example, Detlev Prinz and Manfred Rexin (eds.) *Gewerkschaftsjugend im Weimarer Staat* (Cologne, 1983); Rotraud Tilsner-Gröll, *Die Jugendbildungsarbeit in den freien Gewerkschaften von 1919–1933* (Frankfurt, 1982); Udo Wichert, 'Gewerkschaften und Jugend in der Weimarer Republik', *Gewerkschaftliche Monatshefte*, nr. 3/4, 1981, pp. 144–56.

74. Peter D. Stachura, *Nazi Youth in the Weimar Republic* (Santa Barbara and Oxford, 1975) p. 56.

75. StAB: Bestandsgruppe 3: Senatsregistratur: 3-A. 18, nr. 145.

76. Irmstraud Götz von Olenhusen, 'Die Krise der jungen Generation und der Aufstieg des Nationalsozialismus', *Jahrbuch des Archivs der deutschen Jugendbewegung*, 12, 1980, p. 69.

77. *Arbeiter-Jugend*, 24, 1932, Heft 8, p. 250.

78. Gustav Stolper, *The German Economy. 1870 to the Present* (London, 1967) pp. 110 ff; Wladimir Woytinsky, The Social Consequences of The Economic Depression (Geneva, 1936) pp. 88 f, 94 ff, 137 ff, 164 ff; Eckhard G. Wandel, 'Germany's Political Morale and Morals During the Great Depression', *Leo Baeck Institute Year Book*, XXVIII, 1983, pp. 13 ff.

79. Graf Alexander Stenbock-Fermor, *Deutschland von unten. Reise durch die Proletarische Provinz* (Stuttgart, 1931) pp. 7, 31 ff, 39 ff, 152 ff.

80. Ruth Weiland, *Die Kinder der Arbeitslosen* (Berlin, 1933) *passim.*

81. The percentage of working-class students at universities and other institutions of higher learning during the 1920s averaged no more than 2 to 3 per cent (Lazarsfeld, *Jugend und Beruf*, p. 53), and in 1929–33 their numbers declined even further (Götz von Olenhusen, 'Die Krise der jungen Generation', pp. 64–5).

82. Hertha Siemering, *Deutschlands Jugend im Bevölkerung und Wirtschaft. Eine statistische Untersuchung* (Berlin, 1937), pp. 71–2.

83. *Arbeiter-Jugend*, 22, 1930, Heft 8, p. 175.

84. StAH: Sozialbehörde I: AF 70.01. Reported in *Hamburger Echo*, nr. 98, 21 April 1932.

85. Ibid., Abschrift, Bericht über die ärztlichen Erfahrungen betreffend den Gesundheitszustand der Kinder vom 1.11.31 – 1.4.32, dated 27 April 1932.

86. Ibid., GF 51.02. Letter from Wohlfahrtsamt to Herr Lambach of 5 October 1930; and Niederschrift, Hamburg, 20 November 1930.

87. Taylor, *Youth Welfare in Germany*, p. 120.

88. StAH: Sozialbehörde I: EF 60.13. Report of October 1930, 'Bedroh-

liches Anwachsen ...'; and letter of 28 November 1930 from Jugendamt to Deutscher Verein für öffentliche und private Fürsorge.

89. *Das Junge Deutschland*, 32, 1938, p. 203; Dick Geary, 'Unemployment and Working-Class Solidarity in Germany 1929–1933', paper delivered at University of East Anglia, July 1983, p. 16 fn., 38 (my thanks to the author for sending me a copy).
90. StAH: Sozialbehörde I: EF 60.13. Report of April 1931.
91. Bruno Haken, *Stempelchronik. 261 Arbeitslosenschicksale* (Hamburg, 1932) pp. 68 ff, 72 ff.
92. Weiland, *Die Kinder der Arbeitslosen*, p. 37.
93. StAH: Medizinalkollegium: III W 13, report in *Der Bürobeamte*, nr. 5, 10 March 1927.
94. Hans Kruse, 'Die Straffälligkeit der Jugend in den Jahren 1930–1936', *Monatsschrift für Kriminalbiologie und Strafrechtsreform*, 28, 1937, Heft 11, p. 508.
95. Helmut Asbeck, *Die Jugendkriminalität im Amtsgerichtsbezirk Oberhausen (Rhld.) (1928–1938)* (Düsseldorf, 1940) p. 43.
96. Ehrhardt, 'Die Kriminalität, pp. 670 f.
97. Heinz Jacoby, 'Die Kriminalität der Jugendlichen in den Jahren 1930 und 1931', *ZStW*, LIX, 1935, pp. 95–6; for further relevant details see Elsa von Liszt, 'Die Kriminalität der Jugendlichen in Berlin in den Jahren 1928, 1929 und 1930', ibid., L11, 1932, pp. 251, 256.
98. Bundesarchiv Koblenz (BAK): Deutscher Gemeindetag, R36/1461: Harald Poelchau, 'Kriminalstatistik der Jugendlichen 1927 und 1928', *ZStW*, L, 1930, Sonderdruck.
99. Ehrhardt, 'Die Kriminalität', p. 670.
100. Statistisches Reichsamt, *Statistische Jahrbuch für das Deutsche Reich*, LV1, 1937, p. 591.
101. Jacoby, 'Die Kriminalität', p. 116; 'Entwicklung der Kriminalität der Jugendlichen in den Jahren 1930–1933', *Zentralblatt für Jugendrecht und Jugendwohlfahrt*, 26, 1934–35, p. 127 (Author unnamed).
102. These conclusions are based on evidence presented in Asbeck, *Die Jugendkriminalität*, pp. 25, 28 f, 40 ff; Ehrhardt, 'Die Kriminalität', pp. 667, 685 ff; Jacoby, 'Die Kriminalität', pp. 87, 97 ff; Kruse, 'Die Straffälligkeit', pp. 502, 505, 507: Eugen Schweizer, *Die Ursachen der Kriminalität und Verwahrlosung bei Kindern und Jugendlichen* (Langensalza, 1933) pp. 88 ff; Klaus Seibert *Die Jugendkriminalität Münchens in den Jahren 1932 und 1935* (Leipzig, 1937) p. 41; Herbert Graichen, *Die Kriminalität der Jugendlichen im Bezirk des Amtgerichts Poessneck (1923–1935)* (Jena, 1937) pp. 20 f, 25 f.
103. Kruse, 'Die Straffälligkeit' p. 504; Asbeck, *Die Jugendkriminalität*, pp. 36 ff.
104. Haken, *Stempelchronik*, p. 75.
105. Cf. Herbert Francke, *Das Jugendgerichtsgesetz (Kommentar)* (Berlin, 1926, 2nd edn); Karl Peters, *Jugendgerichtsgesetz vom 16. Februar 1923* (Berlin, 1942).
106. Kindt, *Die deutsche Jugendbewegung*, p. 1479; Asbeck, *Die Jugendkriminalität*, p. 53 ff.
107. StAH: Jugendbehörde I: 99, memorandum to Hamburg Jugendbehörde

from Finanzdeputation, 23 May 1930; HAK: Bestand 903/171, report in 'Kölnische Volkszeitung', 2 January 1932; Siemering. *Deutschlands Jugend*, p. 72.

108. StAH: Jugendbehörde I: 8, Band 5, report in *Hamburger Volkszeitung*, 19 January 1923.

109. *Arbeiter-Jugend*, 24, 1932, Heft 1, pp. 15 f; Ibid., Heft 4, pp. 120 f; HAK: Bestand 903/171, report in *Rhenische Zeitung*, 18 February 1932, in *Stadt-Anzeiger zu Köln*, 17 March 1930, and further in *Rhenische Zeitung*, 15 March 1930. See also Ahlheim *et al.*, *Gefesselte Jugend*, pp. 51–66, 241–86; Peter M. Lampel (ed.), *Jungen in Not. Berichte von Fürsorgezöglingen* (Berlin, 1929); A. Brandt, *Gefesselte Jugend in der Zwangsfürsorgeerziehung* (Berlin, 1929).

110. Justus Ehrhardt, 'Krise der Jugendfürsorge – und was nun?', *Wille und Werk, Pressedienst der Deutschen Jugendbewegung*, nr. 26, Ausgabe A, 2 July 1931; Ahlheim, *Gefesselte Jugend*, pp. 317 ff. An *Arbeitskreis zur Reform der Fürsorgeerziehung* was set up in 1928 by former youth movement members then employed in the system, and the Communist Party also organised a special committee to work for reform.

111. *Arbeiter-Jugend*, 24, 1932, Heft 1, p. 16.

112. Justus Ehrhardt, 'Cliquenwesen und Jugendverwahrlosung', *Zentralblatt für Jugendrecht und Jugendwohlfahrt*, XXI, 1930, nr. 12, pp. 413–18; Hellmut Lessing and Manfred Liebel, *Wilde Cliquen. Szenen aus einer anderen Arbeiterjugendbewegung* (Bensheim, 1981); Lessing and Liebel, 'Jungen vor dem Faschismus', esp. pp. 393–402; Otto Voss and Herbert Schön, 'Die Cliquen jugendlicher Verwahrloster als sozialpädagogisches Problem', in Mennicke (ed.), *Erfahrungen der Jugendlichen*, pp. 69–89; Eve Rosenhaft, *Beating the Fascists? The German Communists and Political Violence, 1929–1933* (London, 1983) pp. 131–6; and same author, 'Organising the "lumpenproletariat": Cliques and Communists in Berlin during the Weimar Republic', in Richard J. Evans (ed.), *The German Working Class 1888–1933. The Politics of Everyday Life* (London, 1982) pp. 179–200, 203 ff., which discusses in detail the connection between the gangs and KPD.

113. Marie Jahoda, P. F. Lazarsfeld and H. Zeisel, *Die Arbeitslosen von Marienthal* (1933, new edn Bonn, 1960).

6 The German Free Trade Unions and the Problem of Mass Unemployment in the Weimar Republic

John A. Moses

The principal strategic objective of the General German Trade Union Federation (ADGB), which united the so-called 'free' trade unions during the Weimar Republic, was to institutionalise participation with both government and management in creating a national economy which would ensure the German working class an existence commensurate with human dignity. This was the aim, despite the ADGB's historic links with the Social Democratic Party (SPD); indeed, in the ADGB's formularies it actually took precedence over socialism. The ADGB guidelines for the future efficacy of the trade union movement (adopted in June 1919) only affirmed that 'socialism' was a higher form of social order than capitalism. The implication was that trade unions were not primarily constituted to work towards socialism as a political goal, although they certainly prepared the ground for the achievement of socialism. Rather, the trade union priority was to protect the work force; and this function would even be necessary within a socialist state.[1]

In the self-perception of the German trade union movement as a whole, the immediate practical concern was, without doubt, to ensure the highest possible rate of employment for the rank and file, and if that were not possible, to ensure that the state would provide the necessary means of subsistence to protect workers and their families from want. The Weimar constitution recognised work as a basic right, and as a corollary to that, acknowledged the obligation of the state to protect the work force as the principal national asset.[2] Given the turbulent political and economic circumstances of the Weimar Republic, however, the trade unions, particularly in trying to mitigate the effects of chronic unemployment, were faced with an unequal task. Their hope to become, within the framework of the new constitution, the agents of 'economic democracy' proved far too optimistic, particularly in view of the presence of powerful enemies not only of the constitution (on both the left and right of politics) but also enemies of the labour movement itself. All of these were out to undermine the constitution and the pillars upon which it rested virtually from its inception. Consequently, the new German republic had little chance of functioning smoothly in an era fraught with complex economic and political problems.

This chapter, then, seeks to outline how the ADGB (as by far the largest trade union organisation) tried to cope with the unemployment problem throughout the Republic's life, whereby, of course, the emphasis has to be on the 'end phase', that is, during the Great Depression. It begins with a précis of the political-economic assumptions by which the leadership was guided, and examines the evolution of their chief techniques of combating mass unemployment, concluding with a brief evaluation of the famous job-creation plan in the 'end phase' of the Republic.

I

As has been explained at length elsewhere,[3] the ADGB was heir to a decidedly pragmatic tradition which had had a stormy history within the over-all German social democratic movement. The 'political wing' had been, since 1891, at least on paper, ideologically committed to Marxism, that is, to the doctrine of inevitable revolution. However, the 'industrial wing', through its umbrella organisation, the General Commission (forerunner of the ADGB), had always insisted on the priority of achieving practical gains for the workers within the existing capitalist system over any reckless (and in their view, counter-productive) attempts to promote the cause of social revolution. Indeed, so deeply ingrained in the German trade union movement was the insistence on the steady achievement of concessions within capitalism that for the greater part it vigorously opposed revolutionary elements within German social democracy both before and during the First World War, and especially during the German revolution 1918–19. In short, the main stream of German socialist trade unionism – not to mention the much smaller Christian and even less significant Hirsch-Duncker (liberal) trade unions – was decidedly anti-revolutionary in the 'pitchfork and barricade' sense or, to use twentieth century imagery, in the 'machine-gun and street battle' sense.

This deep-seated aversion to violent social revolution within the German trade union movement was attributable, first, to the real danger of being outlawed by the Wilhelmine state (as they had been under Bismarck 1879–1890) if the unions became too militant. This explains their extreme caution in using the strike weapon. Added to this was the 'Russian example' of 1917. The economic chaos and political violence unleashed by the Bolshevik revolution were, in the view of the German trade union leadership, horrors to be spared the German people at all costs. Thirdly, and finally, by the time the German free trade unions reconstituted themselves as the ADGB in June 1919, their most articulate leaders had openly embraced the revisionism of Eduard Bernstein, and were convinced that the Marxist doctrine of pauperisation or immiseration had been proved unfounded by both the behaviour of capital, which more recently through 'organisation' had become very resilient and increasingly able to withstand economic crisis, and further, by the ability of the trade union movement itself not only to survive, but to become a major factor in the national economy.[4] Indeed, after 1919, by virtue of the trade union role in the demobilisation process and the creation of the Joint Industrial Alliance (*Zentralarbeitsgemeinschaft – ZAG*) as well as the unique position accorded to organised labour in the new constitution (section on basis rights of social content), it appeared as though the trade unions really had become acknowledged participants with both government and management in the national economic decision-making process. All this meant that the bulk of German trade unionists had no desire to promote revolution, Bolshevik style, and indeed, resolutely opposed all efforts by the German Communist Party (KPD) to advance it. Instead, they chose to work within the capitalist system in the form in which it survived the transition from militaristic empire to democratic republic.

What has been said to this point about the self-perception of the ADGB needs to be complemented by an outline of their predominant economic concepts. It has already been stated that they considered the Marxist notion of 'pauperisation' to have been overtaken by developments. Indeed, it was accepted by 1919 that trade unions functioned to prevent 'pauperisation', and would in time be able to eliminate it. It was the chief trade union task to see that wages and conditions were maintained at a level sufficiently high to prevent the living standard of workers from dropping below the culturally acceptable norm. Consequently, the important thing for unions was a prosperous, buoyant economy in which productivity and wages were kept at an optimal level, and this meant maintaining a high level of purchasing power for the wage earner's mark. This, then, was the ADGB's basic economic assumption. It is, therefore, easy to see that a national economy that was subjected to a series of massive crises provided the ADGB leadership with difficulties on an immeasurable scale. Conditions had forced the unions at the latest since the Kapp Putsch of March 1920 into a defensive position. The idea of continued collaboration with management as in the earliest days of the Republic proved illusory. Instead of being able to pioneer new strategies in genuine partnership with management and government (as envisaged in the 1919 guidelines) they became reduced to a mere *Ordnungsfaktor* in the economy, that is, fulfilling the role of an inadequately armed protector of the work force against a succession of economic crises which were so grave that no government was capable of mastering them to the complete satisfaction of either interest group – labour or capital. However, none of the crises prior to the Great Depression – despite their seriousness – gave any indication of how enormous the problem could become. Whereas to that stage one could speak of more or less chronic unemployment, after 1930 it was a situation of 'mass unemployment' when in the years 1932–3 every third wage-earner was out of work.[5]

As the experience of the early 1920s indicated (particularly in 1918–19 and the winter of 1923–4), large-scale unemployment was becoming a permanent feature of the German economic landscape. The effect of the Great Inflation of 1923 was to undermine for ever the notion that personal savings and trade union support – or even state unemployment benefits – could suffice to tide people over longer periods of stagnation in the labour market.[6] From now on, unemployment meant, not a short period of interrupted income, but a protracted time of real deprivation. Out of this situation early in the Republic emerged the ADGB's demand for a national unemployment insurance scheme that would replace the parish, regional and state authorities' dole systems of mere relief, which would also take account of inflation and give expression to the constitutional precept that the state was responsible for the well-being of the work force. The history of the ADGB's agitation for such a scheme is the history of a struggle for a new kind of Germany. This is to say, in contrast to Bismarckian-Wilhelmine Germany which supported a paternalistic system of social welfare chiefly to keep the working class quiescent (that is, to keep the nation 'governable'), the social democratic and trade unionist champions of the Weimar Constitution wished to reverse the old Hegelian principle that society existed for the well-being of the state. To give concrete expression of this there would have to be a comprehensive system of social welfare insurance central to which would be a scheme of unemployment insurance that was guaranteed by the state.

Two factors of central relevance in explaining the behaviour of the ADGB in the face of atronomical unemployment during the Depression years have to be borne in mind. The first is that the ADGB had always perceived itself as an agency for changing the nature of capitalism, that is, the trade union movement had a 'system-changing' function in Germany. It was assumed that, by virtue of increased organisational strength, the trade unions could indeed become genuine 'social partners' with capital in shaping the economy to achieve a more equitable share of the 'fruits of a higher culture'. As already stressed, the ADGB was not interested in a dictatorship of the proletariat but in real social partnership, in fact what they called 'economic democracy'. The second factor was that capital (or management) in Germany refused to accept the trade union self-perception, almost uniformly regarded such a concept as both economic and political nonsense. Any collaboration between capital and labour that did eventuate during the Weimar Republic had been enforced on capital by external pressures (as in the case of the ZAG). When these pressures receded the spokesmen of capital always insisted that the 'natural' laws of economics be allowed to function without interference either from organised labour or government. Management and trade union views here were, of course, irreconcilably polarised. Hence, the championing by the ADGB of a national unemployment insurance board and labour exchange was energetically opposed by management. The latter's point of departure was that the national economy could not afford further impositions to meet increased social service expenditure.

The ADGB had in mind an unemployment benefits scheme which would dispense with the formerly obligatory means test; indeed, which would pay benefits as a legal right to the unemployed. It was this principle that was subject of a protracted public debate in the mid-1920s. For the ADGB it was essential that no means test be applied and that every worker, having been insured against unemployment should by right receive benefits.

A law to enforce this principle was drafted by the federal ministry of labour (*Reichsarbeitsministerium*) in late 1925, but had to wait until 7 July 1927 to be passed – after many modifications – by the Reichstag.[7] The unemployment insurance and labour exchange law (*Gesetz über Arbeitsvermittlung und Arbeitslosenversicherung* – AVAVG) was regarded by the ADGB as the most significant piece of social legislation yet passed in the Republic. It provided for the uniform administration of unemployment benefits to a maximum of 800 000 jobless by an independent national agency.[8]

As Helga Timm recounts, however, the problem of financing the Federal Board (*Reichsanstalt*) when the 800 000 jobless figure was surpassed after 1929–30 flared up into the greatest socio-political struggle of the post-war period.[9] This is because the AVAVG obliged the Reich government to advance the necessary loans to enable the Federal Board to meet the claims being made upon it in times of crisis. Such a provision, then, linked the finances of the Federal Board directly with the national budget, thus making it a major political issue. In addition, the AVAVG became so controversial because of its significance for wages policy. First, the fact that the Federal Board exercised surveillance over all labour exchanges enabled the government to be more centrally involved in labour market policy. Secondly, its existence in ensuring a minimum income to the work force relieved the wages pressure which the industrial reserve army in times of crisis previously exerted, that is, when the numbers of unemployed forced the worker to accept lower wages. To this extent the AVAVG gave the state an unprecedented ability to interfere in the national economy. It is this factor as well as the major concern of the ADGB to preserve the institution of unemployment insurance which led to the cabinet crisis of March 1930 that heralded the collapse of parliamentary democracy in Germany.

II

The foregoing serves as the framework, both ideological and politico-bureaucratic, within which the ADGB confronted the onslaught of mass unemployment. It did so in two phases. The first was to exert all its influence to save the Federal Board in its pre-1930 constitution and the system of unemployment benefits which it administered under the AVAVG. Secondly, when the salvation of the unemployment insurance scheme proved illusory, the ADGB championed a bold job-creation plan to counter the astronomic unemployment.

The role of the ADGB in the great debate on financing the Federal Board is readily explained. The ADGB leadership saw it as incumbent upon them to be seen fighting to the utmost to preserve the socio-political achievements of the Republic. In fact, this struggle had begun with the sharp rise in unemployment during the winter of 1928–9 which produced 2.6 million on full unemployment benefits.[10] The Federal

Board up to that time had been able to cope by making use of the right to receive a repayable government loan to make up its deficits. And previously such loans could be repaid out of the accumulated reserves of contributions that came in after seasonal unemployment had subsided. From the beginning of 1929 this was no longer going to be possible. Opponents of the scheme loudly proclaimed that the Reich's financial situation – in the midst of a slump and a Reparations crisis – did not permit any further loans to the Federal Board, particularly since the scheme was allegedly abused by work-shy elements. The ADGB immediately responded to these attacks by asserting publicly that the financial plight of the Federal Board had nothing to do with either the reparations question or possible abuses of the scheme. Rather, the over-all economic malaise was attributable to the lost war and international industrial competition in which the German economy was being squeezed out. All this notwithstanding, the ADGB stressed that the unemployment scheme provided only the rock bottom of socio-political standards that had to be maintained at all costs. In order to enable the Federal Board to keep going it was proposed that (1) the government loan be wiped out, that is, not repaid and (2) that the contributions be increased for a one-year period to 4 per cent.[11]

This position the ADGB strenuously advocated for the next twelve months. And since a change in the level of contributions would have necessitated an amendment to the AVAVG, the SPD, the senior party in the Grand Coalition, represented the ADGB position in the Reichstag and cabinet.[12] However, the fact that the ADGB had apparently such leverage at the centre of power (five of their executive were in the SPD parliamentary party) did not mean that they could count on special favours. Rather it brought home the realisation that the balancing of the national budget, the acceptance of the Young Plan on Reparations payments, and the financing of the Federal Board, had all to be considered together.

Meanwhile, a Reichstag committee (*Gutachterausschuss*) had been set up to investigate how to make the Federal Board function independently. It came to the conclusion that an increased contribution of 0.5 per cent would contribute essentially to solving the problem. The ADGB endorsed this recommendation and continued publicly to affirm the absolute necessity for the maintenance of the scheme. Also at this time the ADGB insisted to the SPD that it would not countenance any reduction in benefits.[13] The party should accept no compromise. And this stance was taken in the face of the German People's Party's (DVP) contrary view that the Federal Board should balance its own budget by *reducing* benefits – a view energetically repudiated by the ADGB in mid-June 1929,[14] as were the findings of the so-called 'expert committee for the reform of unemployment insurance' in July 1929, which had been appointed by the minister for labour (*Sachverständigerausschuss*). It was incomprehensible to the ADGB that anyone could choose to balance the budget of the Federal Board by calculating for an unemployment figure – without benefits – of 1.1 million as a long-term solution.[15] However, the Reichstag decision on this was postponed by the findings of the above-mentioned *Gutachterausschuss*.

Meanwhile, the ADGB continued its campaign to have the funding of the Federal Board detached from the financial situation of the Reich and to maintain the existing benefits payments. And to do this the ADGB was now demanding that insurance contributions be raised permanently by 1 per cent, demonstrating that wage-earners were willing to do their part to sustain the system.[16] The ADGB concern now was how cabinet and the Reichstag would actually deal with the issue. That it could split the coalition and turn the SPD back into the wilderness was perfectly clear to them.

A glimmer of hope appeared, though, on 5 March 1930, when the cabinet, despite deep-seated party differences, agreed, apparently unanimously, to shape the budget for 1930. By means of juggling items within the budget 100 million marks for the Federal Board could be found, made up in part by the imposition of a 0.25 per cent increase in contributions.[17] The DVP was, however, not by any means fully committed. The final decision had to wait until agreement on the Young Plan was reached. There was an agreement not to force a cabinet crisis on taxation and financial questions, including unemployment, until the reparations issue had been regulated.[18] By 12 March 1930 that stage had been reached. It was now that the DVP, having moved perceptibly to the right since the death of its leader, Gustav Stresemann (3 October 1929), chose to force the issue, well aware that the SPD had no further room for manoeuvre. They would not tolerate any further burden on the economy; the Federal Board would have to put its own house in order. The DVP had held its party conference (22–23 March 1930) after which it determined to ignore the cabinet agreement of 5 March.

On 27 March the situation seemed quite hopeless when Centre Party leader, Heinrich Brüning, advanced his famous compromise formula. The essential points were:

1. If the financial needs of the Federal Board cannot be fully covered

by contributions and emerging reserves, . . . the Reich will guarantee subsidies, the level of which will be fixed annually in the national budget.

2. The Reich subsidy for the financial year 1930 will amount to 150 million Reich marks, the contribution to the unemployment insurance to be 3.5 per cent.

3. In order to facilitate a balance between income and expenditure, the executive of the Federal Board will take the necessary measures within the administrative machinery. For the same purpose the executive should make proposals to the Reich government as to how the law should be reformed, that is, the AVAVG.

4. If the actual needs of the Federal Board exceed its own resources as well as the Reich subsidy, the Reich will guarantee loans in accordance with article 163 of the AVAVG – however, with the proviso that the Reich government, after having examined further means of saving funds, tables legislation that either enables the repayment of the loans via increased contributions, or achieves a balance between income and expenditure by a reform of the AVAVG, or makes available to the Reich the funds necessary to cover the amounts intended for the loans.[19]

This was indeed a very doubtful 'compromise proposal', as the ADGB rightly judged. It was so hedged about with provisions one could easily see that with the level of unemployment threatening to rise rather than fall, the continued effective existence of the Federal Board would be in grave doubt. All parties in the coalition except the SPD, however, accepted the implicit risks. The DVP made no secret of its views that it was concerned 'to keep alive the will to reform',[20] meaning, of course, that it wished to reduce significantly the benefits payable under the existing legislation. The ADGB reviewed this situation with great bitterness. For them it was a sure sign that the nation to which they were so loyally committed was in the control of a power-drunk élite whose massive pretensions were completely out of proportion to their real social significance.

This became painfully apparent at the cabinet session of 28 March 1930. The SPD, committed as it was to the ADGB, rejected the Brüning compromise by appealing to the earlier government proposal of 5 March. This would have saved the coalition but the DVP was clearly determined at this point to end it, as was the Centre Party. They refused to uphold the cabinet agreement of 5 March.[21]

By standing up for their principles on social policy, that is, by insisting on the state's constitutional obligation to maintain the unemployment scheme, neither the SPD nor the ADGB had imagined they were heralding the end of parliamentary government in Germany. For that matter, at this stage, neither did the DVP by its action envisage the collapse of the Republic. However, with their insistence on primacy of economic over social policy, that is what they initiated. Ironically, though, the ADGB in the period March–September 1930 (that is, between the collapse of the Grand Coalition under Hermann Müller and the appointment of Heinrich Brüning as Chancellor on the one hand, and the September 1930 elections on the other) regarded the DVP and the Centre Party as the chief enemies of democracy. This was because of the attack on the social welfare system and their ruthless intention to balance the national budget at the expense of the working population. A few months later Brüning was regarded as the last bulwark against National Socialism.[22]

The political events of the 'end phase' of the Weimar Republic are well known. When the September elections in 1930 saw 107 Nazis sweep into the Reichstag from a previously insignificant twelve seats, the pre-conditions emerged for an attack not only on the social service system but on the parliamentary system itself. If the SPD and ADGB had imagined that their stance on the social service issue would be applauded in the wider electorate they were to be sorely disappointed. Some sobering conclusions had to be drawn in SPD and ADGB circles as a result of the dramatic right wing upsurge. They were forced into a policy of supporting Brüning's 'presidial' government.

The Chancellor enjoyed President von Hindenburg's confidence as well as that of powerful industrial circles since he pursued an economic policy of ruthless deflation – with which the latter agreed.

In retrospect, the deflation policy can be seen to have been utterly disastrous. In the end it negatively affected every socioeconomic group in the country. The effect of rigorous cuts in public spending was a general and rapid downward spiralling of business, and an even greater rise in unemployment as the Great Depression took hold. The ADGB looked on virtually helpless as its power declined with shrinking membership and funds while everything it worked for was being steadily dismantled. This powerlessness, however, did not produce a state of complete dumbness before the executioner. They were fertile in ideas for remedying the situation. Solving the growing unemployment problem was recognised by the ADGB as an essential prerequisite to overcoming the Nazi peril. The 'Weimar system' had to be made to function in the interests of all Germans. Intellectuals in the ADGB were convinced it could be done provided the rationality of their proposals were taken on board by those with power and influence. By mid-1930 it was abundantly clear to the ADGB that the first priority was to get German industry cranked up to higher production again. This clearly accorded with the ADGB's 'purchasing power' theory, and they tried to persuade leading representatives of German industry at that time of the urgency of reducing unemployment and maintaining the purchasing power of wages.[23] Management, however, continued to insist that the economic malaise was attributable to the high cost of social services in general and so-called 'political' wages. There was no meeting of minds here. The discussion between management and labour reduced itself to a debate whether a cutting of wages or of prices was the key to recovery in the national economy, and was broken off.[24] Meanwhile, the dismantling of the social service system continued and the SPD and ADGB stuck by their policy of supporting Brüning as the 'lesser evil' to the alarming alternative.

Representative for ADGB thinking in this phase was Fritz Naphtali's paper on the economic crisis and unemployment. Here the ADGB intellectual sought to show Brüning's policy of allowing the economy to wind down and 'shrink itself healthy' (*gesundschrumpfen*), in the belief that it would turn itself around eventually, to be fallacious. Such cyclical crises in capitalism were capable of being manipulated in at least some limited respects. They were not fatal events that had to be accepted with resignation. Naphtali recommended, first, a depoliticisation of the struggle between wages and prices so that production would pick up again. The key to the problem was the purchasing power of those classes on fixed incomes and wages, the mass of the population. As Naphtali argued:[25]

> There is no doubt that the working class is acting in the interest of the speedy reinvigoration of the economy and of the reduction of unemployment when it resists the pressure to lower real wages as much as possible. This resistance is today by no means purely economic; it is also a political resistance. Economics and politics are today so entangled that the forces of public opinion have to be invoked again and again to clarify the fact that it is a contradiction to all experience in capitalist circles whenever the industrialists proclaim that the stronger the wages pressure the quicker will the crisis be overcome . . . The opposite is correct. The more the pressure of prices exceeds the wages pressure, the chances of overcoming the

> economic emergency are all the greater. Here is then the point in which the struggle for the maintenance of the basic conditions of life is simultaneously a struggle for a revitalized economy, a struggle for the reintegration of the unemployed labour force into the production process.

Naphtali was doubtless correct in observing that the politics and economics of the day had become so enmeshed that it was difficult to get a dispassionate assessment of the situation and apply a remedy. Nevertheless, the campaign to win over 'the forces of public opinion' continued to be waged by the ADGB. By August 1931 they had published a scholarly volume of essays on *The Forty Hour Week: Investigations into the Labour Market, Wages and Working Time*, which was the main theme of the ADGB Congress at that time.[26] Thereby it was hoped that their convincing arguments would persuade the government that the introduction of the forty-hour week would not only reduce unemployment but also boost the productivity, as well as contribute essentially to the health of the work force.[27]

Brüning remained unimpresssed, despite the fact that he was well aware that his position relied entirely on the support of both the SPD and ADGB. Nothing the latter could do could force the Chancellor to adopt a clear course against the fascist tendencies of the right-wing parties and big business.

Here Social Democrats were forced to watch Brüning defend the parliamentary system by daily eroding the powers of parliament. Political action was thus frustrated. However, they could at least propose ways of restoring the capitalist economy, leaving the ultimate goal of socialism for future struggle. The economist, Gerhard Colm, expressed the attitude of the ADGB when he observed: 'We cannot wait for a reconstruction of the economy in order to be able to reduce unemployment; rather the concern of the moment is to restore the functioning of the capitalist economic process with all its defects.'[28]

Nothing could better illustrate the pragmatism of the ADGB and its attitude to dogmatic socialist theory. Concrete measures had to be taken, and out of the internal union discussion emerged the famous WTB-Plan for creating jobs, the key ideas of which came from Wladimir Woytinsky.[29] The ADGB enthusiastically adopted this job-creation scheme and launched, what must be considered for the time, the most elaborate public relations exercise to persuade the government to implement it. A special 'crisis' trade union congress was convened in the most prominent venue in the nation, namely, in the main auditorium of the Reichstag itself, on 13 April 1932. The aim was to convince Brüning of the political and economic wisdom of the concept.[30] The effort invested in this exercise was, of course, totally unrewarded. The Minister for Labour, Adam Stegerwald, a loyal acolyte of his ascetic and unbending master, remained unimpressed. He merely indicated the government's well-known obsession with the effects of the Great Inflation of 1922–3. Stegerwald was convinced that if the current deflationary policy had not been pursued, the nation would have been once again plunged into an even worse morass of inflation. Given this dogmatic conviction there was no way the government would accept the ADGB advice that it should now, especially because the private sector was impotent, step in and regulate the manipulation of the economy. But the ADGB went even further at their 'crisis' congress. They insisted that steps be taken to restructure the capitalist economy so that such economic catastrophes could in future be avoided. Behind this demand was the wish for a guarantee that mass unemployment which could always occur in capitalism would be rendered impossible. This meant that the government should exert all its powers to organise the economy accordingly.[31]

Here was really a demand for the implementation of a form of socialism, and the ADGB, after the 'crisis' congress had proffered *ad hoc* solutions, published its very last programmatic statement, the so-called memorandum on the restructuring of the economy, 2 July 1932.[32] Of course, if such concepts had no chance of acceptance under the Brüning regime they had even less under the next Chancellor, Franz von Papen, who was out to engineer a veritable 'conservative revolution' and have the Weimar Constitution changed radically. Its socio-political content would have been eliminated and the paternalism of the Bismarckian era of social policy reintroduced. Against the political machinations of the German power élite from von Papen to Schleicher to Hitler, the ADGB – indeed all democratic elements – had ever-decreasing room for manoeuvre. They were crushed by the overwhelming combined forces of the political right, the army and, above all, heavy industry, whose chief priority had been for some time to eliminate the trade union movement from the economic process.[33]

Finally, as an investigation of the key programmatic statements of the ADGB throughout the life of the Republic shows, the basic ideas on social and economic policy never really changed. The state was now constitutionally responsible for social policy in a way fundamentally different from the Bismarckian – Wilhelmine state. The work force was, on paper at least, regarded as the nation's prime asset that must be preserved at all costs. Consequently, it was the state's function to introduce a social and wages policy for that purpose. But beyond this, in the economic conceptions of the ADGB, higher wages were a stabilising factor in the economy and a shorter working day functioned to create jobs and thus activate the business cycle. These, then, were the main economic theories of the ADGB which appeared entirely rational to them and which if implemented would help to combat unemployment and even hasten the advent of socialism.[34]

It must remain one of the bitter ironies of contemporary German history that the concepts which the ADGB generated for combating mass unemployment, especially the WTB-Plan, had provided perhaps the most fruitful source of ideas for the use of the Nazis in their efforts to master Germany's economic crisis after the 'seizure of power'.[35]

Notes

1. See paragraphs 4 and 5 of the 'Guidelines for the Future Efficacy of the Trade Unions', adopted at the Trade Union Congress of the ADGB held at Nuremberg, 10 June to 5 July 1919. English translation in John A. Moses, *Trade Unionism in Germany from Bismarck to Hitler 1869 to 1933* 2 vols (London/New York, 1982) vol. II, p. 459, appendix no. II. For a table of trade union membership during the Weimar Republic, see appendix no. IX of the same work which contains an extensive bibliography. Additional relevant material is listed in F. Deppe and W. Rossmann, *Wirtschaftskrise, Faschismus, Gewerkschaften 1929–1933 – Dokumente zur Gewerkschaftspolitik 1929–1933* (Frankfurt, 1981).
2. Hans-Hermann Hartwich, *Arbeitsmarkt, Verbände und Staat 1918–1933* (Berlin, 1967) p. 12.
3. See note 1.
4. Lothar Erdmann, 'Der Weg der Gewerkschaften', *Die Arbeit* I, 1924, p. 3, and 'Zu den Richtlinien für die künftige Wirksamkeit der Gewerkschaften', *Die Arbeit* II, 1925, p. 388. Both these articles constitute major theoretical statements concerning the self-perception of the socialist trade union movement in Weimar Germany.
5. Thomas Hahn, 'Arbeiterbewegung und Gewerkschaften: Eine Untersuchung der Strategiebildung der Freien Gewerkschaften auf dem "Arbeitsmarkt" am Beispiel des Kampfes gegen die Arbeitslosigkeit mit Arbeitsnachweisen und Arbeitslosenunterstützung bis zum Arbeitsbeschaffungsprogramm in der Wirtschaftskrise Deutschlands 1928–1933' Dissertation (Freie Universität Berlin, 1977) p. 311.
6. Ludwig Preller, *Sozialpolitik in der Weimarer Republik* (Stuttgart, 1949) p. 164.
7. Ibid., p. 369 ff.
8. Helga Timm, *Die deutsche Sozialpolitik und der Bruch der Grossen Koalition im März 1930* (Düsseldorf, 1952) pp. 23–5.

9. Ibid., p. 25.
10. Ursula Hüllbüsch: 'Die deutschen Gewerkschaften in der Weltwirtschaftskrise', in Werner Conze and Hans Raupach (eds), *Die Staats- und Wirtschaftskrise des Deutschen Reichs 1919/33* (Stuttgart, 1967) p. 135.
11. Gewerkschafts-Zeitung (*GZ*) (11 May 1929), p. 294.
12. Timm, *Die deutsche Sozialpolitik*, p. 136.
13. Ibid., p. 138.
14. *GZ* (16 June 1929), pp. 369–71.
15. *GZ* (3 August 1929), pp. 488–9.
16. *GZ* (10 August 1929), p. 503.
17. Timm, *Die deutsche Sozialpolitik*, pp. 171–2.
18. Ibid., p. 154; *GZ* (5 May 1930), p. 221.
19. *GZ* (5 May 1930), p. 220.
20. Ibid.
21. Ibid., p. 211.
22. Hüllbüsch, 'Die deutschen Gewerkschaften', p. 147.
23. *GZ* (14 June 1930), pp. 379–80; *Jahrbuch des ADGB*, 1930, pp. 96, 100–101.
24. Hüllbüsch, 'Die deutschen Gewerkschaften', p. 147.
25. Fritz Naphtali, *Wirtschaftskrise und Arbeitslosigkeit* (Berlin, 1930) p. 27.
26. *GZ* (5 September 1931), pp. 561–2.
27. *Protokoll der Verhandlungen des 14. Kongresses der Gewerkschaften Deutschlands (4. Bundestag des Allgemeinen Deutschen Gewerkschaftsbundes)* held in Frankfurt from 31 August to 4 September 1931, pp. 139–163.
28. Gerhard Colm, 'Lohn, Zins – Arbeitslosigkeit', *Die Arbeit*, VII, 1930, p. 242.
29. Wladimir Woytinsky, *Stormy Passage. A Personal History through two Russian Revolutions to Democracy and Freedom 1905–1960* (New York, 1961) pp 460–72. The initials WTB by which the ADGB plan for job creation was known stand for Woytinsky, Tarnow and Baade, the three ADGB officials who collaborated to produce the plan. See Moses, *Trade Unionism*, vol. II, pp. 385–6. See also Michael Schneider, *Das Arbeitsbeschaffungsprogramm – Zur gewerkschaftlichen Politik in der Endphase der Weimarer Republik* (Bonn – Bad Godesberg, 1975) pp. 74–89.
30. *Protokoll der Verhandlungen des 15. Kongresses der Gewerkschaften Deutschlands (5. Bundestag des Allgemeinen Deutschen Gewerkschaftsbundes)* held in Plenarsaal des Reichtags in Berlin on 13 April 1932 (Krisenkongress) p. 31.
31. Ibid., pp. 70–71, 87.
32. *GZ* (2 July 1932).
33. T. W. Mason, *Arbeiterklasse und Volksgemeinschaft – Dokumente und Materialien zur deutschen Arbeiterpolitik, 1936–1939* (Opladen, 1975) pp. 30–45, *passim.*
34. Hüllbüsch, 'Die deutschen Gewerkschaften', p. 152.
35. Cf. Schneider, *Das Arbeitsbeschaffungsprogramm*, p. 205, and R. A. Gates, 'The Economic Policies of the German Free Trade unions and the German Social Democratic Party, 1930–1933', PhD thesis (University of Oregon, 1970) pp. 289–90.

7 The Development of State Work Creation Policy in Germany, 1930–1933*

Michael Schneider

I

For a long time the lessons to be drawn from the failure of the economic policy of the Weimar Republic had seemed obvious: the claims of the reformist school of economic policy at that time were in many ways regarded as the only promising alternative to the deflationary policy of Heinrich Brüning.[1] As long as the comprehensive theory of an anticyclical economic policy produced by John Maynard Keynes in 1936 enjoyed general acceptance,[2] there was near unanimity among historians and political economists that a deficit-financed work creation policy in 1931–2 would not only have moderated the economic decline, but would have, furthermore, prevented the disastrous social, and above all, political consequences of the crisis. The expectations placed in the efficacy of a deficitary work-creation policy with regards the reduction of unemployment and the stimulation of the economy have in the meantime – in the world economic depression of the 1970s and 1980s – been heavily shaken. This could not fail to have a retrospective influence on the assessment of the economic policy of the early 1930s. The extremely controversial reception of the essay entitled, 'Towards a revision of the traditional view of History', presented by Knut Borchardt,[3] owes much to the topical nature of the political questions which were raised in that context.[4] It is certainly to Borchardt's credit to have reminded us of the circumstances surrounding Brüning's action – the influence of economic problems even of the 1920s, of the prevailing concepts of national economy, as well as obligations regarding foreign affairs, and in particular reparations. Whether Brüning really had no choice in the matter or whether there were other alternatives to his deflationary policy will be exhaustively examined.[5]

*Translation from German into English by Ingeborg Schneider and Peter D. Stachura.

Without doubt, the situation which the Brüning government inherited was not an easy one. Its predecessor, the Cabinet of Hermann Müller (SPD) which resigned in March 1930, passed on to it the unsolved problems which subsequently dominated domestic affairs, namely, the questions of the balancing of the budget, rising unemployment and reparations. Almost no other issue met with such unanimous agreement among the parties of the Grand Coalition than the priority accorded to the balancing of the budget. Sinking revenues were repeatedly the impulse behind ideas aimed at reducing government spending and/or increasing the national revenue by raising rates and taxes. As balancing the budget was of such prime importance, the expenditure policy of the Reich, even under the Müller government, had a restrictive effect on the development of the economy. The lack of financial resources then also determined its attitude to the issue of work creation, as Hermann Müller explained at a meeting of the executive of the SPD Reichstag faction on 13 January 1930.[6] For the government to gain freedom of action, particularly *vis-à-vis* the *Reichsbank*, the precondition was the financial rehabilitation of the Reich; thus 'the Reichstag had to decide as a matter of principle that no expenditure was to be allowed without cover'. This was necessary not only to protect the government and to maintain the stability of the parliamentary system, but also in view of the 'concerns for our currency which must not be jeopardised again as it was in 1924'. Even in the government circles of the Grand Coalition, fears emerged which later were used by the Brüning Cabinet (and the SPD) to reject the work-creation plans. This position determined also the government's attitude to the matter of a productive welfare benefit for the unemployed. Only Rudolf Wissell (SPD), the Reich Labour Minister, advocated the extension of this measure, pointing out that 'not even for 0.9% of the unemployed entitled to unemployment benefit were additional job opportunities yet available'.[7]

This was primarily due to 'the lack of state finance', the provision of which ought not to be further delayed, 'if deep dissatisfaction was not to grip the unemployed and serious political dangers consequently avoided'. Above all, the amount of 55 million marks budgeted by the Reich Finance Minister for productive unemployment welfare in 1930, was thought to be inadequate, and accordingly had to be increased by 25 million marks. The Reich Finance Minister, Paul Moldenhauer (DVP), did not consider it appropriate to give his approval to such a large sum, and asked Wissell to await the outcome of his efforts – aided by the Schröder Banking Corporation in London and New York – to reorganise the financing of the emergency work scheme on the basis of the income from foreign shares. Delays in the implementation of the scheme could hardly be avoided, but could be partly bridged, at least by temporary credits, as soon as progress in negotiations about the planned loan could be demonstrated.[8] The difficulties in arranging a foreign loan were apparently underestimated, for the negotiations lasted well into Brüning's term of office. The fact that no alternative financial strategies were developed, however, can be seen as proof of the feeble economic ambitions even of the Müller government, whose policy was continued by the Brüning administration.

II

The economic and financial measures of the Brüning government are usually summed up under the term 'deflationary policy'. The balancing of the budget and the lowering of prices in Germany were the consistent aims of this policy so that the competitiveness of the German export industry in world markets could be relatively maintained. Above all, the lowering of wages and salaries as well as social welfare payments was seen – in agreement with the demands of the employers' organisations[9] – as an adequate means of lowering industrial production costs which was a pre-requisite for price reductions. Despite the efforts of the Reich Commission for Prices Control (set up in 1931) the price level remained relatively high compared with the forcibly decreased wage level. The lowering of real wage levels illustrates not only the direction imposed upon Brüning's policy, but at the same time touches on the basic issue of deflationary measures, which by way of moderating consumer demand even contributed to the process of economic contraction.

The efforts of the Brüning government to balance the budget despite a decreasing income might be seen as equally problematic. In this regard, measures to augment public revenue (increases in tax and duty) and measures to reduce expenditure (cuts in salaries, pensions, and social welfare) both had an equally pro-cyclical effect, that is, they intensified the deflationary crisis. Cuts in resources available for new buildings, building loans and the like have to be seen in this context. From 1928 to 1931 they were reduced from 2.9 to 0.8 milliards of marks. The spending of the *Reichsbahn* (Railway) on buildings, vehicles and machinery dropped in 1929–31 from 1.2 to 0.7 milliards of marks.[10]

Taking these major political decisions into account, it can be ascertained how far off a deficit-financed work-creation policy by the government was. Prior to 1931 work creation was not explicitly discussed in the Cabinet.[11] Focusing on the most important manifestation of the crisis – unemployment – it instead contemplated and then dismissed ways of making what work there was available stretch further. The proposed measures included reducing hours of work, prohibiting the earning of double wages, and introducing a ninth school session which, it was believed, would keep 250 000 school leavers off the labour market; previously, the authorities had considered finding work for unemployed Germans abroad, as well as banning foreign workers from Germany. Only the schemes for land resettlement (*Siedlungspolitik*) and voluntary labour service (FAD) – due to pressure from the proportionately high youth unemployment – were actually introduced. In October 1931, therefore, resources were made available for suburban resettlement, that is, for the allotments of the unemployed. Such resettlement measures were to be extended also to the agrarian sector because it had to be accepted 'that high unemployment is to be a permanent feature in Germany for the foreseeable future'.[12] The efforts of the resettlement policy to make unemployed industrial workers stand on their own feet reflected a 'feeling' in the Brüning Cabinet 'of giving in to the crisis, the pessimistic attitude that the industrialisation of the past centuries had been "unhealthy" and extreme, against which the decline caused by the Depression revealed signs of a healthy contraction'.[13] It must not be overlooked, however, that even before the work-creation initiative of the Free Trade Unions (ADGB) had forced the government into action,[14] international projects for work creation were under discussion, thus forcing the German government to intimate its position. At the meeting of the Administrative Council of the International Labour Office in January 1931, the Committee for Unemployment had already spoken out in favour of a 'concerted implementation of large-scale international projects'.[15] The German government representative pointed out, however, – in adherence to Brüning's policy – that 'without doubt, a decisive change in the job market could not be expected' as a result of public schemes. He argued that a 'real solution' to the unemployment question 'could not be reached through purely mechanical means, nor through any political, economic or financial techniques: the situation demanded at the same time a thoroughgoing change of attitude, of mentality'.[16] The same hesitant position was taken up by the German government representative at the meeting of the International Labour Office's Administrative Council in April

1931, at the International Labour Conference and in the study committee for the European Union in May 1931.[17]

When the ideas for an international work-creation programme became more definite, the German government was forced to react; on 19 October 1931 the transport and transit organisation of the League of Nations requested that suggestions for public works be submitted by each government by 1 December 1931. Following an inquiry by Herr Weigert of the Reich Ministry of Labour on 13 November 1931,[18] the position of the German government was discussed at a departmental meeting on 23 November. Weigert emphasised at this meeting that Germany could 'if only for tactical and psychological reasons not withdraw from co-operation; the plan ought not to be allowed to fail for lack of German participation' – even though the financing of the works had not yet been finally clarified. Correspondingly, work projects were listed, including the building of canals, roads, agricultural improvements and the electrification of the railways.[19]

Since the League of Nations' body in charge of the suggestions submitted, as mentioned above, was the Committee of Transport and Transit Matters, the Reich Minister of Transport, Gottfried Treviranus (DNVP), thought he could claim the leading role in this matter; the Reich Minister of Labour, Adam Stegerwald (Centre Party), gave in to avoid further delays while pointing out his legal position.[20] This struggle for authority was not without its own meaning because Treviranus – as opposed to Stegerwald – declined to make concrete suggestions to the League of Nations; he ascribed his hesitation – which could not be expressed publicly – to the inability of the German government to afford the interest charges and repayments even if the League of Nations took over the required credits. Contrary to that, Stegerwald, even considering the 'present state of negotiations regarding foreign policy and reparations', believed that 'for tactical reasons Germany had to participate in the work of the committee by making positive suggestions'. This committee had been established with Germany particularly in mind, as was shown by the fact that the Reich railway director (*Reichsbahndirektor*) Julius Dorpmüller had been appointed chairman; thus 'it would not be understood abroad or at home if Germany did not grasp the hand stretched out offering help'.[21]

The activity, shown principally by Stegerwald in Spring 1932, can be explained by looking in particular at the background of trade union and also National Socialist public relations during those months, and the disastrous conditions of the labour market (February 1932: over 6 million unemployed). In this Stegerwald clearly differed from the position of the Cabinet majority as expressed on 25 January 1932.[22] The reason for the preoccupation with the issue of work creation was mainly the deficit of the *Reichsanstalt* for Labour Exchange and Unemployment Insurance and not anything to do with economic policy; correspondingly, these considerations stemmed from the desire to use the means of support productively, that is, as the Minister of Finance Hermann Dietrich (DDP) emphasised, in return for financial support, work should be demanded and obtained. The implementation of labour intensive projects, in particular, appeared to be well suited to this extension of 'productive unemployment welfare'. Dietrich was supported by Treviranus who hoped the 'psychological effect of work creation was going to be very favourable among those sections of the population sympathetic to the radical Right, thus easing the domestic political situation'.[23]

After the question of work creation had been passed on to the Reich Labour and Reich Economic Ministries for further clarification, the topic was again on the agenda at the departmental meeting on 12 February 1932. In his introductory paper *Oberregierungsrat* Wilhelm Lautenbach, true to his longstanding conviction, pointed out the need 'to create additional buying capacity through credit extension'.[24] The representatives of the other departments – excluding the *Reichsbank* – agreed with Lautenbach's exposition, and yet no practical consequences followed, as the cabinet meeting of 20 February 1932 indicated. At this meeting it became very obvious that Brüning had no intention of introducing work creation – neither with additional funds nor even by stimulating the economy; rather, his planning on work creation was linked to his deflationary policy, for he indicated that the workers 'would be prepared to accept decreases in social insurance and other cuts only if they were offered prospects of more employment. Cuts without work creation could not be implemented'.[25]

The hesitant attitude of the Brüning government towards the question of work creation was also made clear by its reaction to the request of the ADGB chairman, Theodor Leipart, on 19 February 1932 for a meeting with Brüning;[26] while trying to clarify the question 'whether the Chancellor should receive representatives of the ADGB', the government emphasised that the *Reichsbank* was only prepared to negotiate the financing of a work creation programme 'if the budget in 1932 was balanced so that the *Reichsbank* did not run the risk of providing funds for the balancing of the budget. The budget can only be balanced, however, if the payments made so far for unemployment and welfare were reduced. It follows that the contributions for unem-

balancing budget

ployment benefits have to be cut. The Chancellor wants resolutions to be aimed in that direction, but not before the Reich Presidential election. Consequently, further discussion of this problem is postponed (as far as the Cabinet is concerned) until further notice'.[27] Accordingly, the *Staatssekretär* of the Reich Chancellory replied to Leipart on 8 March 1932 that 'unfortunately, the present political situation did not allow a reception at the moment. As soon as circumstances had become quieter', he would 'return to the matter'.[28] This made the ADGB resort once again to written petitions; its National Committee endorsed that course of action on 12 April 1932.[29]

In view of the unpopularity of the retrenchment policy further cuts, as well as involvement in work-creation policy, was postponed until after the Reich Presidential election on 10 April or indeed until after the Prussian *Landtag* elections on 24 April 1932. Reich Labour Minister Stegerwald's activities can be seen mainly, therefore, against the background of trade union initiatives for work-creation schemes: the plan sent to the Reich Chancellory by Stegerwald on 3 March 1932 incorporated the following work creation measures:[30] railways (300–400 million marks), postal works (100 million), roadworks (300–400 million), agricultural improvements (200–300 million), waterworks (50 million) and housing construction (200 million), that is, projects costing altogether up to 1.45 milliards of marks. It was not yet clear how these sums were to be provided. In any case, it was expected that with work creation on this scale – with wages lower than official levels – 200 000 jobless could be employed for one year; a further 400 000 were to be given preparatory or ancillary work. Although the plans of the Reich Ministry of Labour were supported by Dietrich, at a meeting on 4 March 1932, their implementation was prevented by opposition from the *Reichsbank*, on whose behalf Hans Luther argued against any form of credit extension.[31]

In consideration of the risks for the stability of the currency, the Reich Chancellory went along with Luther's misgivings.[32] As Köhler has already suggested,[33] this can certainly be explained in part by the fact that Stegerwald's plans were accidentally leaked to the public. Indeed, one would not be wrong in detecting a deliberate indiscretion by Stegerwald, who did not want to appear at the 'ADGB's emergency congress on 13 April completely empty-handed'.[34] In his proposal of 3 March, Stegerwald had explicitly drawn attention to the emergency congress in order to persuade the *Reichsbank* to give in on the question of credit extension. The annoyance of the Reich Chancellory was revealed in a comment by Feßler, who complained that the proposal of

3 March 'was worked out without adequate consultation with the other government departments involved'. At the same time Stegerwald's plan 'appeared to have been developed with the political consideration in mind that the department presenting the proposal had to be seen to be doing everything it could to meet the wishes presented to it – particularly by the unions'. In sum, it has to be stated that the proposal contradicted 'the position hitherto held by the Cabinet and the *Reichsbank*'.[35]

The emergency congress of the unions served without doubt to hasten the formation of the government's attitude to the question of work creation. At a meeting in the Reich Labour Ministry on 1 April 1932, department leader Beisiegel mentioned 'that the Cabinet had to discuss the question of work creation before the emergency congress of the unions took place'. However, in view of the impending negotiations between the Reich Economics Ministry and the *Reichsbank*, it was 'not feasible to assume that a programme costing milliards of marks could and should be implemented'. None the less, the representatives of the Ministry of Transport, the railways, and the postal service, expressed their willingness on 1 April to participate in a work-creation policy, but the financial side of this would still have to be discussed; *Oberregierungsrat* Raps presented Dietrich's view, namely, that not only were measures in the area of house repairs feasible and worthwhile, but also 'it was desirable that agricultural resettlement be encouraged on the basis of a long-term programme and that small-scale suburban resettlement be continued'.[36]

The meeting (announced on 1 April) involving representatives of the *Reichsbank* and the Reich Economics and Finance Ministeries on 5 April was also under pressure from the emergency congress; quick results were required because the Cabinet meetings were to take place on 11 and 12 April, and also because 'on 13 or 14 April the Chancellor and Reich Labour Minister wanted to take part in the union's emergency congress and, if at all possible, make positive announcements there concerning work creation'. Complete agreement was not reached, however; the representative of the *Reichsbank* stuck to his view that he could not 'under any circumstances, agree to the financing of a work creation programme through credit extension'. 'The *Reichsbank* was prepared, however, to examine individual projects favourably at any time with regard to their feasibility and financial suitability'.[37] Given the rigid attitude of the *Reichsbank*, Dietrich presented a programme on 11 April 1932[38] which basically corresponded to Stegerwald's plans and thus attempted to comply with the ideas of the unions, but which also, as regards financing, met the *Reichsbank*'s demands for thrift. The total cost (900 million marks) of the work-creation measures, was – not unlike the ideas of the SPD in this matter – to be primarily covered by the levy of a premium loan; since the profits of such a loan were not estimated to be very high, however, it was suggested that most of the work-creation projects be designated as emergency works, where only half the difference between unemployment benefit and agreed wages was to be paid in cash. That was believed to hold the promise of reducing the over-all requirements by about 200 million marks. The difference which might arise between loan profits and the (reduced) requirements was to be covered by the Reich budget or with the help of the *Reichsbank*. Dietrich's ideas of financing prevailed by and large in cabinet discussion on 12 April 1932 as well.[39] The requirements stipulated by individual government departments – even the *Reichswehr* recognised the opportunity to improve its budget[40] – were limited by Dietrich to altogether 1.4 milliards of marks, which were to be provided through the levy of a premium loan; the matter, however, was not yet finalised.

The very plan of a premium loan seemed to open up a way for work creation while avoiding the feared threat to currency stability. It was hoped to manage without further burdening the national budget provided the loan activated accumulated savings. The fact that this goal could only be reached by extremely favourable loan conditions – low rate of issue, high interest returns – significantly limited the profitability of the loan from the outset; on the whole, the expectations relating to the profits of such a loan could not be assumed to be very high, and this plan, therefore, was no longer discussed after June 1932. Consequently, the only concrete initiative of the Brüning government for work creation turned out to be the programme passed by the Cabinet on 19–20 May 1932, according to which 60 million marks were to be made available for roadworks, 50 million for waterworks and 25 million for agricultural improvements, a total of 135 million marks for the purpose of work creation.[41] It is certainly to be attributed to increasing public approval of work-creation projects that this plan came into being at all – the proposals of the SPD and the Reichstag speech of Gregor Strasser (NSDAP) on 10 May 1932 ought to be mentioned in this regard – but could at the same time be attributed, with some justification by the ADGB, to the pressure exerted by its emergency congress and its own petitions, which repeatedly demanded the quickest possible introduction of a work-creation plan.[42]

Without doubt, the reparations problem in particular contributed decisively to Brüning's reserve *vis-à-vis* the question of work creation. Thus not only was the publication of Stegerwald's work-creation proposal of 3 March 1932 met with concern by the Reich Chancellory for reasons generally connected with reparations policy,[43] but Brüning himself emphasised the connection: 'Foreign countries would believe that Germany was now attempting to improve her economy and get out of her reparations payments by creating artificial credit'.[44] This argument did not lack a certain impact, particularly since transfer problems, which had arisen from inflationary developments probably caused by the creation of credit, could now be detected. Many historians cannot disregard these reasons behind the restraint of Brüning's government in economic policy.[45] The expectation that after the reparations question had been resolved an active campaign against the economic crisis would have begun, might prove deceptive.[46] Besides, Brüning himself did not seem to have expected a quick solution of the reparations question in May 1932. Indeed, although he explained on 27 May 1932 at the Lausanne Conference that reparations should be cancelled, he acknowledged that this demand 'could hardly be met immediately, at least not at this conference'.[47] The unemployed would have been required to be patient for another while before Brüning – after having solved the reparations question – could have made the work-creation plans public. The linking together of the reparations and work-creation questions will thus be seen as very far-reaching planning; it eliminated any thoughts of a large-scale work-creation scheme being introduced in the short term. The view that the Brüning government's orientation towards the primacy of the reparations question – as Köhler suggests – was really 'only' a rationalisation of fears of inflation,[48] might be pushed to an extreme: it could rather be stated that in the policy of the Brüning government a traditionally high regard for foreign policy corresponded with an underestimation of the political explosiveness of social and economic problems, reinforced by bourgeois-liberal theories regarding national economics. Thus, following Brüning's order of priorities, his policy must be judged successful: the willingness to fulfil reparations obligations, even under the most adverse circumstances, could finally convince the creditor of Germany's inability to pay; this might be ascribed to the fact that creditors and debtors agreed in their false estimation of politico-economic needs. Both started out from the same economic theory which was essentially a confirmation of the entrepreneurs' point of view: it was based on the assumption that if state interference in the economic process were reduced to a minimum an 'economic recovery' would not take long to emerge. This theory militated against the development in the end of an active economic policy – even without priority being given to the reparations question.

On the whole, it can be said that the Brüning government did not take any decisive steps towards pursuing an active economic policy. Like the middle-class economists and a large number of entrepreneurs, it undervalued the opportunities for stimulating the economy, as referred to by the ADGB and even more so by the reformist school of economic thought. The commitment to a policy of social reduction, which on one hand seemed to correspond with the short-term interests of the private sector of the economy, and on the other hand showed an inadequate awareness of the social and political consequences of further economic contraction, prevented the government from recognising that the implementation of the trade unions' work-creation plans could contribute importantly to the stabilisation of prevailing economic and social conditions. In other words: 'The formal arrangements of financial policy were consciously used by Brüning and the political and economic interest groups supporting him to undermine the parliamentary system, while financial policy itself served to destroy the social component of Weimar's constitutional order'.[49]

III

Papen:

The government of Franz von Papen took the first steps towards a consistent state work-creation policy.[50] It should not be overlooked, therefore, that in the emergency decree of 14 June 1932, which had been largely taken over from Brüning, there were, alongside measures of social contraction, which generally corresponded with the ideas of representatives of industry, as they intimated to the Chancellor at a meeting on the same day,[51] public works projects in the area of transport and water as well as schemes for agricultural improvement. For the implementation of these projects the sum of 135 million marks, which was insignificant in relation to the number of jobless, was set aside.[52] Stimulation of the economy could certainly not be expected of a work-creation initiative of such scope. This impression cannot be changed by the fact that, in addition to the work-creation measures, further schemes were to be financed: while expenditure for FAD was raised from 22 to 40 million marks (1932), in the areas of small-scale suburban resettlement, and rural resettlement, considerable reductions were planned, from 48 (1931) to 25 million marks (1932) and from 91

Public works started

(not sigf.) see cross re

(1931) to 50 million marks (1932), respectively. To be counted also, of course, is the financial assistance given to German industry for orders in the Soviet Union; the Reich stood security for the sum of 35 million marks, so that with the guarantees also of the state governments (*Länder*), 'Russian orders' for a total of 100 million marks could be accepted.[53]

Within the von Papen government, also, it was apparently realised very quickly that the measures introduced on 14 June were unsatisfactory. As early as 28 June the Reich Labour Ministry – now headed by Hugo Schäffer – demanded an extension of public works by around 150 million marks.[54] Nearly a month passed, however, during which time the reparations question at the Lausanne Conference dominated the political scene, before the issues of economic policy once again took centre-stage. That the Cabinet renewed its concern with the question of work creation on 21 July can be attributed not only to the ending of the reparations problem, but more significantly, to the attempt at distracting attention from the political events of the previous day in Prussia, when the government led by Otto Braun (SPD) was removed from office.[55] The Reichstag elections of 31 July 1932 might also have prompted the government to present a new programme for economic policy. But, at the Cabinet meeting on 21 July Schäffer's suggestions were rejected as going too far: the Finance Minister – Lutz Graf Schwerin von Krosigk – believed that he was unable to authorise more than 200 million marks for work-creation measures, and produced, therefore, a programme costing some 197 million marks, which was extended to 207 million following a meeting the next day at the Labour Ministry.[56] Schwerin von Krosigk thus essentially went along with the *Reichsbank*'s reservations concerning any 'extension of credit which endangered the currency'.[57]

Only the Papen plan, which was discussed and then announced by the Cabinet at the end of August, went beyond the framework established by the Brüning government; it represented a distinct change in economic policy and resulted in the emergency decrees of 4 and 5 September 1932.[58] The funds made available by the state for work creation were increased by approximately 170 million marks. The most decisive measure, however, related to the private sector of the economy, which through a series of tax changes was granted credit worth some 1.5 milliard marks. Moreover, the state paid a wage premium of 400 marks a year for every extra worker employed; altogether, some 700 million marks were laid aside to cover this employment premium.

Petzina was thus correct to point out that the Papen plan '[corresponded to] traditional economic thinking, in so far as state aid was limited to indirect support of private entrepreneurs, that is, help towards self-help in the economy'.[59] It also has to be borne in mind that von Papen's policy did not aim to stimulate the economy by a more powerful extension of public-sponsored economic action; it complied with those interests of the private sector which had been articulated since the mid-1920s.[60] From the perspective of the state's economic policy, tax credits and employment premiums can be seen as measures indirectly stimulating the economy. The support given to these measures by private businessmen was due to the direct profit opportunities that they involved. While the businessmen believed that the restrictions placed on minimum wage levels by the emergency decrees did not go far enough, the trade unions considered the basis of their work to have been shattered. Particularly resented was the opportunity afforded employers by the emergency decree of 5 September, to reduce the agreed wage level by about 50 per cent when employing additional workers; the unions regarded this, as they did the system of tax vouchers, as a subvention of private enterprise at the expense of the employees.[61]

The loss of confidence experienced by the von Papen government was worsened by the failure of the emergency decrees to produce immediate results. The means provided were insufficient to bring about a noticeable reduction in unemployment. The time of year when they were given out (autumn/winter) was an unfortunate choice – if it was a choice at all; in any case, it was difficult to bring about a change in the economy in view of the seasonal increase in unemployment. The long delay in providing the funds was also a factor; there had not only been difficulties in some areas – for example, in the financing of road-building by the *Reichskredit-Gesellschaft*, and in the involvement of towns in work-creation measures – but also problems regarding under-spending of the budget provided by the decrees in June and September 1932 (only 236 million was spent by the end of December out of the 288 million marks available).[62] If Luther is to be believed, this led even the *Reichsbank* to urge the von Papen government on 27 October to allocate the funds more quickly and energetically.[63]

Not least because of the disappointing impact of the measures hitherto carried out, von Papen might have suggested an increase in the funds for work creation to 600 million marks following several meetings with Günter Gereke, one of the most prominent advocates of a public work creation initiative; this plan was not realised, however, because no agreement could be reached in Cabinet.[64] An intensification of the efforts concerning economic policy might have been advisable – after the result of the July election – in view of the impending election in November; the willingness of industrialists' associations to co-operate with the NSDAP, which became apparent from August/September 1932, might have helped induce von Papen 'to seize the bull by the horns'.[65] Although success continued to elude von Papen's work creation policy, his Cabinet managed to break down the resistance of heavy industry to such an emergency policy. This was certainly made easier by the temporary solution to the reparations problem which rendered obsolete a convincing argument against measures of credit extension. None the less, it has to be borne in mind that the von Papen government clearly designed the measures for economic stimulation according to the interests of private enterprise; in this manner, it laid down guidelines which had to be taken up by its successors.

IV

When the administration of Kurt von Schleicher took office on 3 December 1932, it was able to build on a series of measures to combat unemployment which had already been decided upon.[66] They took up a total of 342 million marks of which, however, only 288.7 million marks was secured through the Decree of the Reich President for the Protection of the Economy and Finances of 5 June 1931.[67]

The new course of economic policy resulted in the establishment on 15 December 1932 of a Reich Commission for Work Creation,[68] headed by Gereke, the leading reformist economic theorist; he was also a confidant of Schleicher's.[69] The fact that the work-creation issue now came to the forefront of government policy may have helped ensure that the trade unions did not immediately adopt an oppositional stance towards the new government; the contacts which were aimed at bringing trade union and NSDAP representatives into government may also be seen in this connection.[70] Thus, the hostility of private enterprise was provoked not only by the von Schleicher government's indirect acceptance of greater state intervention in the question of work creation, which meant a departure from the basic principles of liberal economic ideology, but also by the political 'opening to the Left', which became apparent through the replacement of the emergency decree of 5 September by the decree of 14 December 1932 (as demanded by the trade unions).

Contemporary observers were not unaware of the difference in basic concepts between the von Papen and von Schleicher cabinets. Thus, it was stressed in *Der Deutsche Oekonomist* that 'the Papen programme was [based] on an open acknowledgement of the opportunities afforded by the market economy' and amounted 'in essence to a call to the hitherto distrusted readiness for private entrepreneurial action'. On the other hand, the attitudes of the von Schleicher government gave cause for 'serious concern'; even if one could dispense with a wage subsidy – a 'foreign body' – in the market economy, one simply had to warn against schemes which aimed 'to create large-scale public work creation projects, as recommended by the trade unions and the new Work Creation Commissioner, Dr Gereke'.[71]

Gereke demanded an emergency economic programme supported by 600 million marks and carried out by the Reich, provincial and local authorities. It was decided that, in the negotiations planned for 21 December with Luther, Gereke was to insist that the *Reichsbank* provide 600 million marks for an emergency programme; however, there was internal agreement 'that, if necessary, one might settle for 500 million marks'. There was still disagreement, however, particularly over the question of the premiums for additional employment; while Gereke favoured the abolition of these premiums (700 million marks) in order to thus win more room for manoeuvre in negotiations with the *Reichsbank* over credit extension for the proposed direct work-creation measures, his colleagues insisted on the retention, for psychological reasons, of the subsidy measures prescribed by the von Papen government. The von Schleicher government never did come to a decision in this matter.[72]

At the ministerial committee meeting on 21 December, Gereke reported on the discussion he had had with Luther that same day.[73] In accordance with the position already established on 15 December,[74] Luther was only prepared to support a programme costing 500 million marks. Gereke and Economics Minister Hermann Warmbold, who also took part in the discussion with Luther, both stressed that at this point in time no further assistance could be obtained from the *Reichsbank*. While Gereke indicated that as far as he was concerned the emergency programme was simply the beginning of the work-creation policy, Schwerin von Krosigk expressed understanding for Luther's restrictive position since the domestic deficit for 1932–3 amounting to 800 million marks had to be settled with the *Reichsbank*'s help. Hence, Gereke's efforts to obtain a consistent expansion of the work-creation policy almost collapsed even before they had properly begun.

The decrees of 6, 26 and 28 January 1933 reflected these watered-down work creation initiatives.[75] The first decree laid down the method of financing; the *Deutsche Gesellschaft für öffentliche Arbeiten (Öffa)*, and similar institutions, were to extend on favourable repayment terms long-term credit (25 years) to those undertaking individual projects. The decree of 28 January officially fixed the sum available for work-creation measures at 500 million marks; this meant that while the *Reichsbank* advanced the funds, the Reich simply provided security and thus avoided having to touch its budget. In this way – in connection with the framing of the Öffa bill – the blueprint for the work-creation bill introduced on a large scale by the Hitler government with Hjalmar Schacht's assistance was developed. But the von Schleicher government did not stay long enough in office to experience the stabilising effects of its work-creation policy; it collapsed because it lacked a domestic basis of support among socially relevant groups.

V

In contrast to the von Schleicher government, Hitler's Cabinet found support from big business and the large landowners relatively quickly. The *Reichsverband der Deutschen Industrie* (RDI) assured the new government of its willingness to co-operate[76] long before Hitler, at a meeting with representatives of industry on 29 May 1933, had stressed the future importance of private enterprise,[77] and had advocated, at a ministerial meeting on 31 May, a reduction in social expenditure as well as the retention of the tax quota, even when the expected growth of the economy took place.[78] It would certainly be unwise to underestimate the impression which the destruction by terror of the trade unions had on employers, because this laid the foundations for a policy aimed at bringing the workers more and more into line; the rapid curtailment of the rights of parliament should also be seen in this regard.

On the whole, the measures of Nazi work creation, autarky and armaments policies can be separated from one another only to a very limited extent; given the immediate subordination of work creation to the exigencies of rearmament, two phases only – work creation and then armaments – can be discerned in the economic policy of the Nazi regime.[79] Since the work-creation programme initiated in 1932 only came into full operation during the course of 1933, the impression could be given that Hitler's economic policy was completely in line from the beginning with civil work creation. As early as 3 February

1933 Hitler mentioned in a speech to army leaders that the economic crisis could not be solved either by 'internal colonisation' or by increasing exports, but only by an 'expansion of living space'. While this might be regarded as a conciliatory gesture towards the perceived militarist activism of the army leadership, the objectives of the work-creation policy were fixed at a cabinet meeting on 8 February; the public work creation measures were to serve the interests of military preparedness (*Wehrhaftmachung*). The Cabinet decided, therefore, that the armed forces above all were to be alloted sufficient funds; only then was it to be worked out which civil projects could be financed as well. In line with the objectives of Nazi policy, it was decided at the meeting on the same day of the Committee for Work Creation and Rural Settlement (which had been set up by the von Schleicher government), to have participating in future discussions, not only the Chancellor, the Commissioner for Work Creation, and the Ministers of Finance, Economics and Labour, but also the Defence Minister and the Commissioner of Aviation.[80] At a meeting the following day, therefore, the army leadership was able to present their ideas on work creation,[81] which turned out, however, to be far more modest than the Chancellor considered satisfactory; in the discussion about the distribution of the means available under the emergency programme, Gereke advocated the following: 400 million marks to local authorities and state governments, and 100 million marks to the Reich by topping up the figure mentioned before by the sum saved through the abolition of the premiums for additional employment. The army leadership thought it would be satisfied with a share of 50 million marks for 1933. Referring to the position he had taken in Cabinet the previous day, however, Hitler pointed out 'the absolute priority of national defence interests in the placement of state contracts'.

The Labour Ministry played a decisive role in the formulation of work-creation policy. In his proposal of 27 April 1933 the Labour Minister, Franz Seldte, intimated the success of work-creation policy so far;[82] the number out of work had fallen by about 520 000. Through a distribution of funds amounting to betwen 1 and $1\frac{1}{2}$ milliard marks for additional projects, some 470 000 to 700 000 new jobs could be created. Further stimulation of the economy could also be achieved by 'reducing taxes that were too high', by 'eliminating the inflexibility of the system of official wage levels', and by lowering the 'burden of social insurance'. On 10 May Seldte's suggestions were basically approved by the Cabinet;[83] as for the method of financing the work-creation programme, the cabinet meeting on 31 May considered, at the suggestion of the Finance Minister, the issue of treasury bonds worth one milliard marks.[84]

The 'Reinhardt-Programme', which was presented on 1 June, contained not only measures of direct work creation but also a continuation of tax privileges for private enterprise in order 'to make the state work creation programme more acceptable to it'.[85] With this first statute aimed at lowering unemployment, it was expected that approximately 700–800 000 new jobs would be created through the distribution of treasury bonds worth up to one milliard marks, whose effectiveness would be multiplied as grants, loans (for example, marriage loans) or tax credits.[86] The stipulation in the accompanying executive orders, however, that projects were to be labour-intensive whenever possible and that 80 per cent of those taken on were to have been previously unemployed and entitled to benefits, shows the orientation of the work-creation programme towards the short-term objective of reducing the number of jobless; in fact, Schacht, who had succeeded Luther as President of the *Reichsbank*, and the Economics Minister Kurt Schmitt, previously the Director of the Allianz Insurance Society, both believed that such work-creation measures could only make a very limited contribution to a re-stimulation of the economy; instead, economic recovery could be expected to come about through private initiative on the basis of tax relief.[87]

Corresponding to this position was the inclusion in the theory of direct work creation, of which despite its strategic purpose, the Law for the Creation of Motorways (*Reichsautobahnen*) dated 27 June was part, of a series of tax measures;[88] also, the second statute aimed at reducing unemployment (21 September 1933), which made available a further 500 million marks to prevent a seasonal slump in the economy, included provision for grants and tax cuts.

The first signs of economic recovery emerged during the course of 1933. This can be seen as a consequence of the work-creation measures initially introduced by the von Papen and von Schleicher governments, and of the psychological changes caused by the advent of a new government. The number of jobless fell to 4 million by December 1933; industrial production increased noticeably, as did the production even of capital goods.[89] With the implementation of work-creation policies there was a marked increase in the proportion of public investment in relation to the total volume.[90] However, the real breakthrough in the struggle against mass unemployment only came once the armaments measures worked through the economy.

VI

Without wishing to become involved in the controversy over the assessment of Brüning's crisis policy mentioned at the beginning of this essay, it must be stressed in conclusion, however, that the collapse of the Weimar Republic can hardly be explained in economic terms or by the particular difficulties of the Brüning government; overall, the Depression, despite its importance, was certainly not the only factor which brought the Republic to an end.[91] The Brüning government's room for financial manoeuvre was extremely limited not least by economic, financial and social decisions taken during the later 1920s;[92] also, the scope of the crisis and the consequent need for a state-directed counter-taxation policy was fully recognised only after the summer of 1931. That Brüning did not accept the plans put forward by numerous reformist economic theorists was due, not to economic necessity but to his own order of political priorities, as Holtfrerich has convincingly argued.[93] Brüning sought to use the Depression for his own political objectives – the revision of the Versailles Treaty, particularly the obligation of paying reparations. On this basis, domestic political instability was the price that had to be paid. Moreover, it is not to be forgotten that the nature of the Brüning government's economic policy was such that it gave the National Socialists a theme which they were all too capable of skilfully exploiting for their propaganda.

Even if one inclines to the view that the problem of reparations made an early introduction of deficit-financed work creation measures impossible, one has to ask whether this order of priorities, on the other hand, had necessitated such a rigid deflationary policy.[94] Even if, in the light of the most recent research, one were to view with extreme caution the chances of a work-creation policy introduced in 1931–2 being successful, it ought to be stated none the less that Brüning's deflationary policy contributed to an intensification of the social and thus also the political consequences of the crisis. Accordingly, one would need to be very careful about claiming that an active work-creation policy would have strengthened the loyalty of a majority of Germans to the Weimar Republic and perhaps also their trust in the competence of a parliamentary democracy.

Notes

1. See in particular, Wilhelm Grotkopp, *Die große Krise. Lehren aus der Überwindung der Wirtschaftskrise 1929/32* (Düsseldorf, 1954).

2. See John Maynard Keynes, *General Theory of Employment, Interest and Money* (London, 1936).
3. See Knut Borchardt, 'Zwangslagen und Handlungsspielräume in der großen Wirtschaftskrise der frühen dreißiger Jahre. Zur Revision des überlieferten Geschichtsbildes', in Michael Stürmer (ed.), *Die Weimarer Republik. Belagerte Civitas* (Königstein/Ts, 1980) pp. 318–39; and his 'Wirtschaftliche Ursachen des Scheiterns der Weimarer Republik', in Karl Dietrich Erdmann and Hagen Schulze (eds) *Weimar. Selbstpreisgabe einer Demokratie. Eine Bilanz heute* (Düsseldorf, 1980) pp. 211–49.
4. See the supportive reception given to Borchardt's work by Josef Becker, 'Heinrich Brüning und das Scheitern der konservativen Alternative in der Weimarer Republik', in *Aus Politik und Zeitgeschichte*, 22, 31 May 1980, pp. 3–17; Harold James, 'Gab es eine Alternative zur Wirtschaftspolitik Brünings?', in *Vierteljahrschrift für Sozial- und Wirtschaftsgeschichte*, 70, Heft 4, 1983, pp. 523–41. See also the controversy involving Carl-Ludwig Holtfrerich, 'Alternativen zu Brünings Wirtschaftspolitik in der Weltwirtschaftskrise?', in *Historische Zeitschrift* (HZ), 235, 1982, pp. 605–31; Knut Borchardt, 'Noch einmal: Alternativen zu Brünings Wirtschaftspolitik', in *HZ*, 237, 1983, pp. 67–83; Claus-Dieter Krohn, '"Ökonomische Zwangslagen" und das Scheitern der Weimarer Republik. Zu Knut Borchardts Analyse der deutschen Wirtschaft in den zwanziger Jahren', in *Geschichte und Gesellschaft* (GG), 8, 1982, pp. 415–26; Knut Borchardt, 'Zum Scheitern eines produktiven Diskurses über das Scheitern der Weimarer Republik: Replik auf Claus-Dieter Krohns Diskussionsbemerkungen', in *GG*, 9, 1983, pp. 124–37.
5. The following account constitutes a revised version of a chapter from Michael Schneider, *Das Arbeitsbeschaffungsprogramm des ADGB. Zur gewerkschaftlichen Politik in der Endphase der Weimarer Republik* (Bonn – Bad Godesberg, 1975).
6. Müller's comments of 13 January 1930, pp. 2f, 9 (Archiv der sozialen Demokratie, Nachlaß Müller II, 329).
7. Wissell to Staatssekretär in der Reichskanzlei (RK) of 24 January 1930, pp. 1f (Bundesarchiv Koblenz [BAK], R 2, 18 645).
8. Reichsminister der Finanzen (RdF) to Reichsarbeitsminister (RAM) of 31 January 1930 (BAK, R 2, 18 645).
9. The details are in Michael Schneider, *Unternehmer und Demokratie. Die freien Gewerkschaften in der unternehmerischen Ideologie der Jahre 1918 bis 1933* (Bonn – Bad Godesberg, 1975) pp. 118ff.
10. Figures from Paul Jostock, 'Zur Frage des Ausgleichs von Konjunkturschwankungen durch zeitliche Verlagerung öffentlicher Ausgaben', in Institut für Konjunkturforschung, *Beiträge zur empirischen Konjunkturforschung. Festschrift zum 25-jährigen Bestehen des Deutschen Instituts für Wirtschaftsforschung* (Berlin, undated) pp. 231–54, here p. 246.
11. Henning Köhler, 'Sozialpolitik von Brüning bis Schleicher', in *Vierteljahrshefte für Zeitgeschichte* (VfZ), 21, 1973, pp. 146–50, here p. 147.
12. Dietrich to Brüning of 3 September 1931 (BAK, R 43I, 1290).
13. Köhler, 'Sozialpolitik', p. 148.
14. For details see Schneider, *Das Arbeitsbeschaffungsprogramm des ADGB*, esp. pp. 45ff.

15. See 51st Meeting of the Administrative Council of the International Labour Office, Geneva, January 1931, (introductory text), p. 4.
16. Appendix 2 of Weigert's letter to the RdF of 12 March 1931, pp. 3f (BAK, R 2, 18 597).
17. For details, Schneider, *Das Arbeitsbeschaffungsprogramm des ADGB*, pp. 177ff.
18. Weigert (RAM) to Foreign Office, among others, of 13 November 1931 (BAK, R 2, 18 813, nr. 243–8).
19. Notes of the discussion in the RAM on 23 November 1931 (ibid. nr. 251–255).
20. RAM to Reich Transport Minister (RVM) of 18 December 1931 (transcript), (ibid., nr. 256f).
21. Treviranus to Staatssekretär der RK of 22 April 1932 (BAK, R 2, 18 814).
22. Minutes of the cabinet meeting of 25 January 1932 (BAK, R 43 I, 1455). In this connection, Henning Köhler, 'Arbeitsbeschaffung, Siedlung und Reparationen in der Schlußphase der Regierung Brüning', in *VfZ*, 17, 1969, pp. 276–307, here p. 279f.
23. Notes relating to the top-level discussion in the Reich Chancellory under the chairmanship of the Chancellor on 25 January 1932, p. 5 (BAK, R 43 I, 1141, nr. 6–15).
24. Minutes of the departmental meeting of 12 February 1932 (BAK, R 43 I, 2045).
25. Appendix 2 of the minutes of the ministerial discussion of 20 February 1932 (BAK, R 43 I, 1445).
26. Leipart to Brüning of 19 February 1932 (BAK, R 43 I, 2045), nr. 5).
27. Entry of 2 March 1932 (ibid., nr. 6).
28. Staatssekretär der RK to Leipart of 8 March 1932 (ibid., nr. 7).
29. Minutes of the 6th Meeting of the ADGB Committee, 5th Geschäftsperiode, on 12 April 1932 (Berlin, 1932) pp. 87f.
30. Proposal of 3 March 1932 (BAK, R 43 I, 2045).
31. Köhler, 'Arbeitsbeschaffung', p. 281.
32. Entry of 7 March 1932 (BAK, R 43 I, 2045).
33. Köhler, Arbeitsbeschaffung, pp. 281f.
34. See the 'Work Creation Plan of the Reich Labour Minister' in *Gewerkschafts-Zeitung*, nr. 11 of 12 March 1932, p. 161.
35. Feßler's entry of 7 March 1932 (BAK, R 43 I, 2045, nr. 15).
36. Comments on the discussion in RAM on 1 April 1932, pp. 1, 5f (ibid., nr. 29–32).
37. Entry of 6 April 1932, p. 1 (BAK, R 2, 18 646).
38. Dietrich to Staatssekretär der RK of 11 April 1932 (ibid.).
39. Minutes of the ministerial discussion of 12 April 1932, with Appendix (BAK, R 43 I, 2085).
40. See transcript of the letter from Reichswehrminister Wilhelm Groener to Brüning of 13 April 1932, pp. 2, 5 (BAK, R 2, 18 647).
41. Minutes of the ministerial discussion of 19 and 20 May 1932 (BAK, R 43 I, 1456).
42. See, for example: 'Der Arbeitsbeschaffungsplan der Reichsregierung', in *Gewerkschafts-Zeitung*, nr. 19 of 7 May 1932, pp. 294f.

43. Entry of 7 March 1932 (BAK, R 43 I, 2045).
44. Entry relating to the discussion on 28 January 1932 (BAK, R 43 I, 637); previously quoted in Köhler, 'Arbeitsbeschaffung', p. 297.
45. For example, J. Becker, 'Heinrich Brüning', and, fundamentally, Wolfgang J. Helbich, *Die Reparationen in der Ära Brüning. Zur Bedeutung des Young-Plans für die deutsche Politik 1930 bis 1932* (Berlin, 1962).
46. Thus, for example, Werner Conze, 'Brüning als Reichskanzler. Eine Zwischenbilanz.' in *HZ*, 214, 1972, pp. 310–34, here p. 329; Helbich, *Die Reparationen*, pp. 54, 59.
47. Record of the discussions on reparations policy of 27 May 1932 (BAK, R 43 I, 337).
48. Köhler, 'Arbeitsbeschaffung', p. 307.
49. Peter-Christian Witt, 'Finanzpolitik als Verfassungs- und Gesellschaftspolitik. Überlegungen zur Finanzpolitik des Deutschen Reiches in den Jahren 1930 bis 1932', in *GG*, 8, 1982, pp. 386–414, here p. 414.
50. For subsequent developments see especially: Dieter Petzina, 'Hauptprobleme der deutschen Wirtschaftspolitik 1932/33', in *VfZ*, 15, 1967, pp. 18–55; Helmut Marcon, *Arbeitsbeschaffungspolitik der Regierungen Papen und Schleicher. Grundsteinlegung für die Beschäftigungspolitik im Dritten Reich* (Berne and Frankfurt, 1974).
51. In this regard, see the key-words of the Aide Memoire for the discussion with the Chancellor on 14 June 1932 (BAK, Nachlaß Kastl 5).
52. In this connection see Schäffer to Staatssekretär der RK of 28 June 1932 (BAK, R 2, 18 647).
53. See in this regard entry relating to the departmental discussion on 15 June 1932 (ibid.).
54. Schäffer to Staatssekretär der RK of 28 June 1932 (BAK, R 2, 18 647).
55. Petzina, 'Hauptprobleme', p. 21.
56. Entry of the RdF of 22 July 1932 (BAK, R 2, 18 647).
57. See Reichsbankdirektorium (Luther) of 28 July 1932 (ibid.).
58. Cf. Petzina, 'Hauptprobleme', pp. 24f.
59. Ibid., p. 22.
60. In this regard, see Carl Böhret, *Aktionen gegen die 'kalte Sozialisierung' 1926–1930. Ein Beitrag zum Wirken ökonomischer Einflußverbände in der Weimarer Republik* (Berlin, 1966).
61. Minutes of the 9th Meeting of the ADGB Committee, 5th Geschäftsperiode, on 9 September 1932, Berlin 1932, pp. 126ff.; see also 'Die Gewerkschaften und die Notverordnung', in *Gewerkschafts-Zeitung*, nr. 38 of 17 September 1932, pp. 595–9.
62. Leo Grebler, 'Die deutsche Arbeitsbeschaffung 1932–1935 (I und II)', in *Internationale Rundschau der Arbeit*, 15, 1937, pp. 416–35, 816–32, here p. 423.
63. Hans Luther, *Vor dem Abgrund. 1930–1933. Reichsbankpräsident in Krisenzeiten* (Berlin, 1964) pp. 295f.
64. Petzina, 'Hauptprobleme', p. 25.
65. Dirk Stegmann, 'Zum Verhältnis von Großindustrie und Nationalsozialismus 1930–1933. Ein Beitrag zur Geschichte der sog. Machtergreifung', in *Archiv für Sozialgeschichte*, XIII, 1973, pp. 399–482, here pp. 452ff.

66. See note 50.
67. See the list of the RAM of 1 December 1932 (BAK, R 2, 18 649). Regarding the legal safeguards of individual positions see the entry of 9 January 1933 with Appendix (ibid.).
68. The Decree of the Reich President concerning Measures for the promotion of Work Creation and Rural Settlement of 15 December 1932, in *Reichsgesetzblatt*, I, 1932, pp. 543f.
69. Heinrich Brüning, *Memoiren 1918–1934* (Stuttgart, 1970) p. 621.
70. Most recently, Axel Schildt, *Militärdiktatur mit Massenbasis? Die Querfrontkonzeption der Reichswehrführung um General von Schleicher am Ende der Weimarer Republik* (Frankfurt & New York, 1981).
71. Adolf Lampe, 'Reform oder Abbau des Papen-Programms?, in *Der Deutsche Oekonomist*, nr. 50 of 16 December 1932, pp. 1659–64, here pp. 1659f.
72. Entry of 16 December 1932 (BAK, R 2, 18 657).
73. Entry relating to the meeting of 21 December 1932 (BAK, R 43 II, 540, nr. 11f).
74. Vice-President of the Reichsbank Directorate to Staatssekretär Planck (RK) of 15 December 1932 (BAK, R 43 I, 2045, nr. 120).
75. Petzina, 'Hauptprobleme', pp. 28f.
76. RDI (Kastl and Herle) to Schwerin von Krosigk of 24 March 1933, with the Resolution of the Presidential meeting of 23 March 1933 (BAK, R 2, 21 573).
77. Notes of the discussion with industrialists about Work Creation on 29 May 1933, p. 2 (BAK, R 43 II, 536).
78. Petzina, 'Hauptprobleme', p. 47.
79. For later developments see Wolfram Fischer, *Deutsche Wirtschaftspolitik 1918–1945*, 3rd revised edn (Opladen, 1968) pp. 61ff.
80. Notes of the meeting of 8 February 1933, p. 2 (BAK, R 43 II, 540, nr. 32f).
81. Notes of the meeting of the Work Creation Committee of the Reich Government 9 February 1933 (ibid., nr. 35–40).
82. Seldte to Staatssekretär of the RK of 27 April 1933, p. 1 (BAK, R 43 II, 536, nr. 134–46).
83. *WTB-Meldung*, nr. 1118 of 11 May 1933 (ibid., nr. 167).
84. *WTB-Meldung*, nr. 1315 of 1 June 1933 (ibid., nr. 252).
85. Petzina, 'Hauptprobleme', p. 47.
86. 'Gesetz zur Verminderung der Arbeitslosigkeit vom 1. Juni 1933', in *Reichsgesetzblatt*, I, 1933, pp. 323–9. Fritz Reinhardt was Staatssekretär in the RdF from 1 April 1933.
87. See Schacht's statements of 7 April 1933 and Schmitt's of 13 July 1933, quoted in Gerhard Kroll, *Von der Weltwirtschaftskrise zur Staatskonjunktur* (Berlin, 1958) pp. 460ff, 468ff.
88. See the collection of legal measures in L. Grebler, *Die deutsche Arbeitsbeschaffung*, I, pp. 419f.
89. Fischer, *Deutsche Wirtschaftspolitik*, p. 66.
90. As quoted in Grebler, 'Die deutsche Arbeitsbeschaffung II', p. 826.
91. In this regard see Hagen Schulze, 'Das Scheitern der Weimarer Republik als Problem der Forschung', in Erdmann and Schulze (eds), *Weimar. Selbstpreisgabe einer Demokratie*, pp. 23–41.

92. Dieter Hertz-Eichenrode, *Wirtschaftskrise und Arbeitsbeschaffung. Konjunkturpolitik 1925/26 und die Grundlagen der Krisenpolitik Brünings* (Frankfurt & New York, 1982).
93. See Carl-Ludwig Holtfrerich, 'Alternativen'.
94. Ursula Büttner, *Hamburg in der Staats- und Wirtschaftskrise 1928–1931* (Hamburg, 1982) p. 16.

8 Unemployment and the Radicalisation of the German Electorate 1928–1933: An Aggregate Data Analysis with Special Emphasis on the Rise of National Socialism

Jürgen W. Falter

INTRODUCTORY REMARKS

The striking covariation between the rise of the NSDAP and the increase in unemployment between 1928 and 1933 (Figure 8.1) had led many contemporary observers to postulate a causal link between the two phenomena: unemployment was generally regarded as one of the major determinants of Nazi electoral success.

While this may be correct, it is not clear how this causal influence could have worked in detail. Hypotheses, if specified at all, are rather vague in this respect. Did the unemployed themselves flock to the Nazi party in disproportionately large numbers? (One could call this an 'individual effect' of unemployment.) Or did people indirectly affected by unemployment, be it as family members, neighbours, neighbourhood merchants, artisans and pub owners who lost their clients due to unemployment, give their support to the Nazi party? (One could call this a 'contextual effect' of unemployment.) Or did the Nazis draw their support mainly from those who felt threatened by unemployment without being directly or even indirectly affected by it, people who lost faith in the governing bodies and the political parties who ran the

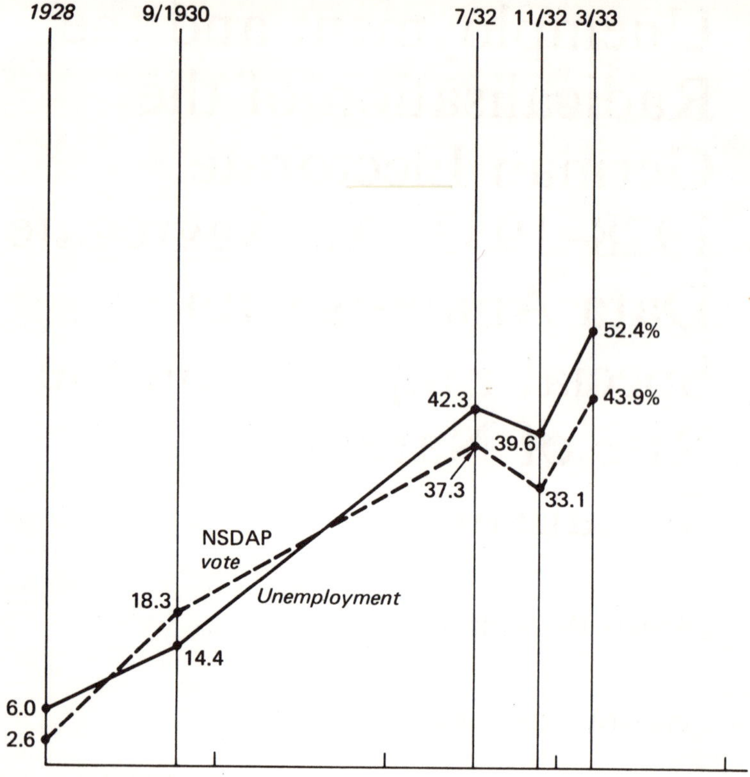

SOURCE Frey and Weck (1981) (as given in note 3)

Figure 8.1 Unemployment and the NSDAP vote, 1928–33 (unemployment quote/percentage of valid vote)

country? (One could call this, according to Zintl, the 'transfer effect' of unemployment.)[1]

Historical electoral research on the Weimar period is confined to aggregate data. The only information available on a vote is on the level of the approximately 1000 counties of the Weimar Republic. We will start with simple bivariate distributions and progress then to more sophisticated statistical models such as multiple regression analysis in order to test for potentially disturbing factors. We will terminate our empirical analysis with an attempt at inferring individual associations from our aggregate data by means of ecological regression techniques.[2]

THE RESULTS OF BIVARIATE ANALYSIS

The results of our bivariate correlation analysis are, at least in the light of received wisdom, quite astonishing: they display a predominantly negative relationship between the percentage of unemployed and the Nazi share of the vote. The correlation for the Communist (KPD) vote on the other hand, is positive. In all Reichstag elections *after 1930* the NSDAP fared, on average, significantly better where unemployment was low and vice versa. The contrary is true for the Communists: their share of the vote went up with unemployment rates (Tables 8.1a, b and Figure 8.2).

In those 551 counties of the Reich where unemployment rates were below average, the NSDAP vote climbed to 41.5 per cent in the July 1932 election, while it fell to 34.6 per cent in those counties which reported above-average unemployment figures. Even if we concentrate on the urban parts of Germany alone (Table 8.2) these associations hold. Thus, in our bivariate correlation analysis we are not able to replicate earlier findings which discerned a positive relationship between unemployment and the Nazi vote.[3] At least for those three Reichstag elections for which we have adequate unemployment data the NSDAP share of the vote was, on average, low where unemployment was high and vice versa; the opposite can be said for the Communist party which fared much better in counties with high unemployment figures.[4]

CONTROLLING FOR OTHER VARIABLES

These associations may well represent so-called spurious correlations, that is, they may be a product of common underlying forces responsible for the negative covariation between the Nazi vote and unemployment as discussed in the preceding paragraphs. Such potentially 'disturbing factors' could be, among others, the religious denomination, the occupational mix, or the urbanisation of the counties. All three are determinants of the Nazi vote well established by prior research.[5] In our next two steps, therefore, we will try to measure the 'pure' effects of unemployment on the Nazi and Communist vote by controlling for these other influencing factors.

One feasible multivariate technique easily understood by the statistical layman is a variety of tree analysis. In this procedure we divide our 865 county units in step no. 1 into two or more subsets which represent

Table 8.1a The correlation of various unemployment variables with the 1930–1933 NSDAP and KPD share of the vote (Pearson's r × 100)

	NSDAP				*KPD*			
	1930	*1932 (July)*	*1932 (Nov.)*	*1933*	*1930*	*1932 (July)*	*1932 (Nov.)*	*1933*
Unemployment rate 1933	(−04)	−24	−23	−44	(75)	77	78	78
Unemployment quota 1933	(−06)	−25	−24	−45	(76)	78	79	79
Unemployed								
Dec. 1930	03	07	07	04	07	06	06	04
Dec. 1931	(09)	−09	−09	−31	(63)	65	65	67
July 1932	(03)	−14	−14	−36	(69)	71	71	73
Oct. 1932	(01)	−17	−17	−39	(69)	71	72	74
Dec. 1932	(05)	−13	−13	−34	(68)	69	70	71
Apr. 1933	(02)	−17	−17	−38	(70)	72	72	73
Welfare unemployed 1930	06	−14	−14	−32	55	54	56	59
Welfare unemployed 1932	(−02)	−20	−19	−41	(70)	72	72	73
Unemployed blue-collar	(−06)	−22	−21	−43	(77)	79	80	81
Unemployed white-collar	(02)	−20	−20	−36	(55)	53	57	58

Table 8.1b The correlation of unemployment figures with the 1928–1933 change of the NSDAP and KPD vote (Pearson's r × 100)

	NSDAP				*KPD*			
	1928–30	*30–32 (July)*	*32 (July-Nov.)*	*32 (Nov.)–33*	*1928–30*	*30–32 (July)*	*32 (July-Nov.)*	*32 (Nov.)–33*
Unemployed								
Dec. 1930	*04*	07	00	−09	*02*	03	−07	−02
Dec. 1931	(10)	*−20*	01	−53	(38)	*−04*	10	−13
July 1932	(04)	*−24*	*05*	−55	(39)	*−03*	*12*	−16
Dec. 1932	(06)	(−23)	*03*	*−52*	(37)	(−04)	*11*	*−17*
Apr. 1933	(04)	(−27)	(05)	*−51*	(38)	(−03)	(09)	*−18*

BASIS 865 county units, adjusted for boundary changes. Cases weighted with their population figures. For definitions of variables see below.

Variable definitions and sources
Unemployment rate 1933: Unemployed × 100/employed and unemployed blue and white collar (Census 1933); SOURCE: StDR, 453–6.
Unemployment quota 1933: Unemployed × 100/employed blue and white collar (Census 1933); SOURCE: StDR, 453–6.
Unemployed December 1930: Unemployed × 100/total labour force (figures only available for those unemployed who were supported by subsidies of labour exchange agencies, the so-called 'Hauptunterstützungsempfänger'; SOURCE: Statistische Beilage zum Reichsarbeitsblatt 1933.
Unemployed December 1931–April 1933: Unemployed × 100/total labour force ('Erwerbspersonen'). Figures based on all people registered as unemployed with labour exchange agencies, including welfare unemployed and unsupported persons (SOURCE: Statistische Beilage zum Reichsarbeitsblatt 1932 and 1933).
Welfare unemployed: Unemployed living on welfare × 100/total labour force; SOURCE: StDR, 421.
Unemployed blue collar: Unemployed blue-collar workers × 100/all blue-collar workers (Census 1933); SOURCE: StDR, 453–6.
Unemployed white collar: Unemployed white-collar workers × 100/all white-collar workers (Census 1933); SOURCE: StDR, 453–6.
NSDAP (KPD) 1930, etc.: NSDAP (KPD) vote × 100/total electorate.
NSDAP (KPD) 1928–30, etc.: NSDAP (KPD) 1930 − NSDAP (KPD) 1928, etc.
Catholic: Catholics × 100/population (Census 1933))
Urban: Percentage of people living in communities with more than 5000 inhabitants; SOURCE: StDR, 401.
Blue collar: Blue-collar workers × 100/total labour force (Census 1933); SOURCE: StDR, 453–6.
StDR = Statistik des Deutschen Reiches, Neue Folge, vols 421, 453–6.

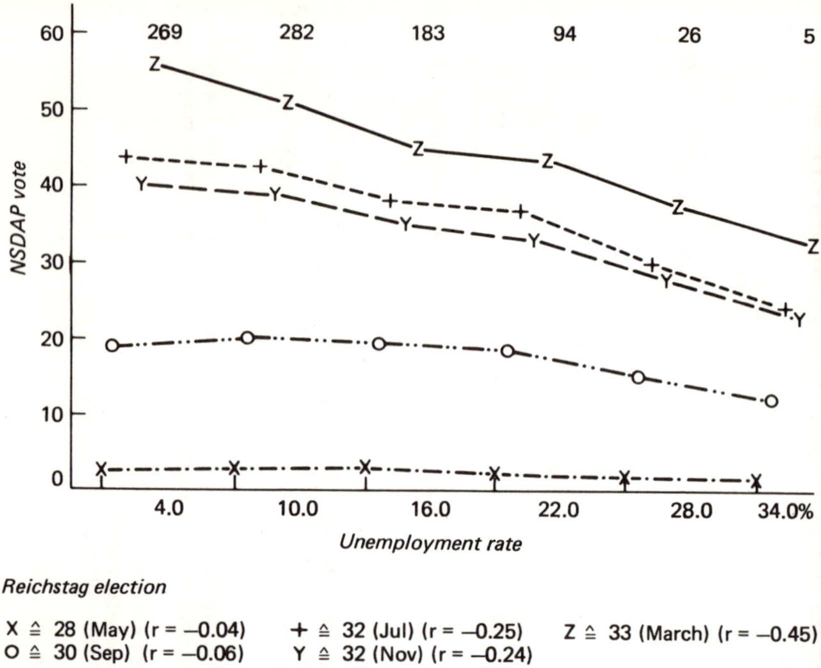

Figure 8.2 NSDAP vote in counties with differing unemployment rates (NSDAP vote/unemployment rate)

different value ranges of the first independent variable, in our case 'religious denomination' (as measured by the percentage of Catholics living in each county). We thus get a first set of contrasting groups of counties for which we calculate the average value of the dependent variable, that is, the Nazi or Communist share of the vote. In step no. 2 we repeat this procedure, now dividing up our two or three denominational subgroups into several more subsets according to our next explanatory variable, the percentage of blue-collar workers, and again we determine the NSDAP and KPD share of the vote for these new subgroups and so on. The last variable we introduce in this way (in our fourth step) is unemployment.

Thus, we obtain 24 subgroups of counties ranging from predominantly Protestant with an above-average blue-collar population and urbanisation and a disproportionately large percentage of unemployed, to predominantly Catholic rural counties with a below-average share of blue-collar workers and low unemployment rates.

Table 8.2 The correlation of some unemployment variables with the NSDAP share of the vote in rural, mixed and urban regions

County type	*1930*	*1932 (July)*	*1932 (Nov.)*	*1933*
Rural counties				
Unemployed blue collar	—	−09	−03	−22
Unemployed white collar	—	−29	−29	−13
All unemployed	11	02	05	−18
Mixed counties				
Unemployed blue collar	—	−17	−13	−29
Unemployed white collar	—	10	12	−02
All unemployed	09	−08	−06	−24
Urban counties				
Unemployed blue collar	—	−18	−15	−24
Unemployed white collar	—	−13	−06	−13
All unemployed	−07	−35	−29	−41

NOTES: Same variable definitions as in Table 8.1.
Urban counties: >66 per cent living in communities with more than 5000 inhabitants;
Mixed counties: rest;
Rural counties: 0 per cent living in communities with more than 5000 inhabitants.
Pearson's r × 100. Unemployment data, with the exception of the 1930 figures, from Census 1933. In this and the following tables unemployment rates are operationalised according to the above definitions (see Table 8.1).

Having done this, we discover at first glance a very strong effect of the denominational variable on the NSDAP election results. In July 1932, in the Protestant parts of Germany, the Nazi share of the vote almost doubled that of the Catholic counties. The confessionally-mixed regions fell in between these two contrasting groups. Even after introducing the other three independent variables the differences between the Catholic and Protestant counties prevail. Thus, in counties with a below-average percentage of blue-collar workers, unemployment, and urbanisation, the NSDAP share of the vote climbed up to 56.2 per cent in the Protestant parts of Germany while it fell to 22.8 per cent of the valid vote in Catholic regions.

Furthermore, a quite interesting effect emerges after the introduction of the blue-collar variable as a second independent factor: in the predominantly Protestant and confessionally-mixed areas there is a clear negative effect of the blue-collar variable in regard to the Nazi vote. The higher the percentage of blue-collar workers, the lower, on average, the NSDAP share of the vote; in Catholic counties this effect does not seem to exist. Even after the additional control of urbanisation and unemployment this striking discrepancy between Catholic counties on the one hand, and confessionally-mixed and Protestant counties on the other, persists.

The influence of unemployment on the Nazi vote (but not on the Communist!) thus seems to be restricted to the two non-Catholic branches of our explanatory tree. Here, however, its effect is rather clear-cut: where unemployment was low, irrespective of urbanisation or the percentage of blue-collar workers, the NSDAP share of the vote in July 1932 was consistently higher than in counties of this branch of the tree with an above-average number of blue-collar workers and unemployment. By means of a magnifying glass we may even discover a reverse, but negligible effect in the Catholic counties.

This pattern seems to have emerged as early as September 1930 and it prevailed, at least in essence, until the last principally free Reichstag election of March 1933. A comparison of trees for the July 1932 and March 1933 elections, however, shows that the differences in Nazi voting between the Catholic and the non-Catholic areas of the Reich considerably shrank. In other words, in 1933 the NSDAP managed to augment its share of the vote disproportionately in the Catholic counties, especially those with a relatively low percentage of workers and unemployed. In these constituencies its increase of the vote almost doubled that of the non-Catholic parts of Germany. Even then, however, Catholic Germany was far less overwhelmed by Nazism than the country as a whole (Figure 8.3). The Communist electorate, finally, concentrated in exactly the opposite types of counties as the Hitler movement (Figure 8.4).

As a result of our tree analysis we may keep in mind that, at least in the Protestant and confessionally-mixed parts of Germany, that is, in about four-fifths of the country, the NSDAP vote was low where unemployment was high and vice versa while the Communist vote rose and fell with unemployment, irrespective of the denominational character of the region.

MULTIPLE REGRESSION ANALYSIS

The outcome of research techniques such as tree analysis, which are extremely plausible intuitively, but by no means very sophisticated statistically, depends, when dealing with aggregate data, to a certain

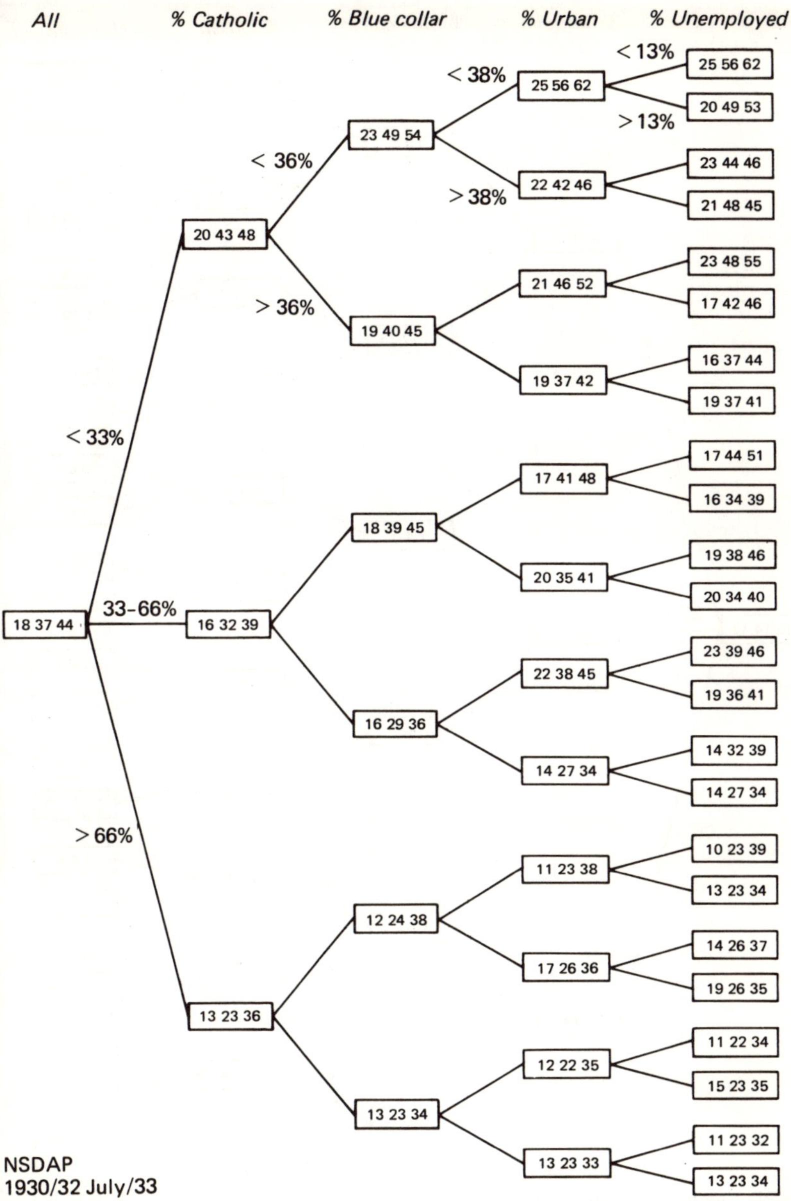

Figure 8.3 A tree analysis of the NSDAP vote, September 1930, July 1932 and March 1933

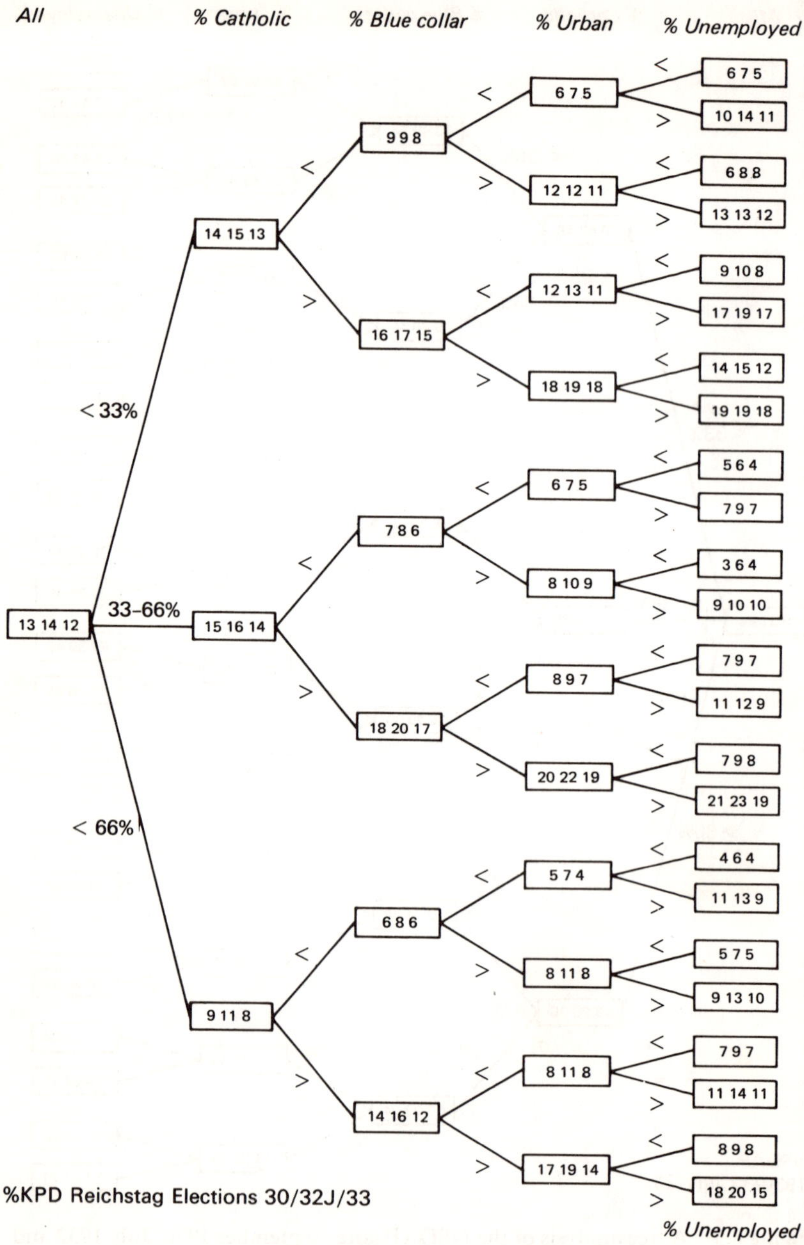

Figure 8.4 The KPD vote 1930–33

degree, on the choice of cutting points, that is, the definitions of categories of an originally continuous variable. It seems to be advisable, therefore, to try to replicate its findings by means of other multivariate statistical techniques, such as multiple regression analysis, which does not depend on the choice of cutting points (but which has, of course, other shortcomings).

The results of our tree analyses, as reported above, could indeed be replicated by a series of multiple regression analyses which we ran in order to test for the effects of several model specifications. Again, the confessional factor, which typically explains more than four-fifths of the total variance of the Nazi vote, proves to be of prime importance. It is no surprise that its explanatory power diminishes considerably during the March 1933 election. All other findings of the tree analysis are corroborated as well: the percentages of blue-collar workers, urban dwellers and unemployed, with the exception of the 1930 Reichstag election, consistently exert a negative influence on the Nazi and a positive one on the Communist share of the vote.

In regard to beta weights, that is, the standardised regression coefficients, the unemployment variable typically shows up as the second- or third-best predictor of the 1932 and 1933 Nazi vote (and as the strongest predictor by far of the Communist constituency). On the other hand, the additional explanatory power of unemployment in a hierarchical regression model where unemployment is introduced as the last variable is, in the case of the Nazis, rather small: in the case of the Communists, however, it is of major importance. While in the Nazi case it only accounts for about 2 to 4 per cent of the total explained variance, it is responsible in the Communist case for about 20 per cent of the variance, that is, the explanatory power of the model (Table 8.3).

If we differentiate between unemployed blue-collar and white-collar workers the regression coefficients display surprisingly consistent differences between the two groups: coefficients for unemployed blue-collar workers are negative while the corresponding values for white-collar workers are positive in sign. Where blue-collar unemployment was relatively high the Nazi share of the vote tended to fall below average and vice versa. Where white-collar unemployment was high the Nazi vote tended to come out above average.

Surprisingly enough, the association between both blue-collar and white-collar unemployment and the Communist vote turned out to be positive. It should be pointed out again that these coefficients are already controlled for religious confession, urbanisation, percentage of blue-collar workers, and percentage of either blue-collar or white-collar

Table 8.3 Multiple regression analysis of 'Tree variables'

	NSDAP				KPD			
	1930	*1932 (July)*	*1932 (Nov.)*	*1933*	*1930*	*1932 (July)*	*1932 (Nov.)*	*1933*
% Catholic	−55	−78	−73	−65	−66	01	−04	−09
% Blue collar	−04	−09	−11	−12	−12	34	32	28
% Urban	−04	−14	−20	−19	−39	−05	−04	−02
% Unemployed	01	−21	−13	−34	−15	65	66	68
Explained var. (%)	28	64	57	60	56	69	70	71
R^2–change through unemployment (%)	0.0	1.4	0.6	3.6	0.01	13.6	13.9	14.4

Hierarchial regression analysis with unemployment entered as last variable. Standardised regression coefficients × 100. Same definition of unemployment variable as in Table 8.2. Counties weighted by numbers of inhabitants. For unstandardised regression coefficients see Jürgen W. Falter, Andreas Link, Jan-Bernd Lohmöller, Johann de Rijke and Siegfried Schumann, 'Arbeitslosigkeit und Nationalsozialismus. Eine empirische Analyse des Beitrags der Massenerwerbslosigkeit zu den Wahlerfolgen der NSDAP 1932 und 1933', *Kölner Zeitschrift für Soziologie und Sozialpsychologie*, 35, 1983, pp. 525–54.

unemployment. In contradistinction to the Nazi vote, the Communist vote thus profited from both types of unemployment (in a, however, admittedly quite disproportionate way) while the NSDAP made only very small gains above their Reich mean in regions with high white-collar unemployment, losing heavily at the same time where blue-collar unemployment prevailed (Table 8.4).

A CLOSER LOOK INTO THE TEMPORAL DIMENSION

Up to this point the analysis has been purely cross-sectional, dealing only with the covariation between unemployment and the Nazi vote at a given point in time. Its main finding, so far, is a consistently negative association between the two variables, which even increases over time. In March 1933, the NSDAP vote thus fell about half a percentage point when the over-all rate of unemployment of a county increased by one percentage point.

On the other hand, there is an extremely strong positive statistical association between the development of the Nazi vote and the increase of unemployment figures between 1928 and 1933 at the Reich level. The impact of unemployment on the Nazi vote thus seems to have been slightly negative from a cross-sectional, and strongly positive from a longitudinal, point of view. How can these apparently contradictory results be reconciled?

There are two ways in which we will try to cope in this section with the puzzle: (a) by means of a pooled regression analysis, that is, a combination of longitudinal and cross-sectional data in one regression equation, and (b) by means of a longitudinal path analysis introducing lagged variables as predictors of the NSDAP vote. To control for the influence of other factors not yet considered, such as turnout, the regression models will be specified somewhat differently from those above.

Pooled regression analysis, where geographical distributions and their longitudinal developments are considered simultaneously, discerns the same pattern of influence as our separate cross-sectional analyses do: unemployment rates correlate negatively with the NSDAP vote and covary, on a much higher level, positively with the Communist vote (Table 8.5). It may be interesting to take a closer look at the turnout variable: turnout seems to have indeed favoured the electoral successes of the Nazi party, as postulated by so many impressionistic historical and sociological studies.[6]

Table 8.4 Multiple regression analysis with unemployed blue and white-collar workers

	NSDAP			*KPD*		
	1932 (July)	*1932 (Nov.)*	*1933*	*1932 (July)*	*1932 (Nov.)*	*1933*
%Catholic	−78	−72	−62	03	−02	−08
%Blue collar	−16	−16	−25	51	48	46
% Urban	−20	−26	−27	06	08	10
% Unemployed BC	−14	−11	−39	33	33	38
% Unemployed WC	04	08	19	16	17	11
Explained variance (%)	63	56	60	66	67	67
R^2–*change through unemployed BC*	0.6	0.1	2.8	10.2	10.0	10.5
R^2–*change through unemployed WC*	0.03	0.1	0.7	0.5	0.5	0.2

Hierarchical regression analysis with the two unemployment variables entered as last variables. Standardised regression coefficients × 100. For unstandardised regression coefficients see Falter *et al.*, as given under Table 8.3.
NOTE: BC = Blue collar; WC = White collar.

Table 8.5 Unemployment and the percentage change of the NSDAP and KPD vote 1930–1933 (pooled multiple regression analysis)

	Unemployed	*Catholic*	*Urbanisation*	*Turnout*	R^2 (%)	*Pearson's* r w. *unemployed*
NSDAP	−17	−37	−18	43	42	−0.12
KPD	60	−10	13	−09	50	0.70

Standardised regression coefficients × 100.

Finally, in our longitudinal path model, where we look at the interplay of several theoretically relevant factors over time, we again find a negative influence of unemployment on the electoral growth of the National Socialist movement: where unemployment was high the rise of the NSDAP in July 1932 and March 1933 was slowed down. The positive correlation between unemployment and the November 1932 vote, however, does not fit into this trend; it could be interpreted, perhaps, as a statistical artifact, that is, as a result of the shifting trend of unemployment and the Nazi vote. The other variables of the model 'behave' as expected: the percentage of people working in the agricultural sector is positively, and the percentages of Catholics and blue-collar workers are negatively, associated with the Nazi share of the vote in 1930 and its increase in July 1932 (Figure 8.5).

BUT HOW DID THE UNEMPLOYED THEMSELVES VOTE?

So far we have amassed some strong evidence that the association between unemployment and the Nazi vote between 1930 and 1933 was indeed negative at the county level: above-average unemployment rates not only tended to lower the NSDAP vote but also slowed down, on average, its stupendous growth in the July 1932 and March 1933 elections. This does not necessarily imply that the unemployed did not vote in disproportionately high numbers for the Hitler movement. Hitherto, we have been talking exclusively about relationships on the level of the approximately 1000 counties and cities of the Reich.

It is, of course, individuals and not geographical areas who go to the polls. From the theoretical viewpoint it would therefore be much more desirable to give information about individual or group voting behaviour, instead of talking about minor or major civil divisions and their propensity to vote for certain parties. Unfortunately, the obstacles to inferences from aggregate to individual relationships are almost insurmountable.

Under very special circumstances, however, it is possible to infer, by means of ecological regression analysis, individual or group behaviour from aggregate data. One of the main assumptions of this technique is that there are no systematic contextual effects. Catholics voting for the Centre Party should do so, for example, with about the same probability, irrespective of the denominational context, the occupational mix of their community, and so on. Only random variation is acceptable. Unfortunately, the electoral historian is not able to determine

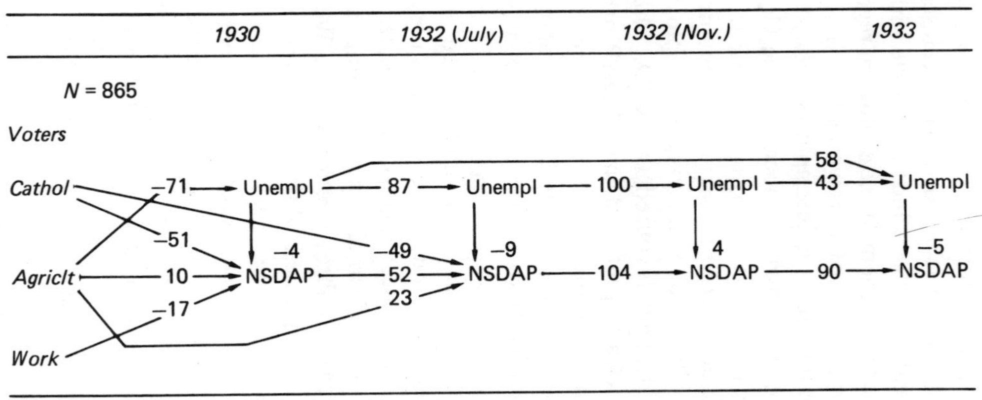

Figure 8.5 A longitudinal path model of the NSDAP vote, 1930–3

from aggregate data alone if this assumption is always true. The results of ecological regression analysis, therefore, are permanently endangered by hidden biases. This danger may be somewhat reduced (but by no means totally eliminated) by the inclusion of potentially biasing factors into the regression equations as so-called moderator variables.[7] Since, on the other hand, there is no better way so far to make inferences from the aggregate to the individual level it seems justified, at least for theoretical reasons, to conclude the article with some findings of an extended series of different multiple ecological regression analyses of the affinity of unemployed voters towards the National Socialists.

According to these findings, the unemployed indeed appear to have voted in disproportionately high numbers for the Communist party while they tended to keep away from the NSDAP in 1932 and 1933 (Table 8.6). There is, however, a theoretically quite interesting difference between blue-collar and white-collar unemployment. Laid-off blue-collar workers strongly favoured the KPD, while unemployed white-collar workers clearly preferred the NSDAP over the KPD. It should be pointed out, however, that the latter seem to have voted for the KPD somewhat above average as well. This cannot be established, in turn, for the propensity of unemployed blue-collar workers to vote for the Nazis.

Since more than four-fifths of all unemployed were blue-collar workers they determine, of course, the voting figures for the whole group. Supposing our ecological regression estimates are, at least in essence, correct, this would imply that a strong majority of the unemployed, during the last three elections of the Weimar Republic, favoured the two socialist parties, while only a minority of them was affected by the spell of Nazism. The radicalisation of the German electorate in reaction to the economic crisis of the 1930s took the form of client behaviour, not (or only to a minor degree) of reward and punishment. Voters tended to choose those extremist political alternatives which were close to their socio-political milieu, that is, unemployed workers tended to opt for the Communists, unemployed with a middle-class background flocked to the Nazis.[8] Astonishing as these results may be, they are in perfect agreement with our earlier findings on the aggregate level. By now it should be beyond reasonable doubt that a high level of unemployment in a county tended to reduce the National Socialist electoral success, and that it did so because of the unwillingness of the great majority of the unemployed themselves to vote for Adolf Hitler and his party.

Table 8.6 The propensity of unemployed blue collar and white collar to vote for the NSDAP or KPD

	NSDAP (%)			*KPD (%)*		
	1932 (July)	*1932 (Nov.)*	*1933*	*1932 (July)*	*1932 (Nov.)*	*1933*
Unemployed blue collar	13	12	10	29	34	30
Unemployed white collar	28	30	43	13	16	14
All voters	31	27	39	12	14	11

Percentage of total electorate. Values based on multiple ecological regression analyses with religion and urbanisation as moderator variables. For further details see Falter articles as given in notes 5 and 8.

CONCLUDING REMARKS

How are we to interpret these findings? Do they really imply that the rise of National Socialism was not (or only to a minor extent) affected by mass unemployment? This would portend that the extremely close covariation between the rise of unemployment and the increase of the National Socialist vote over time on a national level were merely spurious. In regard to a multitude of biographical and personal accounts on this time period, which almost invariably connect the decision to vote for Hitler or his movement in some way with the economic hardships of the time in general and the apparent impotence of the democratic state to fight unemployment in particular, one feels compelled to reject such an interpretation.

The relation between mass unemployment and Nazi electoral successes was indirect; the causal links between the two phenomena were considerably more complicated than usually spelled out in the historical literature about the Weimar Republic. We are now in a position to determine that neither individual nor contextual effects can account for the major impact of unemployment on the rise of Hitlerism. Individual effects would imply a greater than average affinity of the unemployed towards the NSDAP. As we have seen, this is probably not the case. Contextual, that is, neighbourhood effects, on the other hand, would require a positive relationship betwen unemployment figures and the NSDAP vote on the county level. Again, we are able to rule out this possibility.

Thus, the impact of unemployment on the rise of National Socialism could have possibly worked only as a so-called transfer effect: voters for National Socialism must have been mainly people who felt threatened by unemployment and the radicalisation of many unemployed towards the left, even without being individually or contextually affected by the fate of unemployment themselves.

Mass unemployment and the other manifestations of the severest economic crisis experienced in Germany in at least 50 years led to a general climate of fear and despair. Even voters from regions where unemployment, if not economic hardship as such, was low, were affected by this mental state of depression and hopelessness. When losing their confidence in the problem-solving capacities of the government and the democratic parties, they tended to radicalise towards the right, following their traditional voting habits and group norms which in better times had favoured the Conservatives and other right-of-centre parties. The unemployed, as well as many employed, blue-collar workers, in turn, tended to vote for the Communist party as the left-wing radical alternative of their urban social environment.

In the course of the economic crisis, however, the Nazis proved able to increase their share of the vote in both settings, as could be seen in ecological regression analyses reported above and elsewhere.[9] It should be kept in mind, therefore, that the landslides won by the Nazis occurred 'across the board', that is, almost irrespective of regional unemployment, leaving the cross-sectional patterns of negative aggregate association between the Nazi vote and local unemployment more or less intact. The transfer effect of rising (or permanent) mass unemployment did not make the unemployed more favourably disposed towards the Nazis when compared to other voters (in fact, the distance between unemployed and employed in respect to Nazism even increased over time). On the other hand, this 'transfer effect' did not transform the Hitler movement's most fertile fields (with comparatively low regional unemployment) into barren land. Instead, against the background of (almost) stable cross-sectional associations the propensity of all voters to turn out in favour of the Nazi party increased.

Mass unemployment thus indeed furthered the rise of National Socialism. But it did so in an unexpectedly indirect way. Theories about the radicalisation of the German electorate after 1928, therefore, may not have to be totally rewritten, but they certainly ask for specification and differentiation.

Notes

1. Reinhard Zintl, 'Zur politischen Wirkungsweise von makroökonomischen Variablen: Ein Problemaufriss', in Dieter Oberndörfer, Hans Rattinger and Karl Schmitt (eds), *Wirtschaftlicher Wandel, religiöser Wandel und Wertewandel* (Berlin, 1985) pp. 45–59.
2. The data used and the computations run for this analysis are the result of a larger research project devoted to the Nazi electorate in Weimar Germany and Austria's First Republic. The project is financed by a grant from the Volkswagen Foundation. The results reported are the product of the collaborative efforts of the whole research group which includes, besides the author, Jan-Bernd Lohmöller, Johann de Rijke, Andreas Link and Siegfried Schumann.
3. Samuel A. Pratt, *The Social Basis of Nazism and Communism in Urban Germany*, M. A. Thesis (Michigan State University, 1948) p. 175ff; Loren K. Waldman, *Models of Mass Movements. The Case of the Nazis*. Ph.D. thesis (University of Chicago, 1973) pp. 70, 74; Bruno S. Frey and Hannelore Weck, 'Hat Arbeitslosigkeit den Aufstieg des Nationalsozialis-

mus bewirkt?', *Jahrbuch für Nationalökonomie und Statistik*, 196, 1981, pp. 1–31; Werner Kaltefleiter, *Wirtschaft und Politik in Deutschland. Konjunktur als Bestimmungsfaktor des Parteiensystems* (Cologne, 1968) pp. 21ff.

4. To our knowledge, there are no complete unemployment figures available on a county or labour-agency district level before December 1931. Since it does not make too much sense to predict the 1930 vote of the two extremist parties from unemployment rates tallied some 15 months later we make use of some earlier, if somewhat incomplete, unemployment data in Tables 8.1 to 8.3. The December 1930 figures called upon in these tables refer to 'Hauptunterstützungsempfänger' only, that is, persons receiving unemployment relief payments from their regional labour exchange agency. They form but a (however substantial) part of the total number of unemployed (2 832 738 out of 4 383 843). The correlation coefficients for the December 1930 unemployment rate and the September 1930 NSDAP and KPD share (and percentage increase) of the vote are close to zero. In other words, in the 1930 Reichstag election there was no systematic linear relationship between unemployment and the rise of Nazism at the county level. Such a relationship, negative in the case of the Nazis, positive in the case of the Communists, first developed for the July 1932 election.
5. Jürgen W. Falter, 'Die Wähler der NSDAP 1928–1933. Sozialstruktur und parteipolitische Herkunft', in Wolfgang Michalka (ed.), *Die nationalsozialistische Machtergreifung 1933* (Paderborn, 1984), pp. 47–59.
6. Jürgen W. Falter, 'Radicalisation of the Middle Classes or Mobilisation of the Unpolitical?', *Social Science Information*, 20, 1981, pp. 389–430.
7. Jan-Bernd Lohmöller, Jürgen W. Falter, Johann de Rijke and Andreas Link, 'Unemployment and the Rise of National Socialism. Contradicting Results from Different Regional Aggregations', in Peter Nijkamp (ed.), *Measuring the Unmeasurable* (The Hague, 1984), pp. 357–70.
8. For the different theories underlying these concepts and their application to Weimar or Bonn elections see Jürgen W. Falter, 'Politische Konsequenzen von Massenerwerbslosigkeit', *Politische Vierteljahresschrift*, 23, 1984, pp. 275–95; Zintl, 'Wirkungsweise'; Hans Rattinger, 'Politisches Verhalten von Arbeitslosen. Die Bundestagswahlen 1980 und 1983 im Vergleich', in Oberndörfer *et al.*, *Wirtschaftlicher Wandel*, pp. 97–130.
9. Falter, 'Die Wähler', Lohmöller *et al.*, 'Unemployment and the Rise of National Socialism'.

9 Unemployment and Left-Wing Radicalism in Weimar Germany, 1930–1933*

Conan J. Fischer

I

Calamitous economic collapse, a sharp rise in the level of unemployment, and an upsurge in political radicalism occurred simultaneously in Germany during the early 1930s. On the political Right the splinter parties, small liberal parties and, to a large degree, the conservative DNVP saw their voters switch to the NSDAP. On the political Left the republican Social Democratic Party (SPD) vote declined whilst the revolutionary German Communist Party (KPD) vote increased. This trend was accompanied by mounting political violence in town and country which, by 1933, had left a trail of death, injury and physical damage through Germany. By the time Hitler became Chancellor in January 1933 the substance of democratic republicanism had long since been destroyed.

Historians have often argued that the economic catastrophe and political radicalisation not only coincided, but were causally linked. Thus, when writing of developments on the Left, Mason argues that economic crisis contributed significantly to intensified class conflict and to the KPD's rising fortunes between 1928 and 1932.[1] Earlier observers had reached similar conclusions, with Preller noting the appeal of Communist slogans to youthful activists[2] and Kuczynski commenting on the mounting despair fostered by unemployment, particularly in working-class circles.[3] It is therefore understandable that most of the KPD's expanding, youthful membership during the early 1930s was

*I am very grateful to the Wolfson Foundation and the German Academic Exchange Service for their support which made possible the research for this article.

unemployed while within the SPD the unemployed were in the minority.[4]

None the less, the growth in unemployment had not created German radicalism. The political attitudes of the younger generation in particular were becoming more radical even before the First World War, and youth tended to eschew parliamentary politics throughout the Weimar era, preferring activist and paramilitary forms of political expression. It might seem, therefore, that unemployment accelerated the process of radicalisation and helped radicalise broader sections of the German population rather than giving birth to the phenomenon.

Against this stands the oft-repeated observation that far from fostering radicalism, mass unemployment induces political apathy and, on a personal level, resignation or cynicism. This might suggest that radicalisation in late Weimar Germany occurred in spite of, rather than because of, unemployment or other facets of economic catastrophe. Much of the recent sociological and psychological work in this field tends to the anecdotal, relying for its theoretical basis on a number of important studies completed during the 1930s.[5] Among these the writings of Bakke, Eisenberg and Lazarsfeld, and Jahoda, Lazarsfeld and Zeisel have been particularly influential. Bakke's study of the London borough of Greenwich in the early 1930s concluded that most men and their families manage to adjust to unemployment and that in Britain most had. Only the particularly harsh circumstances faced by a small minority or the flaws in the character of a few others had led some jobless on the road to political radicalism.[6] More recently, Bakke has argued that lengthy unemployment can, temporarily, disrupt family life most severely, but that most households eventually adjust to their changed circumstances.[7] Eisenberg and Lazarsfeld believed that unemployment had a similar effect on the individual. After initial shock, an active, optimistic search for work will, if unsuccessful, be followed by anxiety, pessimism and distress. Then, 'the individual becomes fatalistic and adapts himself to his new state with a narrower scope. He now has a broken attitude'.[8] The study by Jahoda, Lazarsfeld and Zeisel of the Austrian industrial village of Marienthal during 1931 seems to confirm these findings. Political and social activity decreased with the persistence of high unemployment levels and resignation prevailed within most unemployed households.[9] It would therefore be ill-advised automatically to ascribe the rise in left-wing radicalism in late Weimar Germany to unemployment. Indeed Geary, discussing the impact of unemployment on working-class solidarity in late Weimar Germany, argues that boredom and apathy, above all else, characterised unemployment.[10]

However, such findings only represented one side of the 1930s studies which were more equivocal than many recent authors would suggest. Eisenberg and Lazarsfeld found that unemployment undermined people's emotional stability, resulting in mounting fear, a loss of sense of proportion and a collapse in self-esteem. When everything else is considered, some of the unemployed were consequently more suggestible politically than the employed, with a propensity to follow 'any political group or leader who appealed directly to their needs'.[11] Unemployment may not have increased any sense of class consciousness – despite the more recent claims of some historians – but Eisenberg and Lazarsfeld believed that it could engender a less-clearly-defined criticism of the social order. Thus a good quarter of the unemployed remained unbroken by their experience, being 'unresigned, aggressive individuals who are far from content with their present situation, who will not give up and sometimes go so far as to try to change the social order'. Membership of this vociferous minority was, apparently, determined by age. Men older than 30 were fairly readily broken by unemployment, but the jobless young were seen as more receptive to the social questions posed thereby.[12] Unemployment, therefore, may have contributed to the decisive youthfulness of the paramilitary Left and Right in Weimar Germany.[13]

Admittedly the Marienthal study reaches different conclusions. In the little Austrian town, apart from the deadening impact of unemployment, compassion survived the onslaught on material fortunes to the extent that the authorities and neighbouring farmers were reluctant to stamp out widespread pilfering by the cold and hungry villagers. The latter, with the partial exception of youth, retained fond memories of better times rather than developing grandiose revolutionary projects.[14] However, the authors were careful to avoid claiming universal applicability for their findings and were at particular pains to distinguish the experience of Marienthal from developments in Germany:

> This [trend], which contrasts markedly with all the developments in the German Reich, can probably be attributed to the fact that in little Marienthal everyone, regardless of party membership, has experienced the same fate. However, throughout this study it must be borne in mind that the national characteristics of the Austrians

> might play a role. These are different in northern Germany and could therefore lead to a different turn in events.[15]

Certainly, many of Jahoda's German contemporaries believed that unemployment had contributed decisively to the upsurge of political radicalism in their country. Neumann wrote of the KPD's attraction for 'youth and groups who have despaired in the present, but remain militant and who expect everything from tomorrow',[16] while Rosenberg noted a fractious Communist programme of agitation which 'was aimed entirely at the needs of the utopian-radical unemployed'.[17] Wunderlich argued that a qualitative difference between Weimar, and earlier, unemployment produced this distinctive political reaction. In pre-war Germany unemployment rates had varied between 1 and 5 per cent, with about 100 000 long-term unemployed. With defeat in 1918 a trail of privation and disaster included significantly higher unemployment levels. For the first time this unemployment scourged wide sections of society such as the skilled workers and white-collar staff who were not prepared to regard this as part of their lot. Furthermore, the surge in unemployment levels, particularly from 1929, resulted in increasingly long periods spent out of work. In Munich, for instance, half the unemployed had been without work for more than two years by 1932. Wunderlich regarded this growth in long-term unemployment as particularly damaging. Weimar's social insurance system was not geared to supporting the long-term unemployed who were thrown back on meagre local authority relief payments. This material hardship was intensified by the diminishing prospect of re-employment as the time spent out of work increased. Employers and the victims of unemployment alike knew that the latter's skills and experience were being 'dissipated in idleness'. They seemed 'condemned to professional death' with unemployment 'an inevitable fate, a continuing state, if not to say a profession'. The unemployed eventually lost their links with society as economic resources evaporated and because, in Wunderlich's words, an individual's 'job determines his social position; it is his emblem of respectability'.[18] Thus Furtwaengler, Director of the Workers' Academy in Frankfurt-am-Main, could argue that 'the working class broke into two fundamentally different parts, those in work and the unemployed'.[19]

Unemployed youth in particular became outcasts as their life prospects faded, their apprenticeship training became useless or, if they were school-leavers, they confronted a world into which they had never been socialised through holding a job. Wunderlich argued that the seeds of radicalisation rather than apathy lay in this degrading process. As poverty at home drove unemployed youth on to the streets, devoid of either money or self-respect, they became ready recruits for street gangs which, in turn, were manipulated by extremist political parties.[20]

> In the last few years the radical political parties gathered up these groups for their storm troops. There the unemployed found what they needed. Uniforms gave them the feeling of superiority which compensated for their feeling of inferiority. They could march in file with the companions of their fate. They could fight against an enemy, they learned how to shoot and kill and they found an outlet for the painful tension of hate and resentment.[21]

Rosenhaft's recent study of Communist paramilitary politics in late Weimar Berlin confirms these earlier findings, although she too reminds us that rising unemployment did not create political radicalism as such, but, rather, enhanced it and led to it adopting new forms.[22]

The critical factor in Germany's case, therefore, would appear to have lain in the previous existence of well-established radical organisations and traditions on the Left, and Right, of the political spectrum. These were able to channel and exploit the vaguely defined criticism and deep resentment, described by Eisenberg and Lazarsfeld, with devastating effect. Recent studies of unemployment in interwar Britain confirm that individual responses were not necessarily significantly different from those in Germany, but angry despairing individuals in themselves hardly pose a significant threat to any political system, and seem ill-equipped to organise themselves to pose such a challenge. Thus a South Wales miner commented of the slump: 'It has definitely lessened my interest in politics, because it has led me to believe that politics is a game of bluff, and that these people do not care a brass farthing for the bottom dog; it is only power which they seek'.[23] In contemporary Britain with its high unemployment, feelings can be similar, as a recent study has shown.[24] In interwar Britain, as in Germany, the experience of mass unemployment fractured working-class society. Constantine comments; 'a single working class society divided into two communities – the employed and the unemployed; their occupations and life styles differed and kept them apart'.[25] In twentieth century Britain, however, there has never been a major party fundamentally opposed to the existing constitution and therefore able to appeal on that basis to the long-term unemployed. Weimar Germany, by contrast, possessed the KPD on the Left and the NSDAP on the Right.

II

The KPD, as a radical critic of the prevailing socioeconomic and political order, found itself favoured, therefore, by the severe strains which mass unemployment had imposed on German society. The character of Weimar politics further strengthened the KPD's potential attraction for the unemployed. Social democratic or labour parties in much of western and northern Europe certainly operated within the institutional framework of bourgeois society, but could claim that their purpose in so doing was the reform and ultimate transformation of these societies. However, the Weimar Republic was not created by bourgeois parties or a bourgeois revolution, but by the SPD itself. During the Imperial era the Social Democrats had regarded the absence of a sovereign parliament as a crucial obstacle to the creation of a socialist society and, accordingly, made the creation of a parliamentary state their first priority in 1918 and 1919. Thus, during the Weimar era, the SPD, sometimes with misgivings, was charged with defending its parliamentary republic within a capitalist society which inflicted a fair deal of material hardship on the working class. The SPD had become an establishment party and Communists noted SPD officials' willingness to take harsh measures against the radical Left in defence of the Republic. In these circumstances, it has been observed, the description of the SPD by the KPD as a 'Social Fascist' party might not have been entirely nonsensical from the latter's point of view.[26] During the early 1930s the worsening economic climate saw the SPD ensnared into an assault on the material conditions of the unemployed in particular. Wickham comments that the Social Democrats' prominent role in local government compelled them 'to directly participate in the onslaught on the conditions of the unemployed, enforcing those cuts and administrative tightenings-up in local social welfare payments which central government policy ordained'.[27] While this judgement seems harsh, it does explain to some degree how many of the unemployed came to regard the SPD as actively hostile to their interests at that time. This, it has been argued, fostered political radicalisation of the jobless and no doubt benefited the KPD.[28]

The SPD's problems were compounded by its attitude to youth who, as noted, are most prone to radicalisation through the experience of unemployment and who, in Germany, were disproportionately affected. Well before 1929 a highly bureaucratised SPD had come to regard time-serving as the normal road to advancement within the party, thus alienating ambitious and capable younger members at a time when its parliamentarianism in any case exercised little appeal for the young. They were treated essentially as 'second class colleagues'[29] and while the SPD's left wing and the activist *Reichsbanner* units did attract some young workers, Social Democracy became distinctly middle-aged.

Under the circumstances, however, the KPD's success during the depression was relatively modest. While it almost trebled its membership from 130 000 in late 1928 to over 300 000 during 1932 and increased its (already rising) share of the national poll from 10.6 per cent in 1928 to 16.9 per cent in November 1932,[30] unemployment affected many more people than that. Registered unemployment reached 33 per cent by late 1932 and the real rate was probably nearer 50 per cent.[31] Thus, even remembering the specific appeal of political radicalism for unemployed youth, the KPD's membership returns are not overly impressive. It is tempting to set the 6 million Communist voters of November 1932 against the 6 million registered unemployed, but electoral support for the KPD cannot be so characterised. It had substantial support in some particular industrial regions before the advent of mass unemployment and retained this support during the depression years.

Even so, more jobless Germans came into direct contact with the KPD than its membership figures initially suggest, for the party suffered from an exceptionally high turnover rate of paid-up members. Thus, during 1930, membership rose from 133 000 to 180 000, but the KPD achieved this gain by recruiting 143 000 new members while 95 000 – no doubt often the same people – resigned or drifted away. A similar scale of turnover during 1931 has been noted [32] which suggests that well over half a million people belonged to the party at some stage during the early 1930s. Taking Communist ancillary organisations into account, even more of the unemployed must have associated themselves with Communism during the depression years, however briefly.

Clearly, though, the instability of the KPD's membership constituted a major weakness and prevented the party from mounting a serious revolutionary challenge to Weimar. This situation was in part forced upon the KPD. The collapse of work had, as noted, left many of the young divorced from the labour process, and for these youths the relationship between labour and capital, which essentially informed Marxian ideology, was less relevant than for earlier working-class generations. Some undoubtedly found the KPD's radicalism and activism appealing, but outside those urban communities where the KPD had earlier struck root, the ideology which underlay this radicalism was less pertinent. As Rosenberg comments, 'With rising unemployment the KPD won a certain following among those unemployed who wished, above all, to have their misery proclaimed far and wide. But that does not provide the basis upon which a revolution can be achieved and a socialist community built.'[33] The KPD appreciated that the dispossessed alone would not make a Marxist-Leninist revolution and accordingly ascribed the central role therein to the factory-employed proletariat who would topple capitalism through a general strike and a subsequent uprising. The unemployed movement was therefore to be linked with the Communist factory movement to lend the former a revolutionary significance.[34] However, except in a few localities, the employed industrial proletariat stood by the SPD and, therefore, by the Republic. Whatever its feelings on the matter, the KPD found its wider constituency during the depression among the unemployed youth on the streets and even in the countryside.[35]

This demanded political strategies which reflected the growing rootlessness of the radical unemployed, but simultaneously destabilised the KPD itself. Rabble rousing speeches at meetings may have served as the most successful means of recruitment, but as Neumann observed, these were 'based on the momentary enthusiasm found at meetings which, in contrast to a gradual, systematic and rational conversion, does not last; above all not if membership of various Communist organisations results in a commitment of time and in a continual, heavy financial burden'.[36] The need repeatedly to rally its unstable membership doubtless also contributed to the ferocity of its verbal onslaught on the Republic and SPD and to a spate of demonstrations against the authorities' imposition of welfare cuts. However, in the end this agitation, which was badly organised, 'merely stressed what the unemployed already knew – the bleakness of their situation'[37] and in Berlin at least, left 'fewer and fewer people becoming more and more disposed to violence'.[38]

In some areas the KPD attempted a more constructive approach to the problems of unemployment. The capably led Offenbach KPD was able to negotiate with the authorities on behalf of the unemployed, became involved in community work, and showed a willingness to co-operate with the SPD to these ends.[39] Similarly, while the Ruhr KPD continued to be active in street politics, these were either combined with, or supplemented by, a growing emphasis, from mid-1930, on improving the material conditions of the unemployed. In essence this involved resisting cuts in benefits, as in Herne in May 1931 when the KPD extracted welfare concessions from the authorities by combining debate inside the city parliament with demonstrations outside. However, the Prussian government's ability to impose cuts through its local government commissioners, and the appalling financial difficulties faced by local government, deprived the KPD of much significant success. Even when the Papen government's spending cuts combined with particularly severe unemployment after mid-1932 to enhance markedly the level of social unrest, Communist activity among the unemployed in the Ruhr was characterised by futile demonstrations, petitions, and fights with rivals and the police.[40] There is evidence to suggest that KPD activity among the unemployed did become more coherent as the year 1932 passed by,[41] but Hitler's accession to power put an end to this. Attempts by the KPD directly to provide welfare relief were hampered by the party's meagre resources which compared unfavourably with those of the better-endowed Nazi movement.[42]

Thus, at the end of the day the KPD's principal attraction for the young unemployed lay in its paramilitary formations which could compensate for the bitter experience of unemployment in the manner described by Wunderlich, and which provided the party with a means of dominating the streets where the unemployed were forced to spend their days.[43] If the factory had constituted the focal point of working-class politics hitherto, high unemployment had greatly enhanced the political significance of the neighbourhood.[44]

However, while paramilitarism and street politics provided the KPD with an organisational focus of last resort among the unemployed, the party's effectiveness, even in this sphere, was limited. The banning of the paramilitary Red Front after clashes between it and the police in Berlin on May Day 1929 posed obvious problems which were compounded by the latitude sometimes afforded by the authorities to the Stormtroopers (SA) of the NSDAP. A deeper problem lay in the ambivalent character of that radicalism fostered by severe unemployment. It is true that the KPD had always attracted youthful casualties of economic crisis[45] and that its ideological contortions during the 1920s have attracted scathing comment from some historians,[46] but for much of the Weimar era the KPD had a relatively solid base of support. Industrial workers in certain parts of Germany did favour the KPD rather than the SPD and its ideology did have solid roots within pre-war Social Democracy. It was manifestly a revolutionary socialist party with many class-conscious members. By 1927, it is true, Arthur Rosenberg saw fit to warn the party that its meagre support in large factories had placed it on the periphery of the working class,[47] but the position worsened markedly during the Depression. By 1932, with almost 90 per cent of its membership out of work, the marginalisation of the KPD had assumed chronic proportions and the nature of its grass roots radicalism had altered fundamentally.[48]

III

It is doubtful whether the radicalism of unemployed rank-and-file Communists, many of whom only remained briefly within the party, could meaningfully be described as left wing. Its basis lay not in any constructive vision of a just social order, but at best in an ill-defined quasi-socialist millenarianism, and more often in a simple rejection of, and despair in, the existing society.[49] This was often tempered by a predisposition to find scapegoats which, then as now, could assume racialist overtones.[50] The tendency of communities afflicted by severe unemployment to blame outsiders for their plight or for 'stealing' those jobs available[51] contrasts markedly with the internationalism of socialism and might, arguably, find greater resonance in fascist social policy. Interwar psychologists certainly regarded the radicalism of unemployment as inherently fascist rather than socialist. Writing of the low-paid victims of unemployment, Eisenberg and Lazarsfeld commented:

> It seems likely that they are sympathetic to fascism because, having practically nothing, they will support a system which promises them an easy way out of their distress, that is, if they are uncritical. At this historical moment they are less likely to support a communist program, which also promises to aid them in their distress but which also requires much more active support which this group, because of its apathy, is not prepared to give.[52]

This accords with Neumann's explanation for the KPD's rapid turnover of members[53] and while it could be judged a *post hoc* rationalisation of fascist successes, some modern analysts, although writing in an age when fascism appears less immediate a threat, have reached similar conclusions. Notable is Gorz, who argues that power in industrial society is no longer exercised by people who hold it. An impersonal bureaucracy wields power, even dispenses misery, while denying responsibility for its actions. Yet, Gorz argues, 'the subject of this power is untraceable, which is why the dominated masses tend implicitly to call for a sovereign whom they could hold responsible and to whom they could present their demands or appeals'.[54] This search for a charismatic Führer, who would sweep away the perceived injustices and corruption of modern capitalism, is not regarded as an explicitly reactionary middle-class phenomenon:

> The themes of fascist ideology can be found permanently, if in diffused form, among all levels and classes of society, especially among the popular classes . . . But only in exceptional circumstances (such as an economic crisis blocking social mobility) and with a charismatic leadership can these themes and the masses who spontaneously propagate them give rise to a radicalised political movement.[55]

Applying Gorz's provocative analysis to late Weimar Germany, the economic crisis and potential charismatic leader were present. The oft-repeated Nazi promise to sweep away the impersonal Weimar 'System' can be understood in this light and, when everything else is considered, it seems that Nazism should have found greater resonance among the unemployed than did Communism. Many young, unemployed workers were attracted to Nazism, and to the SA in particular, which worried the KPD in parts of Germany very deeply indeed. Thus, in late 1931 the Revolutionary Trade Union Opposition's Central Council was warned that the KPD had taken for granted support from the unemployed with disastrous results. In a characteristic instance, a single Fascist in Frankfurt-am-Main had succeeded in organising 1600 of the jobless while the local Communists stood by.[56] However, the socialist traditions of many urban working-class communities blunted the initial Nazi onslaught in the larger towns. In the Communist strongholds the KPD retained a strong, relatively stable following among the unemployed until the collapse of Weimar. Elsewhere matters were more complex. Older unemployed workers seem to have remained loyal to Social Democracy, as the KPD itself was forced to confess.[57] Younger workers, who were more easily radicalised on becoming unemployed were probably predisposed towards the KPD in the first instance if they lived in largely socialist communities, and the approximate correlation between the fall in the SPD's vote and the rise in that of the KPD can be taken as indicative of this. Even so, it is clear that the KPD could not sustain many recruits' interest for very long,[58] which raises the question of their subsequent political behaviour. Some transient Communists doubtless became apathetic, although they may still have voted KPD,[59] but others switched to the Nazi movement; again notably to the SA.[60] While this transfer of loyalties occurred in both directions, those from the Communist to the Nazi movement probably predominated, which suggests that the process was not entirely haphazard. It was not that the KPD's leaders neglected co-operation with, and recruitment of, working-class Nazis. As early as June 1930 the Central Committee saw in the economic crisis an excellent opportunity for detaching proletarian elements from the NSDAP, and similar observations and exhortations to local officials to act accordingly continued until Hitler's takeover.[61] By late 1932 there were signs that this policy was paying off. In December 1932, at the first national conference of the illegal Red Front, it was observed that; 'among the proletarian elements of the SA there exists a strong desire to work with us. Upon receiving orders to undertake terror actions against us, they are declaring that they will not take part in attacks on the Commune any longer'.[62] However, Hitler's takeover put an end to all that, and up until the autumn of 1932, when the Nazi movement was in disarray, success had been limited for the most part. The few Communist party figures available suggest that perhaps 0.5 per cent or 0.75 per cent of entrants during 1931 were former Nazis.[63] Any detailed figures pre-dating 1933 for transfers in the opposite direction are unavailable, but the tenor of official reports and reports from within the Nazi movement indicate a higher rate of transfer.[64] Perhaps equally significant was the substantial transfer of former Communists to the Nazi movement, especially to the SA, after Hitler's takeover, since it was not matched by a comparable transfer of former Socialists.[65]

While this could be taken to indicate the apparent perfidy of Communist as against Socialist supporters, the very high proportion of unemployed members within the KPD was probably the significant factor.[66] The Nazi paramilitary organisations, which were competently led by First World War veterans, overshadowed the KPD's paramilitary wing. The NSDAP, while not awash with funds, was able to offer the destitute better welfare benefits than the KPD and these complemented the political appositeness of Nazism's well-developed paramilitarism. Street marches and fights, rudimentary accommodation, soup kitchens, and handouts of used clothing met a variety of the unemployed's needs,[67] but clearly these were of little interest to workers still in employment. When, in 1933, the NSDAP could add to this the allure of political power and the expectation of socioeconomic redress for the unemployed, the KPD's position became hopeless. Its loyal core of class-conscious members were subjected to terror and persecution while much of the remaining membership melted away or transferred to the Nazi movement.[68] The latter process evidently did not involve any Pauline conversion on the road to Damascus. As before Hitler's takeover, it constituted a search for the most convincing outlet for a radicalism which lacked any precise ideological content, despite the intensity of feeling which underlay it.

IV

In conclusion, the character of the KPD's expanding membership during the early 1930s does not support the contention that unemployment led to a radicalisation of class politics as this concept is normally understood. In those particular communities which the KPD had dominated politically throughout the Weimar era, political radicalisation did benefit the KPD during the early 1930s, but this was probably incidental. In such communities the KPD was the obvious first port of call for any radicalised, unemployed worker, however inchoate his radicalism.

Some commentators, accepting that mass unemployment did not create an upsurge of explicitly left-wing radicalism, have consequently suggested that unemployment was not responsible for radicalisation at all. Instead, the loss of a job resulted in apathy. The older generation of unemployed clearly did become apathetic but, among the young, things were different. However, their radicalism differed from that of people in work since the former's ideology was not located in the labour process. It derived from their estrangement from the labour process and, therefore, from society. This created a very aggressive form of political radicalism, but of a free-floating nature.

The KPD profited from this state of affairs, as demonstrated by its expanding membership and improving electoral performance, but its new recruits were not convinced Communists, and were almost as ready to leave the party as they were to join. The KPD's activism and opposition to Weimar were appealing, but National Socialism was certainly no less appealing, indeed possibly more so to the unemployed, than Communism. These Nazi recruits evidently possessed an insufficient grasp of their movement's ideology to be described as right-wing radicals but equally, while unemployment boosted the paper strength of the main left-wing radical party between 1930 and 1932, it created relatively few left-wing radicals. The radicalism of that era was a distinctive phenomenon in its own right.

Notes

1. T. W. Mason, 'Zur Entstehung des Gesetzes zur Ordnung der nationalen Arbeit vom 20. Januar 1934: Ein Versuch über das Verhältnis "archaischer" und "moderner" Momente in der neuesten deutschen Geschichte', in H. Mommsen, D. Petzina and B. Weisbrod (eds), *Industrielles System und politische Entwicklung in der Weimarer Republik* (Düsseldorf, 1977) p. 332.
2. L. Preller, *Sozialpolitik in der Weimarer Republik* (Düsseldorf, 1978) pp. 179–80.
3. J. Kuczynski, *A Short History of Labour Conditions in Germany, 1800 to the Present Day* (London, 1945) p. 251.
4. R. J. Geary, 'Jugendarbeitslosigkeit und politischer Radikalismus in der Weimarer Republik', *Gewerkschaftliche Monatshefte*, May 1983, p. 305.
5. For consideration of this question see A. Sinfield, *What Unemployment Means* (Oxford, 1981) pp. 37–8; A. Sinfield, *The Long-term Unemployed* (Paris, 1968) pp. 51–2.
6. E. W. Bakke, *The Unemployed Man* (Nisbet, 1933) p. 149.
7. E. W. Bakke, 'The Cycle of Adjustment to Unemployment', in N. W. Bell and E. F. Vogel (eds), *A Modern Introduction to the Family* (Glencoe, Ill., 1960) pp. 113, 121.
8. P. Eisenberg and P. F. Lazarsfeld, 'The Psychological Effects of Unemployment', *Psychological Bulletin*, 1938, p. 378.
9. M. Jahoda, P. F. Lazarsfeld and H. Zeisel, *Die Arbeitslosen von Marienthal* (Bonn, 1960 – first published Leipzig, 1933) pp. 37–41, 54.
10. R. J. Geary, 'Unemployment and Working Class Solidarity in Germany, 1929–33', unpublished manuscript, p. 1.
11. Eisenberg and Lazarsfeld, *Unemployment*, pp. 359, 364.
12. Ibid., pp. 369–72, 375, 384.
13. Cf. Sinfield, *What Unemployment Means*, p. 68.
14. Jahoda *et al.*, *Die Arbeitslosen*, pp. 22–3, 37–8, 64.
15. Ibid., p. 42; cf. J. Wickham, *The Working Class Movement in Frankfurt-am-Main during the Weimar Republic*, D. Phil. Dissertation (University of Sussex, 1979) p. 218; S. Constantine, *Unemployment in Britain between the Wars* (London, 1980) p. 38, where similar points are made.
16. S. Neumann, *Die Parteien der Weimarer Republik* (Stuttgart, 1977) p. 87.
17. A. Rosenberg, *Geschichte der Weimarer Republik* (Frankfurt, 1980) p. 199.
18. F. Wunderlich, 'New Aspects of Unemployment in Germany', *Social Research*, I, 1934, pp. 97, 99, 100–4.
19. Quoted in C. Severing, *Mein Lebensweg* (Cologne, 1950) vol. 2, p. 357; cf. Wickham, *The Working Class Movement*, p. 189.
20. Wunderlich, 'New Aspects of Unemployment' pp. 105, 108; cf. Geary, 'Jugendarbeitslosigkeit', p. 307.
21. Wunderlich, 'New Aspects of Unemployment', pp. 108–9; cf. Sinfield, *What Unemployment Means*, p. 68, and Bundesarchiv Koblenz (BAK) R45IV/39, 'Schluß mit dem SA Terror' (Herausgegeben von der Roten Hilfe Deutschlands) pp. 4–5; 'Die wahren Schuldigen'. Here the KPD

explains the SA's success in recruiting so many workers in remarkably similar terms to Wunderlich.

22. E. Rosenhaft, *Beating the Fascists? The German Communists and Political Violence 1929–1933* (Cambridge, 1983) p. 49; cf. R. J. Geary, 'Radicalism and the German Worker' in R. J. Evans (ed.), *Society and Politics in Wilhelmine Germany* (London, 1978) p. 274; Geary, 'Jugendarbeitslosigkeit', p. 306.
23. Constantine, *Unemployment in Britain*, p. 43.
24. J. Seabrook, *Unemployment* (London, 1982) p. 2.
25. Constantine, *Unemployment in Britain*, p. 38.
26. R. J. Geary, 'The Failure of German Labour in the Weimar Republic' in M. Dobkowski and I. Wallimann (eds), *Towards the Holocaust* (Westport, 1983) p. 182.
27. Wickham, *The Working Class Movement*, p. 217.
28. Geary, 'Radicalism', p. 274.
29. Geary, 'Jugendarbeitslosigkeit', pp. 304–5.
30. O. K. Flechtheim, *Die KPD in der Weimarer Republik* (Frankfurt, 1969) pp. 347–8.
31. *Statistisches Jahrbuch für das deutsche Reich, 1934* (Berlin, 1934) IX, 307, Table 11; Kuczynski, *Labour Conditions*, pp. 235–7.
32. S. Bahne, *Die KPD und das Ende von Weimar. Das Scheitern einer Politik 1932–1935* (Frankfurt, 1976) p. 16.
33. Rosenberg, *Weimarer Republik*, p. 200.
34. Staatsarchiv Bremen (St.AB) 4, 65/251/46. Zentralkomitee der Kommunistischen Partei Deutschlands. Sekretariat. Brief des Zentralkomitees an alle Betriebs- und Straßenzellen (Berlin, beginning of June 1930), p. 3. St.AB 4, 65/260/49. Abschrift. Der Polizei-Präsident in Bochum. Politische Nachrichtensammelstelle für die Provinz Westfalen. Betrifft: Pionier des Bolschewismus (Bochum, 5 October 1932); Cf. Rosenhaft, *Beating the Fascists?* pp. 43, 49.
35. Wickham, *The Working Class Movement*, pp. 248–9; Rosenhaft, *Beating the Fascists?* p. 45; Geary, 'Failure', p. 185.
36. Neumann, *Die Parteien*, p. 88.
37. Wickham, *The Working Class Movement*, p. 195.
38. Rosenhaft, *Beating the Fascists?*, p. 52.
39. Wickham, *The Working Class Movement*, pp. 194–5.
40. B. Herlemann, *Kommunalpolitik der KPD im Ruhrgebiet 1924–1933* (Wuppertal, 1977) pp. 91, 175, 178f, 186; cf. Flechtheim, *Die KPD in der Weimarer Republik*, p. 279.
41. BAK R45IV/28. KPD Unterbezirk Bautzen. An die Bez. Leitung Sachsen. Betr.: Bericht über die Schaffung von Einheitsausschüssen (18 June 1932). BAK R45IV/44. 'Wir lauten die Sturmglocken zum Millionen-Angriff! Genosse Thälmanns Kampfruf für das Massenheer der hungernden Erwerbslosen' (November 1932). St.AB 4, 65/261/49. Abschrift. Der Polizei-Präsident in Bochum. Politische Nachrichtensammelstelle für die Provinz Westfalen. Part I, nr. 13/33, Betrifft: KPD (Bochum, 23 January 1933).
42. Rosenhaft, *Beating the Fascists?*, p. 52; cf. C. Fischer, *Stormtroopers: A*

Social, Economic, and Ideological Analysis, 1929–35 (London, 1983) p. 209.

43. Rosenhaft, ibid., p. 43. cf. Wunderlich, 'New Aspects of Unemployment', p. 108.
44. Rosenhaft, ibid., p. 45. cf. Wickham, *The Working Class Movement*, p. 218.
45. Cf. R. Wheeler, 'Zur sozialen Struktur der Arbeiterbewegung am Anfang der Weimarer Republik. Einige methodologischen Bemerkungen' in H. Mommsen, D. Petzina and B. Weisbrod (eds), *Industrielles System und Politische Entwicklung in der Weimarer Republik* (Düsseldorf, 1977) p. 184; Geary, 'Radicalism' p. 274.
46. For instance, F. Borkenau, *World Communism. A History of the Communist International* (University of Michigan, 1962) chapter XIV; Flechtheim, *Die KPD in der Weimarer Republik*, esp. chapter 5.
47. Quoted in Flechtheim, ibid., p. 241.
48. Cf. Wickham, *The Working Class Movement*, p. 189.
49. Rosenberg, *Weimarer Republik*, pp. 199–200; Wunderlich, *New Aspects of Unemployment*, pp. 108–09.
50. Fischer, *Stormtroopers*, pp. 196, 215; cf. Sinfield, *What Unemployment Means*, p. 122.
51. Constantine, *Unemployment in Britain*, p. 21; Sinfield, ibid., p. 121.
52. Eisenberg and Lazarsfeld, *Unemployment*, p. 370.
53. Neumann, *Die Parteien*, p. 88.
54. A. Gorz, *Farewell to the Working Class. An Essay on Post-Industrial Socialism*, trans. M. Sonenscher (London, 1982) pp. 58–9.
55. Gorz, ibid., p. 62.
56. For instance, St.AB 4, 65/278/55. 'Einige Schwächen der RGO-Arbeit. Rede des Genossen Heckert auf der Tagung des Zentralrats der RGO', *Arbeiter Zeitung*, nr. 5 (7 January, 1932). See also St.AB 4 65/280/55. Der Polizei-Präsident in Bochum. Politische Nachrichtensammelstelle für die Provinz Westfalen. Part I nr. 124/32. Betrifft: 3. Ruhrkongress der RGO Ruhrgebiet (Bochum, 8 May 1932). Abschrift e. Entwurf. Entschliessung zur Lage. BAK R45IV/11. KPD Bezirk Halle-Merseburg. An das Zentralkomitee der KPD, Sekretariat (Halle, 19 May 1932).
57. St.AB 4, 65/278/55. It should also be remembered that some younger unemployed Social Democrats joined the activist Schufo units of the Reichsbanner; K. Rohe, *Das Reichsbanner Schwarz Rot Gold. Ein Beitrag zur Geschichte und Struktur der politischen Kampfverbände zur Zeit der Weimarer Republik* (Stuttgart, 1965) pp. 272–3.
58. Cf. K. Duhnke, *Die KPD von 1933 bis 1945* (Cologne, 1972) p. 30.
59. Cf. Geary, 'Unemployment', p. 12.
60. Fischer, *Stormtroopers*, pp. 146, 151–3, 206, 211–17; cf. Bahne, *Die KPD und das Ende*, p. 16; W. Böhnke, *Die NSDAP im Ruhrgebiet, 1920–1933* (Bonn-Bad Godesberg, 1974) p. 154, note 73.
61. St.AB 4, 65/251/46. Abschrift IAN 2160/1.8. Zentralkomitee der KPD. Sekretariat (Berlin, 17 June 1930). Rundschreiben Nr. 10, p. 3; see also St.AB 4, 65/253/47. Der Reichsminister des Innern. IAN 2160d/31.10. Betreff: KPD – Kampf gegen Faschismus (Berlin, 7 November 1930).

St.AB 4, 65/257/48. Zentralkomitee der Kommunistischen Partei Deutschlands. Rundschreiben an alle Leitungen der Betriebszellen, Straßenzellen, (Berlin, 8 December 1931) p. 11. St.AB 4, 65/260/49. Zu IAN 2162/11/10. Bericht von der Agitprop-Konferenz (16 September 1932). Appendix 1.

62. BAK R134/76 (86–89). Abschrift IAN 2166a/31.1. Appendix 1. Reichskonferenz des Rotenfrontkämpferbundes. Referate! Kamerad Paul! Fischer, *Stormtroopers*, pp. 209–11.

63. St.AB 4, 65/255/47. Aus L. B. Stuttgart, Nr. W.8 – N. Stelle nr. 2325/31 geh. (17 June 1931) p. 18. BAK R45IV/21. 'Ergebnisse des Aufgebots der 100 000' [April? 1932] Figures for Thüringen. BAK R45IV/25. Bezirksleitung Südbayern. An das Zentralkomitee, Abt. Org. und Sekretariat (München, 19 May 1932).

64. BAK R134/58 (207). Deutsche Nachrichtenkonferenz in Berlin am 28 and 29 April 1930. Regierungsrat Bach – Darmstadt, 'Die Entwicklung der nationalsozialistischen Bewegung in Hessen, besonders im Odenwald'. St.AB 4, 65/259, 49. Die Lage in der KPD (Munich, 20 April 1932). BAK NS26/1404. Berichte der Staatspolizei Württembergs zur politischen Lage (25 November 1931). Fischer, *Stormtroopers*, pp. 211–12.

65. Fischer, *Stormtroopers*, pp. 56–7, and Table 3.11; cf. St.AB 4, 65/284/56. Polizeipräsident Recklinghausen. Politische Nachrichtensammelstelle für die Prov. Westfalen. I. Geheim Nr. 83/33. Betrifft: R.G.O. Recklinghausen (18 April 1933); see also Bahne, *Die KPD und das Ende*, p. 54 and I. Buchloh, *Die nationalsozialistische Machtergreifung in Duisburg. Eine Fallstudie* (Duisburg, 1980) pp. 36, 151–3, for a discussion of the factory council elections in early 1933.

66. However, Geary, 'Unemployment', p. 3, attacks the notion that the KPD and NSDAP were in competition for the same unemployed. It is perfectly plausible that this was the case in certain places. However, national and local KPD reports do indicate considerable direct competition between the KPD and NSDAP in many localities. For instance, see the sources cited in notes 61, 62 and 64. An interesting description of the Nazi recruitment of children in a working-class quarter of Zwickau is found in: BAK R134/86 (167–68). Abschrift. IAN 2167/15.4. Appendix 1. Zentralbüro der Roten Jungpioniere. Material zum Kampf gegen Kindergruppen der Nationalsozialisten (Berlin, 18 November 1930).

67. Fischer, *Stormtroopers*, chapters 5–7; Rosenhaft, *Beating the Fascists?*, p. 52.

68. Cf. note 65; see also R. Diels, *Lucifer ante Portas. Zwischen Severing und Heydrich* (Zurich, 1949) p. 153; Bahne, *Die KPD und das Ende*, pp. 41, 43–4, 53; Fischer, *Stormtroopers*, p. 58.

Index